CW00829482

GOING OFFSHORE

GOING OFFSHORE

How to Boost Your Capital and Protect Your Wealth

LEO GOUGH

FINANCIAL TIMES

Prentice Hall

DISCLAIMER

This book is intended only as a general guide to offshore investment. Anyone who is considering investing offshore should seek professional advice. While every effort has been made to ensure accuracy, no legal responsibility or liability can be accepted by the author or the publisher for any errors or omissions.

PEARSON EDUCATION LIMITED

Head Office:
Edinburgh Gate
Harlow CM20 2JE
Tel: +44 (0)1279 623623
Fax: +44 (0)1279 431059

London Office:
128 Long Acre, London WC2E 9AN
Tel: +44 (0)171 447 2000
Fax: +44 (0)171 240 5771

First published in Great Britain in 1995
as *The Investor's Guide to Offshore Investment*
Second edition published 1998

© Leo Gough 1998

The right of Leo Gough to be identified as author
of this work has been asserted by him in accordance
with the Copyright, Designs and Patents Act 1988.

ISBN 0 273 63115 2

British Library Cataloguing in Publication Data
A CIP catalogue record for this book can be obtained
from the British Library.

3 5 7 9 10 8 6 4 2

Typeset by Pantek Arts, Maidstone, Kent.
Printed and bound in Great Britain by
Biddles Ltd, Guildford and King's Lynn

*The Publishers' policy is to use paper manufactured
from sustainable forests.*

ABOUT THE AUTHOR

Leo Gough is a financial journalist. He worked as an expatriate in the international film and television industry for ten years before returning to the UK. He is the author of ten books, including:

- *The Financial Times Guide to Business Numeracy*
- *How the Stock Market Really Works,* and
- *The Finance Manual for Non-Financial Managers* (with Paul McKoen),

all published by Pitman, and contributes regularly to newspapers and financial periodicals.

To Arieh Eilan,
a true cosmopolitan

CONTENTS

INTRODUCTION

This book is for people who are ready to take responsibility for their own lives. Investment is an activity where success is dependent on your capacity to assess risks, and to live with losses. If you are terrified of ever making a loss, you are likely to keep your cash on deposit at home, and to buy those heavily marketed financial products that promise security above all. Tax, inflation and high charges will eat away at these savings over time, but the hapless savers will be assured that this is because of the 'state of the economy', and that everyone else is in the same boat. As consumers, we are virtual captives in a market which is rigged against us. The alternative? Make your own plans, diversify abroad and become the master of your own destiny; in short, become an offshore investor.

> **Investment is an activity where success is dependent on your capacity to assess risks, and to live with losses**

Some may find these views controversial, so perhaps I should describe something of my own background. There have been expatriates in my family for over 150 years. My parents and their siblings all worked abroad, and some have emigrated permanently. My father worked as an academic in the Middle East for 35 years, and I was brought up there. Living with insecurity seemed entirely natural; coups, small wars and turbulent economies were a part of life, and nobody ever expected the state to protect the individual. The notion of a benevolent state, so dear to British hearts, is an illusion. Regulations, social contracts, pension schemes and political moods change frequently and no-one can afford to assume that the status quo is permanent.

> **Make your own plans, diversify abroad and become the master of your own destiny; in short, become an offshore investor**

Societies are in a constant state of flux, and wealth is always moving from one social group to another. It can be argued that every 60 years or so a large part of the middle and upper classes are wiped out financially. At the poorer end of the minority who possess any net worth at all, people tend to have small cash deposits, some equity in a house and a few wasting assets such as cars. At the upper end, the majority of assets are in good-quality securities, directly or indirectly; in effect, they are invested in the productive side of the world's economy. Investing off-shore is old news for the very rich, and this book is not likely to teach them anything. For the rest, I hope that it will be useful as a manual to help you design your own long-term financial programme and bring it to fruition. How much money do you need to go offshore? It depends; the more that you have, the more possibilities are open to you, but even if you have nothing at all, you can apply some of the ideas presented here. Topics covered include:

- *The varieties of offshore investor.*
- *Tax havens* – what they are, and why countries become tax havens.
- *Tax havens and the EU* – working across the 'Euro curtain'.
- *Tax* – legal ways of minimizing the tax you pay.
- *Becoming an expatriate* – how to get the best deal from your employers, and what to do with your tax-free savings.
- *The stock markets of the world* – an overview of the global financial markets.
- *Offshore companies* – how they are used to minimize tax and to trade internationally. The use of the Netherlands as a corporate base.
- *Trusts* – what they are, how they are used, and how to avoid trouble.
- *Banking overseas* – techniques to use, and the problem of confidentiality. The horror stories – the collapse of BCCI, and the world of money laundering.
- *Foreign exchange* – the collapse of the Bretton Woods system, the floating rate system, and how to deal in foreign currencies.
- *Going international* – how to obtain dual nationality, and profit by it.
- *The tax havens of the world* – details of the main offshore centres around the globe.

INTRODUCTION
TO THE SECOND EDITION

People are interested in offshore investment for a great variety of reasons. Your perspective on the subject depends largely on your circumstances, so a course of action which might appear obvious to one person could be salvation to another. While this book cannot offer a completely exhaustive guide to every wrinkle in the vast complexity of the competing regulatory regimes, it can, hopefully, be useful as an introduction to the offshore scene and as a resource from which to obtain ideas which you must then investigate for yourself. It should also be helpful in reducing the amount of money you spend on obtaining professional advice as many long hours are spent unnecessarily in specialist lawyers' offices, listening to introductory explanations which are better and more cheaply obtained by reading books such as this.

Writing a book of this kind makes one conscious of the perpetual friction between the centralizing, oppressing forces of state bureaucracy and the drive for independence within many individuals. A word of advice; 'rendering unto Caesar that which is Caesar's' – in other words, staying within the law and avoiding, rather than evading, taxes – is a practical necessity. Far too many people attempt, with inadequate knowledge and resources, to outwit the machinery of the state on every possible occasion. This can lead to a paranoiac, stress-filled existence and, at worst, to becoming like a hunted animal, scrambling in ever-decreasing circles towards its doom. Make your goal prosperity and financial independence, and be prepared to compromise with authority rather than become an anti-regulation crusader; the latter course often ends in tears.

> **Staying within the law and avoiding, rather than evading, taxes is a practical necessity**

Take a lesson from 'old money' and accept that co-operation and passive resistance are often better tactics than confrontation.

Equally, though, no one should feel entirely defeated by regulatory burdens; working for a few years in a low-tax or no-tax country is an excellent way to accumulate capital, whether you simply have the humble ambition to be able to purchase a house on your return home or aspire to greater things, such as running a successful international business.

> **Working for a few years in a low-tax or no-tax country is an excellent way to accumulate capital**

Offshore company formation is not for inexperienced businesspeople; to make it work, you need to have a good understanding of accounting and company law and have strong practical abilities. Thus, neophyte entrepreneurs are advised to keep things simple and not to place too much confidence in paper companies and what they have been told about regulations – wait for a few years before attempting to build your vast network of interlocking offshore companies!

There are no easy answers in offshore investment, and you should be suspicious of any 'one decision' packages which promise to solve all your problems. Not only are the regulations constantly changing, but also there are some loopholes which it would be a shame to publicize as this could lead to their closure. Careful readers should be able to divine promising areas for further investigation by reading between the lines herein.

ACKNOWLEDGEMENTS

I would like to thank the professionals who generously gave of their knowledge during the writing of this book, and who have asked not to be named, to Sean Gabb for his help on the UK's anti-money-laundering laws and to Aggie Morrison of Profile for her invaluable help in using the Profile system. The opinions and any mistakes herein are mine, not theirs. Lastly, readers who have any corrections or suggestions for future editions are welcome to write to me care of the publishers.

1
TAX HAVENS

In this chapter we will examine the basic considerations for offshore investors. Topics include:

- The varieties of offshore investor
- Tax havens and offshore centres
- The European Union
- The Ruding report
- The EU and value added tax
- Mergers
- Groups of companies
- Company law
- The Lome conventions
- The EU and tax havens
- Ireland
- Luxembourg
- Overseas departments of France
- Spanish territories in Africa and the Atlantic
- Madeira and the Azores
- The Isle of Man and the Channel Islands
- Gibraltar
- The Vatican
- San Marino
- Andorra
- Malta
- Monaco
- The Dutch Antilles
- Aruba
- Cyprus
- European enclaves
- Campione and Samnaun (Switzerland)
- Christiania (Denmark)
- Kleinwalsertal (Austria)
- Os de Civis (Spain)
- San Marino and Valle San'Anastasio (Italy)
- The offshore investor
- Languages
- Offshore trusts and companies – are they worth it?
- Spotting the sharks
- Dual nationality

'The optimum population,' said Mustapha Mond, 'is modelled on the iceberg – eight-ninths below the water line, one-ninth above.'

'And they're happy below the water line?'

'Happier than above it. Happier than your friends here, for example.' He pointed.

'In spite of that awful work?'

'Awful? They don't find it so. On the contrary, they like it. It's light, it's childishly simple. No strain on the mind or the muscles. Seven and a half hours of mild, unexhausting labour, and then the soma ration and games and unrestricted copulation and the feelies. What more can they ask for? True,' he added, 'they might ask for shorter hours. And of course we could give them shorter hours. Technically, it would be perfectly simple to reduce all lower-caste working hours to three or four a day. But would they be any happier for that? No, they wouldn't. The experiment was tried, more than a century and a half ago. The whole of Ireland was put on to the four-hour day. What was the result? Unrest, and a large increase in the consumption of soma; that was all. Those three and a half hours of extra leisure were so far from being a source of happiness, that people felt constrained to take a holiday from them. The Inventions Office is stuffed with plans for labour-saving processes. Thousands of them.' Mustapha Mond made a lavish gesture. 'And why don't we put them into execution? For the sake of the labourers; it would be sheer cruelty to afflict them with excessive leisure. It's the same with agriculture. We could synthesize every morsel of food if we wanted to. But we don't. We prefer to keep a third of the population on the land. For their own sakes – because it takes longer to get food out of the land than out of a factory. Besides, we have our stability to think of. We don't want to change. Every change is a menace to stability. That's another reason why we're so chary of applying new inventions. Every discovery in pure science is potentially subversive; even science must be sometimes treated as a possible enemy. Yes, even science.'

ALDOUS HUXLEY, *Brave New World*, p. 176, 1932

THE VARIETIES OF OFFSHORE INVESTOR

There are many kinds of offshore investor. They range from the world's biggest international companies and institutions, through families with 'old money', small- and medium-sized businesses, all the way to the small-time tax evader with a few thousand in undeclared cash. For many people, a spell working abroad is the only time in their lives when they are able to accumulate enough capital to make a difference to the way they live. These different types of offshore investor have little in common with one another – their motives and aims vary considerably, not just in proportion to the worth of their assets, but also according to their individual 'philosophies'. The small-time tax evader, for example, may have his heart set on a numbered Swiss bank account out of bravado; he may not appreciate the high costs of Swiss banking, nor that, had he arranged his affairs differently, he might have had a fully declared, tax-paid nest egg which could be left safely at home. Expatriates may be unsophisticated about investment, and opt for financial products which they would have avoided had they had better advice. The world of the multinationals and institutions may be a grander place, with daily trade in foreign currencies and huge pension and investment funds held offshore, but they too have their risks and difficulties.

Irrespective of their financial resources, all offshore investors have widely varying attitudes towards their home country. For some, there is no question of leaving their home country permanently, and the ability to repatriate capital will always be essential, while for others the idea of emigrating or becoming completely 'international' is very appealing. Inheritance Tax is a major concern, especially for the elderly. If your assets far exceed the UK's £215,000 Inheritance Tax threshold, the use of offshore trusts and a planned schedule of giving can ensure that more of your estate goes to the people you want to give to rather than to the government. Anyone running a small business can save tax and open up new markets by forming an offshore company, and, as popular fiction tells us, no self-respecting tycoon appears to be without a complex network of anonymously owned companies, culminating in a parent entity in Liechtenstein or the Cayman Islands.

3

Whatever their reasons for investing offshore, all these groups are taking advantage of the anomalies that exist between the financial and tax regimes of the different nations of the world. Many people are surprised and disturbed that there should be such differences. From childhood we absorb our own country's attitudes and habits towards money, and the fact that other countries offer different, or, worse still, more favourable conditions for investment seems unfair. Nevertheless, it is true. Economic power can move from one trading bloc to another in a few decades, and political ideologies can transform a country within a few years. Yesterday's enemies are today's friends, and physical and economic barriers between nations can evaporate suddenly – the collapse of the USSR, for instance, seemed unthinkable only a few years ago.

I believe that as an investor it pays to be neutral. If you can legally drive from England to France and return with a van-load of cut-price beer, are you cheating or somehow being unpatriotic? Is it wrong to make money by investing in the booming economies of the Far East? In my view, making the most of opportunities abroad is only common sense; any moral inhibitions a person may have about investments seem to be better applied to the way in which money is specifically put to use, rather than to the political colour of a government or its particular tax rules.

It is also something of a revelation to discover just how little sense international fiscal laws make. One may have the impression that there is somehow a vast, harmonious network of revenue authorities across the world, all working to the same rule book in full co-operation with one another and with a scrupulous devotion to fairness, like some taxman's Interpol. Nothing could be further from the truth; the reality is that while tax and exchange of information treaties between some countries do exist, there is no international system of co-operation on tax collection, enforcement, or even the setting of tax rates.

Whatever kind of financial arrangements you make overseas, it is important to spend time on research and in the preparation of your plans. Some of these arrangements may involve long-term commitments, and the 'architecture' of your plan must be as well-designed as possible. Study all the tax havens before narrowing down to a short list of two or three. You will need professional advice, but remember that the more information you can obtain through your own efforts, the less time and expense will be incurred in having advisers explain things to you. Different professions have different areas of expertise, and you will need to develop relationships with bankers, brokers, accountants and solicitors; one or more of these may also be an investment adviser. Personal relationships are important, because if an adviser does not understand you, he or she may be forced into a position of trying to please you rather than guiding you into a sound investment structure. As an investor you are your own worst enemy, in the sense that if you don't have full confidence in your advisers you are likely to meddle. This does not mean that your advisers must be with you for life; people and circumstances change, and you may find even better advisers in the future as your assets and expertise grow. If you are using a firm, try to stick with one member of it, and ask for the firm's internal policies and philosophies so that you understand how they work.

The more you have, the more you have to lose, and your portfolio should be monitored and kept up to date regularly. With offshore investments this means that you should always have access to your brokers and advisers, and that you need to spend time each week reviewing your progress. If you have a large portfolio, it makes sense to invest principally for growth, only taking out a fixed amount each year for living expenses, in the most tax-efficient way. Investment advisers may not be able to help you outperform the markets consistently, but they can certainly save you from making expensive elementary mistakes.

Tax considerations aside, it still makes sense to invest internationally. Ultimately, any investment will lose its value. Wars and political changes wipe out some of them, while others simply die a natural death as markets and technologies change. Diversifying across countries helps to guard against these risks. Political stability isn't everything – one can have perfect stability in a stagnant economy that is inhibited by heavy regulations and high taxes. The really big booms tend to happen in under-regulated environments, and although this may mean taking more risk in the short term, your long-term prospects for growth may be better in such countries. These days, few people are likely to make their fortunes in Britain; investors must look further afield if they are to prosper in the future. Venture capital schemes, however, are best avoided by most people, particularly those in far-off countries. The success rate tends to be low, and unless you are an active businessperson yourself, you will be unlikely to be offered the most interesting deals yourself – these tend to go to specialists. The quality of management is the most important factor in any venture capital scheme; unless the people who are making the business work are capable and dedicated to the shareholders' interests, even the best ideas are unlikely to produce a good return.

5

TAX HAVENS AND OFFSHORE CENTRES

Not all low-tax countries like to be called tax havens, and although even professionals use the name, it is not a very precise one. Switzerland, for example, is not a low-tax country, but its sophisticated banking facilities and tradition of conservatism and confidentiality makes it an important feature of the offshore world. The exclusive urban paradise of Monaco does not have much in common with the remote islands of Vanuatu, yet both have their financial attractions. Some tax havens specialize in the forming of offshore companies, while others have highly developed banking facilities. Most of them are small countries (quite a number are islands), and look to offshore business as an important part of their economies, but none of them can afford to pull up the drawbridge entirely – not only are they in strong competition with one another, but also they are dependent in varying degrees on the policies and practices of the dominant trading nations of the world.

Most of the money going into tax havens comes from the big trading countries of the developed world, all of whom take steps to limit the flow of these transactions, and tax havens must take this fact into account when designing their own laws. It is a principle of international law that every sovereign nation must regulate its own economy, and can set its own tax rates, so the right of a country to become a tax haven is well-established. Despite the adverse publicity that tax havens get – they are an easy target for onshore politicians – it would appear that it is not in the interests of the developed nations to close tax havens down entirely. Tax havens are, as it were, the gas which gives the international economy its fizz. There are bureaucratic and ideological forces which would wish that such anomalies did not exist, but, short of a world government with the power to harmonize taxes into one global system, it is difficult to foresee a time when tax havens will not have their part to play in the international economy. Even in the EU, where attempts are being made to harmonize company taxation in member states, there have been no moves to set universal standards for personal taxation because of the enormous legal and political difficulties in doing so. For nationals of EU countries, the offshore jurisdictions which are physically close to the EU and have special tax arrangements with the community, offer benefits which are not available at home.

Until recently, the post-war period has been characterized by political and economic barriers to the free movement of money around the world. We have now entered an era of globalization, but hitherto people living in high-tax countries had powerful motives to go offshore. If, like the Beatles, you had been taxed in the 1960s at 98p in the pound, the arguments for emigrating to a country with lower taxes would have been powerful indeed. Societies go through cycles in which wealth periodically shifts from some groups within a country to others – this was the case after the war with the drive towards the redistribution of wealth and the establishment of quasi-socialist states in much of the developed world. Individuals from a class of people who are under economic threat have often been drawn to the use of tax havens as a route to salvation. In the 1960s, though, there were problems of communication; many havens were physically isolated and lacked the sophisticated telecommunications and banking facilities which we expect today.

Since the general abandonment of exchange controls and a lowering of the tax rates on high-earners, people are less inclined to take drastic steps to preserve their wealth. Tax havens have, in some ways, become more respectable; the multinationals use them for in-house pension and insurance schemes, many sound investment funds are based offshore, and international offshore subsidiaries of ultra-respectable banks abound – and all these are active in trading in foreign currencies offshore. Nor is it illegal in the UK to have a bank account in a tax haven, but you must declare it to the Inland Revenue, and you will probably have to pay tax on it. Businesses investing in unstable parts of the world will often use tax havens as a base for their operations. This gives them the flexibility and protection they need.

Not all tax havens are independent countries. Labuan, for instance, is a small territory in Malaysia and Ireland's International Financial Services Centre is a district in the Dublin docklands. How much tax you pay often depends upon where you are doing business; quite a number of jurisdictions exempt companies from tax if they are doing business abroad, while subjecting domestic businesses to high tax rates. Others, notably Holland, have special rules for international holding companies while possessing double-taxation treaties with the developed world which allow international corporate groups to avoid tax. Modern tax havens have good communications and well-developed banking and legal systems. Worldwide action against money laundering (see Chapter 7) has meant that many tax havens co-operate to some degree with the state authorities in other countries. Today, offshore investors must be as sophisticated as the global financial world allows, while taking a long-term view. As economic power shifts to the Far East, there is the possibility of a return to trade barriers, and having an offshore network in place beforehand could be an advantage. Offshore investors don't simply deposit money in an offshore bank account; they use offshore centres as a base or a conduit for the investment of their funds internationally. London is possibly the best market for equity investors and has special attractions in such areas as Eurobonds; many investors balance their offshore portfolios by investing in onshore markets, often by means of an offshore vehicle.

THE EUROPEAN UNION

The European Union has taken its time in creating its single market, and new obstacles may arise. EU financial business is a significant part of the EU's economy, and barriers to the flow of money between member states have been lifted. Institutions which are permitted to operate in one member country may now trade in any or all of them, and have an advantage over EU branches of non-EU groups. Banks within the EU are highly regulated and lack confidentiality.

The Ruding report

The Ruding Committee was formed in 1991 to design a harmonized system of taxing companies within the EU. Headed by chairman Onno Ruding, the Committee was given a wide brief and allowed to consider all possibilities. It advised that the existing system could be extended, and made the following recommendations:

- Double taxation between member states should be abandoned.
- Double taxation treaties with non-member states should use the OECD Model Treaty
- A minimum rate of corporation tax should be instituted across the EU.
- Businesses which are not companies should be taxed as companies.
- Holding companies and parent companies should all suffer corporation tax.
- Mergers between EU businesses, whether or not they are companies, should not suffer Capital Gains Tax (CGT).

8

- Transfer pricing (transactions between companies which are under common control, see page 90) should not be doubly taxed by two member states, and affected companies can now appeal to an advisory committee. This is covered by the Transfer Pricing Arbitration Directive.

Some of these recommendations have now been implemented, while others are the subject of negotiation between member states.

The EU and value added tax

The most progress has been made in harmonizing value added tax and customs duties. Goods are taxed in the member state into which they are imported, but when the new system is in place, they will be taxed in the country of origin. Businesses trading with non-EU states have a harsher VAT system to deal with, and may use certain tax havens associated with the EU (see pages 10–13) to mitigate this.

Mergers

Businesses in different countries within the EU are allowed to transfer assets and shares, merge and demerge without automatically suffering Capital Gains Tax. This means that in the UK such transactions will not be subject to the normal rule of valuing such transfers at the market rate for CGT purposes.

Groups of companies

Dividends paid between groups of companies in different EU countries are no longer liable to double taxation. A parent company is defined as a company owning more than a quarter of a subsidiary, and the country in which a parent company is situated must allow it tax relief on its subsidiaries' profits.

Company law

All businesses in member states must be allowed to move or set up branches in other member states. Directives on company law are regularly produced and amended, and attempts are being made to harmonize accounting methods, valuation, credit and share ownership across the EU.

The Lomé conventions

A large number of Third World countries supply the EU with commodities and raw materials. These African, Caribbean and Pacific (ACP) countries have signed a series of conventions with the EU at Lomé which adjust trade agreements according to circumstances. International debt has become a more pressing problem than food scarcity in ACP countries, and the EU has promised to support ACP states in developing their economies; help includes technical support and free financial aid as well as loans. The EU treats the ACP as a favoured trading bloc, but does not demand free access to ACP markets. Ways of encouraging private investment in ACP countries are being explored, and the ACP has agreed not to discriminate between EU member states. The Fourth Lomé Convention was designed to allay fears of 'fortress Europe' by establishing firm ties with the ACP nations, whose total population exceeds 250 million.

The EU and tax havens

As was mentioned earlier, there are a number of states and territories within the EU which have an anomalous relationship with the EU. Some are associates of the union, others are full members, and others have transitional status; most of them have tax advantages, and can be used as bases from which to trade within the community. The full members are Ireland and Luxembourg.

Ireland

Although it is a full member of the EU, Ireland offers a wide range of tax incentives to outside investors which include a 10 per cent tax rate on manufacturing and licensing companies. It has two low tax zones, one in Dublin, the International Financial Services Centre, entry to which is now limited and is designed for multinationals and financial institutions, and the Shannon Free Zone which encourages inward investment. A wide range of soft loans are available and it is possible to set up a non-resident company in Ireland which is exempt of tax on overseas earnings.

Luxembourg

The tiny principality of Luxembourg is a popular location for holding companies and investment companies which can reinvest profits from foreign countries tax free. Banking services aspire to rival those of Switzerland. Some other member states treat Luxembourg holding companies unfavourably for tax, however, and complex group structures may be necessary to take advantage of Luxembourg's tax breaks. Banking secrecy is not assured. Luxembourg is the centre of the massive trade in Eurobonds, which are issued in bearer form.

Territories within or dependent on member states
These include:

- overseas departments of France
- Spanish territories in Africa and the Atlantic
- Madeira and the Azores
- the Isle of Man and the Channel Islands
- Gibraltar.

French overseas departments
These include Guiana, Martinique, Réunion and Guadaloupe. They are part of the EU through their status as parts of the French republic and are subject to EU directives.

Spanish territories
There are two Spanish towns in North Africa, Melilla and Ceuta, which are subject to the EU but are not included in the EU customs territory and are excluded from the EU's policies on trade. The Canary Islands were treated in the same way until 1991 when it was agreed that they should be incorporated within the customs union. The Canaries are to keep their own tax arrangements for a transitional period.

Madeira and the Azores
Parts of Portugal, Madeira and the Azores get special EU economic support. Madeira is expanding as an offshore centre, and has created a special free zone which gives tax advantages to companies importing from countries outside the EU.

The Isle of Man and the Channel Islands
These are possessions of the British Crown but are not part of the United Kingdom. They are not full members of the EU, and are

exempted from customs duties and trade levies. The territories are well-established tax havens.

Gibraltar

Gibraltar is a dependency of the UK, but is exempt from EU regulations on customs and VAT. Gibraltar offers a number of tax advantages to companies and individuals.

Territories close to the EU

These are:

- the Vatican
- San Marino
- Andorra
- Malta
- Monaco
- the Dutch Antilles
- Aruba
- Cyprus.

The Vatican

The Vatican is excluded from the EU and is treated as a foreign country.

San Marino

San Marino is an independent republic within Italy, but has a customs union with it, and is thus included in the EU customs union. Although it has many arrangements with Italy, San Marino is not an EU member.

Andorra

Andorra is jointly ruled by the Bishop of Urgel and the President of France. Situated in the Pyrenees, it is not an EU member and is well known as a duty-free zone. Andorra is a difficult country in which to form offshore companies, but it does have tax advantages for those that are able to establish a connection there.

Malta

Malta is an independent country and is an associate member of the EU. It has joined the customs union, and hopes for full membership, but provides low tax rates for offshore companies and residents.

Monaco

Monaco is an independent principality with customs union with France, and thus with the EU. It is not a member of the EU, and is a tax haven for all except French nationals.

The Dutch Antilles

The Dutch Antilles are islands off the coast of Venezuela ruled by the Dutch Crown. They have a special associate relationship with the EU, and are an important centre for offshore companies.

Aruba

Aruba is an independent island which was part of the Dutch Antilles. It is ruled by the Dutch Crown and is thus associated with the EU, but has more of the characteristics of the other Caribbean tax havens than do the staid Antilles.

Cyprus

Cyprus is an associate member of the EU, but is also an important tax haven for individuals and companies.

There are also many other smaller territories around the globe which are associated with the EU and are subject to the same rules.

EUROPEAN ENCLAVES

Enclaves are simply territories which, through their geography and historical accident, are 'foreign territories' surrounded by another country or which can only be reached through another country. They often have regulatory anomalies by virtue of their being within a state to which they are not subject. Europe has many; the Continent's bloody past has ensured the creation of many little districts which have sought to protect themselves from political turmoil by adopting a strategy of camouflage and anonymity. Despite the best efforts of the EU, they still exist today, and offer the adventurous offshore investor with various interesting opportunities. The following list is not exhaustive, but gives an indication of some of the areas which Continental Europeans use in order to avoid regulatory burdens. The author would be glad to hear from any readers about their experiences in these, or other, European enclaves – the information can be included in the next edition of this book with an appropriate credit.

Campione (Switzerland)
Campione is a tiny (2.6 square km) piece of Italian territory which is entirely surrounded by Switzerland. There are no visible borders or customs barriers between Campione and Switzerland, and it has, for many years, been a place of interest to offshore investors, particularly Germans seeking to escape their own country's draconian fiscal laws.

Campione is on the edge of Lake Lugano. As part of the EU, any EU citizen is theoretically entitled to take up residence there, which entitles one to, among other things, Swiss licence plates for your car ('TI' for Ticino). Liechtenstein is a mere two hours' drive away,

Although, as part of Italy, Campione residents are subject to Italian tax laws, it appears from anecdotal evidence that non-Italian residents are largely ignored because of the practical enforcement difficulties posed on the authorities by Campione's location.

The main drawback to this fiscal paradise is the scarcity of property – in recent years prices have escalated dramatically, many new apartments are poorly constructed and rented property is hard to find.

Samnaun (Switzerland)
Samnaun is a valley in Engadin, Switzerland (Postcode CH 7551). It is attractive to investors in precious metals and gems because, unlike anywhere else in Europe, there is no sales tax on these commodities. After making your purchases, you can keep them in a safe deposit in a local bank for a small annual fee.

Christiania (Denmark)
Christiania is a small district (34 hectares) in Copenhagen which was taken over by hippies in the 1970s and declared a 'free state'. With a shifting population of about 750 people, Christiania is a feature of a tourist holiday in Denmark and attracts some 50,000 visitors a year to sample the delights of its wholefood cuisine and to wander through the market where drugs are openly sold.

14

The Danish authorities have chosen to tolerate its existence, and an agreement has been reached whereby the residents have promised to maintain the buildings (of which there are more than 100) and pay their utilities bills. Taxes, however, are not collected.

Christiania is reminiscent of the pirate havens of the Caribbean in the sixteenth and seventeenth centuries. Among its denizens are groups of Scandinavian Hell's Angels who conduct murderous raids on their peers as far away as Sweden – recently a bazooka was fired into the crowd at a disco, killing several. The area even has its own breed of dog, which is a dangerous but obedient beast. Arms dealers, drug addicts and people on the run find Christiania a safe place to live, as would those who can adapt to a 'hippie' ethos. Oddly enough, its dangerousness actually makes Christiania a safe place for one whose face fits.

Kleinwalsertal (Austria)

This 97 square km valley in Austria (population 5,000) is actually part of Germany and is two hours' drive south of Munich. Some of the banks in the district allow the Austrian practice of opening 'Sparbuch' accounts – roughly equivalent to a UK building society account – which are truly anonymous numbered bank accounts. Further deposits can be made to such accounts from anywhere in the world by bank transfer, but withdrawals can normally only be made in person by presenting the passbook. The passbook is the only proof of ownership of the account, so keep it safe!

Os de Civis (Spain)

This picturesque village is about 10 km outside Andorra and, although it is in Spanish territory, it can only be accessed through Andorra, with which there are no border checks.

While EU citizens are generally restricted on their purchases in duty-free Andorra, the location of Os de Civis effectively removes this difficulty. The village is cut off by snow in winter, except via the access road, so Spanish officials rarely visit and the Andorran authorities have no jurisdiction in the area. Thus, this remote piece of Spain has, *de facto*, most of the benefits of Andorra without any of the difficulties of obtaining residence or setting up a company there.

San Marino and Valle San'Anastasio (Italy)

San Marino, the oldest republic in Europe, is an independent state surrounded entirely by Italy with which it has a customs union and is thus subject to EU regulations. Tax rates are low and there are no double-taxation treaties. Company formation is possible, but only with a local representative. Obtaining residence is extremely difficult. This country has some potential as a base from which to operate companies trading elsewhere in the EU.

Valle San'Anastasio is a village bordering on San Marino with a population of 150 which seeks to become part of San Marino. By obtaining residence in the village (setting up an accomodation address and registering with the police), one might obtain the much-coveted San Marino citizenship if the village is ever handed over.

THE OFFSHORE INVESTOR

Investors who have accumulated enough capital to have the increased choices, and increased responsibility, that go with wealth use offshore centres. If your net worth is less than £150,000, active overseas investment is probably not for you – yet. In fact, overseas investment becomes a necessity rather than an option as an individual's wealth increases. Once you are in possession of a large amount of capital, your thoughts inevitably turn to how to keep it safe from all the unrelenting forces that are continually trying to take bites out of it. The world looks different to the wealthy; they are much more interested in international political and economic patterns than most people as these have a bearing on the future of their money. Obviously, it is vital to be as well-informed as possible, but before we look at the benefits of moving money around the world, we should consider the reservations that many people have about taking a step outside the conventions of their own country. People often think that there is something wrong with investing abroad, but there is nothing necessarily odd or improper about doing so – in fact, it is an essential part of the international economy.

Unlike Continental Europe, where centuries of wars, revolutions and expropriations have made people wary of their own countries, in Britain and the United States the popular view is that one is better off keeping one's money at home. This perception is sustained by a variety of commercial and political lobbies in whose interests it is that the public continue to think this way. Most countries want to keep their citizens' money where they can control it; inside their own borders. Sometimes laws are passed that prescribe dire penalties, even death, for individuals

16

holding investments outside their own borders. When the situation is that bad, citizens are often not allowed to leave their own countries, except with the greatest difficulty; they must resort to drastic measures to remove themselves and their money to freer places, often running the risk of reprisals against their relatives and friends who they leave behind. Less drastically, there are often situations like the one at present in Hong Kong, now part of the People's Republic of China. Despite Chinese assurances to the contrary, many Hong Kong nationals think that life will get harder for them, and are seeking to emigrate. This is difficult, because many desirable countries will only let a few Hong Kong nationals in, often basing their immigration policy on the amount of money the immigrant has. Latin America, Asia and the Middle East abound in regimes that limit the amount of money their nationals can take abroad, while the wealthy rack their brains to find ways of getting money out. Even clean, civilized Sweden is the enemy of the rich, with its draconian tax laws, and many wealthy Swedes have found it necessary to leave permanently.

Most people, perhaps, would like to keep their money at home, all things being equal. The reason people take their money abroad is generally to protect it, rather than out of greed for more; having everything in one place makes it vulnerable, as history has proved over and over again.

The important thing to remember about tax havens is that they are vulnerable to change. Simply putting your money in a tax haven and forgetting about it is unwise; you have to keep on top of developments that may affect your investments. Each tax haven has different laws and different prospects, and all are vulnerable to pressure from foreign governments. To make a tax haven work for you, you generally have to be resident there, or to form a company based there. This doesn't mean that you have to live there all the time; you can usually qualify by simply renting a property on a long lease. Holding an investment portfolio through a bank or trustee in a tax haven, and keeping the physical securities in another country, gives you the benefit of low or no taxes, freedom from any future currency controls and protects you from the dangers of expropriation. Thus, as your deal-making and income-earning abilities are likely to be confined to a higher-tax country, the best time to make the move is when you can afford to live off your investment income indefinitely – hence the large numbers of retired people in tax havens. Tax havens offer some opportunities to people who are still trying to accumulate capital, but it is expensive and can be difficult legally, especially if you find that you have to return home permanently at some point.

If you are intrigued by tax havens and want to investigate further, it is worth visiting them in person; detailed information is easier and cheaper to obtain on the spot, rather than going to consultants in other countries, and many schemes and wrinkles cannot be advertised in the countries where they are of the most interest. Remember that many countries don't tax money held abroad unless it is 'repatriated', so if you spend income from your overseas assets abroad you may not need to move to a tax haven.

Languages

People who don't speak another language are shooting themselves in the foot; the best opportunities are for the multilingual investor, so take the trouble to learn a language or two, and don't be afraid to go to countries where they don't speak your native tongue.

OFFSHORE TRUSTS AND COMPANIES – ARE THEY WORTH IT?

I believe that the short answer for smaller investors is generally 'No'; hordes of parasitical professionals exist who are only too keen to set you up with any number of paper organizations which have a curious tendency to be expensive to run. Usually you must appoint company officials and trustees who are resident in the tax haven concerned, and while you can make every effort to ensure that such individuals are *bona fide*, they may be vulnerable to outside pressure in a crisis. If your objective is principally to protect your capital, and you are prepared to live a fairly mobile life, it is generally cheaper and safer to keep control of your assets by, as far as possible, gaining domicile in a tax haven, understanding the tax regimes of the countries where you spend your time, and carefully diversifying your portfolio, trading through banks and brokers situated in tax havens other than your own. Trusts are examined in detail in Chapter 6; if you are committed to remaining in your own country there is a case for having a trust in a tax haven in favour of dependants in order to avoid inheritance tax.

Avoiding the sharks

People who are trying to evade tax illegally in their own countries are the prime targets of sharks. The reason is simple; if a shark steals their money, the tax evaders can do nothing about it without inviting the attentions of their tax authorities. Some people are always trying to be too clever, and are suckers for complicated schemes that they don't really understand. Changing your domicile is a far cheaper, safer, and above all, legal, move than setting up over-complex schemes that may not be accepted by the tax collectors.

Dual nationality

All the countries that are members of the UN have agreed to its 'Universal Declaration of Human Rights', issued in 1948 which states that no one should be arbitrarily denied the right to change his nationality. While countries and passport officers don't particularly like it, dual nationality gives the private investor enormous scope for 'arbitrage', in the sense that it is possible to exploit differences in the regulations between different countries. The US is one of the few countries where it is usually illegal to hold dual nationality, which some regard as a disgraceful attack on civil liberties. There are many ways to obtain a second passport; the cheapest methods are through marriage, ancestry and religion. Specialist immigration lawyers can advise on your particular needs and opportunities. Clearly, some passports are worth more than others – try travelling around the world on an Israeli, Lebanese or Syrian passport, or one from an African country if you want to experience how the less-advantaged half of the world lives! Many people are eager to get US nationality, but while it may be better than being, say, from Paraguay, my view is that most other First World passports are an infinitely better bet. Most countries are hypocritical enough to give passports to people who are able to pay for them, often by 'investing' in the country concerned, and this may be worth while as a last resort. This fascinating area is covered in detail in Chapter 9.

2
TAX ON INDIVIDUALS

There is a simple way for British people to avoid direct tax completely; leave the UK forever with all your assets and move to a tax haven. The trouble is that most people don't want to do this. Tax havens are not necessarily the most desirable places to live, and many people have responsibilities at home which they feel they cannot abandon. If you are prepared to leave the country forever though, you don't have to stay in a tax haven all the time. For adventurous types, becoming a perpetual traveller is an option (see Chapter 9). Even those who are not prepared to leave may be able to save tax by using offshore centres; it just means that life is more complicated.

Tax is a burden on everyone in society, from the richest to the poorest, and the rules are Byzantine in their twisted incomprehensibility. Use an accountant, even if you don't have much money; a good one – often these are provincial, and charge very reasonable fees – will stop you getting into a mess and should be able to save you substantial amounts of money. Some people think that you can monkey with the Inland Revenue in the way that you can with some other government departments. Don't – you won't have a prayer. When it comes to collecting its revenue, the state apparatus loses its kindly, socialist face and gets very tough indeed. Nevertheless, there is scope for considerable tax saving if you are prepared to study the rules. This chapter can only scratch the surface of the subject, but it should give you some food for thought. Remember, though, that the rules are always changing, so always take professional advice. In this chapter we will look at:

- Tax avoidance and tax evasion – why avoidance is legal and desirable
- The Ramsay doctrine, which is applied in the UK to prevent blatant tax avoidance moves
- Tax-planners' tactics

- Residence, ordinary residence and domicile – how these different categories affect your tax status
- Double-taxation treaties
- The UK as a tax haven

- Income tax – the current allowances and reliefs in the UK
- Tax relief on investment income
- Capital Gains Tax (CGT) – how to reduce your liability
- Offshore trusts and CGT
- Inheritance Tax – why it is never too early to make a will, and some ideas on how to plan for passing on your estate
- Lifetime gifts
- Husbands and wives
- Husbands and wives with foreign domiciles of origin
- Estate planning
- Deeds of variation
- Trusts and IHT
- Reservation of benefit
- Tax avoidance through starting a limited company
- Working abroad

> 'If everybody minded their own business', said the Duchess in a hoarse growl, 'the world would go round a deal further than it does.'
>
> LEWIS CARROLL, *Alice's Adventures in Wonderland*

TAX AVOIDANCE AND TAX EVASION

Tax avoidance is when you make efforts to legally reduce or avoid paying tax by exploiting the complexity of the rules. Tax evasion is exactly the same thing, except that you break the law. The right to avoid tax is well-established and, to paraphrase Lord Clyde's comments in a famous tax case of 1929, a person does nothing wrong by arranging his or her affairs to take advantage of the rules, so long as they are not broken. The extraordinary complexity and unfairness of tax legislation means that in practice there are many circumstances in which a layperson could not possibly tell the difference between avoidance and evasion. Nevertheless you should make sure you use the very best adviser you can find, and do all that you can to stay within the law.

The Ramsay doctrine

The Ramsay doctrine is a set of principles in dealing with tax avoidance. It sets out the rule that when making arrangements to reduce tax, no artificial steps can be taken. This relates to the situation where no fraudulent steps are taken which could be construed as tax evasion, but the primary motive overall is to avoid tax. However, you can avoid the doctrine if you arrange the steps so that either they are not under your control the whole time, or that someone else receives a partial benefit from them during part of the sequence.

Tax-planners' tactics

For well-to-do people who have no intention of ever leaving the UK, the principal worry is Inheritance Tax (IHT). Many people avoid IHT by getting their assets out of the country before death (see page 32), which may also be beneficial when it comes to receiving state health benefits. In the UK, there is an iniquitous trend towards pauperizing the old – if an old person has to go into a state nursing home, for example, their assets will be used to pay for the service until they are used up entirely. If such a person had transferred assets abroad into an offshore company or a trust, the DSS may have difficulty in enforcing this rule as their powers are far more limited than those of the Inland Revenue. This also throws up an interesting idea; in cases where the Inland Revenue disputes avoidance measures and is taking steps to try to prove evasion, one of the main tests of whether a crime has been committed is the dominant motive of the accused. If it could be shown that the dominant motive of the accused was DSS avoidance, rather than tax evasion, it could keep the accused out of jail!

Really good tax lawyers can be worth their fees; the reality of the British tax regime is that the Inland Revenue's interpretation of the laws is not always the same as that of the courts, and although a prolonged court battle may be something of a Pyrrhic victory, if enough money is involved it may be worthwhile in making IHT avoidance plans with this contingency in mind. A tax lawyer will set up a good position which can be strongly argued and which is of such complexity that it creates a kind of smokescreen that requires many years to work out, with a good chance of reaching a favourable settlement.

RESIDENCE OUTSIDE THE UK

If you are legally resident outside the UK, you only have to pay UK tax on income arising in Britain. Tax havens charge their residents little or no tax, and wealthy people have often found it necessary to move to a tax haven for this reason. Residence has nothing to do with nationality or passports. Currently (1997) anyone who works outside the UK for more than 365 days will not normally pay UK Income Tax, provided they do not visit the UK for more than a sixth of this period.

Ordinary residence

'Ordinary residence' is a strange notion, quite distinct from residence. As it is the main criterion for CGT, it is important to get the Inland

Revenue to agree that you are 'not ordinarily resident' before you make a capital gain, if you want to avoid the tax. You can be resident in more than one country at the same time, but 'ordinarily resident' in only one country at a time. It's relatively easy to work through this nonsense if you are leaving for ever, but it can cause serious problems if you return to the UK within three years as the Inland Revenue may decide that you were ordinarily resident in the UK for the whole time you were away, and ask for the CGT on any capital gains you made during that time.

Domicile

Domicile is another strange notion, quite distinct from 'residence' or 'ordinary residence'. If you are not domiciled in the UK, you are not liable for tax except on the money that you bring into the country. There are two kinds of domicile; 'domicile of origin' and 'domicile of choice'. Your domicile of origin is usually the country where your father was domiciled when you were born. If you have a domicile of origin outside the UK, you can live in the UK for a long time without ever having to pay UK tax.

Domicile of choice is more tricky; you have to be resident in a country and have 'the intention of permanent or indefinite residence' there. If you want to change from a UK domicile, you must intend never to return for anything more than brief, infrequent visits, or the Inland Revenue will say that you haven't changed your domicile.

Unlike many other people, the British have a curious fear of emigrating. It really is not as bad as it sounds – life in many other countries can be better than in the UK, especially if you are affluent and capable of adapting. Nor will you lose out on culture or modern conveniences; in fact, you may find more of them in other countries than there are in Britain.

DOUBLE-TAXATION TREATIES

A double-taxation treaty is an agreement between two states designed to mitigate the effects of tax on people and companies that do business in both countries. If two countries do not have a treaty, income arising in one country may be taxed there under a withholding tax rule, and then taxed again when it arrives in another country. Although there is a model international agreement, there is great variation in the details of different treaties. Strong trading countries have superior bargaining power and are generally able to force agreements which are favourable to them. Treaties may exempt withholding tax entirely from income going abroad, or they may mitigiate it. A general principle is that no country will collect another country's taxes, and, in general, will not enforce another country's tax regulations. Individuals are rarely extradited for tax evasion in a foreign country, although it does occur. For well-established concerns that lack the flexibility to switch jurisdictions quickly, international tax planning is done to make the best use of double-taxation treaties rather than to avoid them; it is, after all, better to have high profits that are taxed tolerably than to have low profits that are not taxed at all.

THE UK AS A TAX HAVEN

For people with a foreign domicile of origin, the UK has some of the characteristics of a tax haven. This presents tax-saving opportunities for UK-domiciled people who have a foreign-domiciled spouse. For instance, a British man with, say, a Chinese wife can transfer all of his savings into her name and invest the money offshore. If the wife is living in the UK, the income from the investment will only be taxable if it is brought into Britain. If you have to import some of the money, carefully arrange the investments so that they are separated into capital and income, and only bring in capital, which is not subject to tax. In addition, if income is withdrawn just before the end of a tax year and transferred into a UK non-interest-bearing account after the beginning of the new tax year, it will not be subject to Income Tax. This is because income is only taxable if the source of the income exists in the tax year in which the income is imported. Another possibility is that the Chinese wife can give the money to her husband by transferring it into an offshore account in the name of the husband, who can then import the money free of tax as it is a gift between spouses and not income. The husband is not allowed to spend the money on his wife as it would not then be treated as a gift.

INCOME TAX

The Income Tax rates often change; the 1997/98 rates are 20 per cent on taxable earnings of £4,100 or less, 23 per cent, known as the basic rate, on earnings between £4,101 and £26,100, and 40 per cent, the higher rate, on earnings above £26,100. People who are employed are taxed at source through the PAYE (pay as you earn) system.

The allowances are:

- **Personal Allowance.** Everyone, including children, has an annual personal allowance, £4,045, which is free of tax.
- **Married Couple's Allowance.** A married man can claim an extra annual allowance of £1,830 or transfer it to his wife.
- **Age Allowance**. If you are aged between 65 and 74 and earn less than £15,600, you get a personal allowance of £5,220, and if you are aged 75 or over, you get a personal allowance of £5,400. The married couple's allowance is £3,185. For people over 75, the personal allowance is £5,400 and the married couple's allowance is £3,225. Age allowances are reduced by £1 for every £2 of income in excess of £15,600, but are not reduced below the normal personal allowances.
- Single parents get an extra allowance of £1,830.
- There are other allowances for the blind and for a widow in the first year after her husband's death.

As well as the allowances, there are also 'reliefs' on the following:

- The interest you pay on the first £30,000 of a mortgage on your main home is eligible for tax relief.
- The interest on a mortgage to purchase rental property can receive relief, but check the rules with your accountant.
- Interest on a loan to be used for a business.
- If you sign a covenant to give money annually for more than three years to a charity, you can deduct tax at your rate, and the charity can reclaim the deducted tax.
- A one-off gift to charity of over £250 is treated in the same way.
- If you are over 60, you may be able to get tax relief on private medical insurance; check the rules with your accountant.

- Within certain limits, pension contributions get tax relief.
- If you are self-employed, you can claim a wide range of business expenses against tax. If you are employed, it may be possible to do this, but it is much more difficult in practice.

Tax relief on investment income

Interest, which is taxable if you are a taxpayer, is paid gross on the following:

- Bank deposits and building society deposits, if you register as a non-taxpayer.
- Gilts purchased through the National Savings Stock Register.
- National Savings Bank investment accounts.
- National Savings Bank Capital Bonds.
- National Savings Bank Income Bonds.
- Some offshore accounts.

Interest is paid net of tax on the following:

- Bank deposits and building society deposits, if you do not register as a non-taxpayer.
- Shares and bonds.
- Unit trusts and investment trusts.
- The income portion of annuities.

You get tax-free income from the following:

- TESSAs
- PEPs
- SAYE and National Savings Certificates growth.

A checklist for the essentials of income tax saving

- Check your assessments carefully, and claim all your entitlements. Even low earners can benefit by using an accountant.
- Keep up to date with the tax-free investments available, and make an annual review where you consider how much you should be investing in them.

- **Higher taxpayers should consider using trusts** (see page 103).
- **Use mortgage relief if possible.**
- **If you are self-employed, make sure you claim all your business expenses.**
- **Take advice on how to use your company car.**
- **Take advantage of benefits in kind offered by your employer.**

'HIDDEN' TAXES

As well as Income Tax, Capital Gains Tax and Inheritance Tax, there are also all kinds of taxes on things that you buy, such as VAT. They don't seem to be taxes, because they are included in the price, but they are. Spend your money in lower-tax countries where possible.

CAPITAL GAINS TAX (CGT)

CGT is tax on the profits you make on an asset, charged at different rates according to your income. Almost all assets will be chargeable to either Income Tax or to CGT. However, it is possible through tax planning to influence how money is treated, to take advantage of the different reliefs which apply to the two taxes. Gambling winnings and damages awarded for defamation are tax free. Cars are also exempt from CGT as most cars are sold at a loss. If you invest in classic cars, and can convince the Inland Revenue that you are not trading in them, you can keep your profits from their sale tax free.

Everyone has an annual exemption from CGT of £6,500 (1997/98), but this only applies to a particular year and cannot be carried forward. Thus, if you make no profits for four years and then make a profit of £25,000 in the fifth year, you will have to pay CGT, while if you had made £5,000 profit a year for five years you would have avoided CGT altogether.

If you are going to realize a gain that is subject to CGT, you can take advantage of timing. Disposing of an asset just after 5 April (the end of the tax year) will give you a whole year before you have to pay over the CGT, so you can benefit from the use of the money, and the interest it can earn, during that time. The 'date of disposal' of an asset is a thorny subject; the Inland Revenue say that it is the date of the contract, not the date on which you received payment, so if, for example, you signed a contract to sell a company where you received payment over a period of years, you would be liable for CGT on the whole amount in the first year. One way around this is to arrange for 'cross options' between you and a purchaser, where you sell an option to buy the asset and the purchaser sells you an option to insist on the sale – great care must be taken over the wording of such a deal.

Gifts between husband and wife are tax free as long as they are genuine, which can help you to take advantage of two amounts of annual exemption rather than one. The gift cannot be made after the sale of the asset. You can also take advantage of your children's annual exemptions (even if they are babies), but the rules are trickier; once again, the gifts must be absolutely genuine.

Capital gains that you make through inflation are given 'indexation relief' to take the decreasing value of cash into account. In addition, if you are selling an asset which you bought before 31 March 1982, the gain is calculated on the difference between the 31.3.82 value and the sale value, and then you can claim indexation relief on top. There is also some indexation relief for capital losses, but the government are tightening up on the rules.

If you are a higher-rate taxpayer, you can reduce the amount of CGT payable by transferring an asset into a trust which can then sell it and pay CGT at the lowest rate. The proceeds can go to your children, for example, but not to you or your spouse, or the CGT will be charged at your tax rate, not the trust's.

Your main residence and up to half a hectare of its garden is exempt from CGT. If you move and have trouble selling your old house, you have up to three years in which to sell it without losing any CGT relief. If you normally own two houses, you can switch main residences from time to time, which can reduce CGT when you combine it with the three-year rule.

Suppose your house has grounds that are much larger than half a hectare. You may still obtain exemption on the excess if you can show that it is necessary for 'the reasonable enjoyment' of the house.

If you use part of your house as an office or other business premises, you may be claiming some of the running costs against Income Tax. This can cause a problem when you sell as the Inland Revenue may claim that the business part of your house is subject to CGT. If, however, you can show that no part of your house was used exclusively for business, you will be exempt from CGT.

If you own a business and sell it, the proceeds are usually subject to CGT, but if you are over 55 you can get retirement relief. Otherwise, you could transfer the business from the company to a new one and then sell it, which can reduce the amount of CGT.

Another relief for businesses is 'rollover relief'; if you sell certain categories of business assets and use the money to replace them, you can deduct the gain on the old asset from the price you paid for the new one. The new assets could be for a completely different kind of business – they don't have to be identical to the ones you sold. If you sell a business to your spouse, you will not have to pay CGT on the money you receive, while your spouse may claim rollover relief on the price paid. Groups of companies are like husbands and wives in this respect; you can transfer assets from one company to another, avoiding tax and getting rollover relief. To obtain rollover relief, the new assets must be bought between one and three years after the old ones were sold. If you are planning to move abroad permanently, rollover relief can be used to buy foreign assets, delaying CGT until you have become exempt from it as a foreign resident.

CGT on stocks and shares

You must keep complete records for all your share dealings. If you buy shares in the same company at different times, the indexation and CGT is worked out on the cost of the 'pool' of shares (i.e. the total number of shares you have bought). Get your accountant to show you how this works and, in particular, the tricky calculations for enhanced scrip dividends, where a company buys back scrip issues at a good price.

For the sale or gift of unquoted shares, the Inland Revenue will accept your valuation of any 'arm's length' deal, where the two parties are not closely associated, but otherwise they may insist on valuing the shares themselves.

You can use your annual exemptions to the full if you own shares by selling enough of them at the end of each year to realize a CGT-free gain and then immediately buying them back at the beginning of the next year. This technique is called a 'bed and breakfast operation'.

Some securities, such as gilts, are exempt from CGT.

If you are married, take full advantage of your exemptions by dividing your shares accordingly.

Offshore trusts and CGT

Before 1991 the CGT rules regarding offshore trusts were not strict, and many UK residents were able to use them to avoid paying this tax. The principle applied that if the trustees were not resident in the UK, capital gains made by the trust assets were not taxable, although UK beneficiaries were taxed on distributions. Keeping the value of a distribution low would mitigate the tax, and beneficiaries could receive loans from the trust or have the use of assets belonging to the trust while paying a lower amount of tax. Sadly, the rules have changed and it is now more difficult to benefit in this way from offshore trusts. Since 1991 trust assets have been subject to an exit charge when they leave the UK. Furthermore, if the settlor has 'an interest in the trust', where the settlor, the settlor's spouse, their children or their children's spouses, can benefit from the trust, then the trust's assets will attract CGT. The settlor's parents, grandparents and siblings are not included in this rule, so it is possible to create offshore trusts using such relatives and avoid the exit charge, although CGT will be payable on distributions to beneficiaries in the UK. Offshore trusts that are created by a will can also avoid the exit charge.

INHERITANCE TAX (IHT)

If you care at all about the people you will leave behind when you die it is extremely selfish not to make a will. Intestacy, or dying without a will, causes a great deal of expenditure and unnecessary suffering for your heirs – the state and the professionals will profit at their expense. Despite this, a very large number of people with assets die intestate, often because of a superstitious feeling that making a will may somehow hasten death. Making a will is inexpensive – there are even standard forms you can buy that will do the job – so it is really inexcusable not to make provision for how your possessions will be divided up after your death. It is advisable to use a solicitor when drawing up a will, because it is easy to make a mistake which renders it technically invalid; the fee should not usually be more than £100.

Key points to remember when drawing up a will

- **Choose executors who you trust.** An executor is a person who agrees to take the responsibility for seeing that the legal formalities of dividing an inheritance are done properly. I believe that you should never appoint a solicitor, bank, or some other professional as an executor; their fees are likely to be out of all proportion to the value of the work they do, and in the despair of bereavement no one will want to fight them over their fees. It is quite extraordinary how often estates are shamelessly ransacked in this way. Any reasonably responsible person can do the executor's job, and a solicitor can always be engaged (at a much lower rate) to advise on technical matters. Have at least two executors, to avoid problems if one dies at the same time as you, or is too busy to do the work.

- **Think long and hard about who you want to leave your money to.** Don't try to play God, punishing the 'bad' ones of your family and rewarding the good – this often results in disputes. If possible, leave everything to one person, such as your spouse, who you can rely on to care for the others who you want to help.

- **Plan carefully to legally avoid as much Inheritance Tax as possible.** This is discussed in more detail below; the main point to remember is that proper planning can massively reduce the bite the state will take out of your money. Regularly review your will with an accountant and a solicitor, and adjust it to take any new legislation into account.

- **Have a substitute beneficiary in your will** in case the first ones die at the same time as you do – in a car crash, for example.

A dead person's assets (the 'estate') is taxed in three ways, through Inheritance Tax (IHT), Income Tax and Captial Gains Tax. Inheritance Tax must be planned for; it is a tax not only on the 'final disposal', which is the amount you leave when you die, but also on some gifts made during your lifetime. It's no good handing over all your money to your heirs on your death bed to avoid IHT – it won't work.

IHT is currently (1997) charged at 40 per cent on disposals totalling more than £215,000. If your estate, including chargeable lifetime disposals, comes to less than this, no IHT is payable. Valuations of property must be agreed with the Inland Revenue, and the rules are complex. Woodland and agricultural property get special relief, as can the transfer of an interest in a business.

Lifetime gifts

- Gifts up to £3,000 per year are exempt, and can be carried forward for one year.

- Gifts of up to £250 per year, per donee are also exempt, in addition to the £3,000 mentioned above. Thus, you can give away £250 a year to, say, ten people.

- Gifts between spouses are exempt if both are domiciled in the UK.

- Normal, regular spending out of income is exempt.

- Wedding gifts of cash up to certain limits are exempt.

- Charitable and political gifts are exempt, with no upper limit.

- Family maintenance payments are exempt.

- Gifts, however large, which are made more than seven years before your death are exempt.

- Some gifts and payments into some kinds of trusts are exempt only if the donor lives for seven years after the gift is made. These are called Potentially Exempt Transfers (PETs). There is a sliding scale of tax rate depending on the length of time between the gift and your death if you die within seven years.

- Gifts into discretionary trusts are fully chargeable.

- Gifts with a Reservation of Benefit (GROBs) can catch people out; if you give away your house but go on living in it, it is a GROB, and chargeable. The rules governing GROBs are nightmarish, so professional help is necessary.

Husbands and wives

As was mentioned above, gifts between spouses who are both domiciled in the UK are exempt of IHT; this includes gifts made upon death. For high net worth individuals this may create other problems as the surviving spouse may have less time and less ability to take steps to avoid IHT on their own death. The first step is usually to give £215,000, the IHT-free alowance, to someone who is not your spouse or to put it in trust for the benefit of your spouse. Ideally, both spouses should have £215,000 each in their estates to take full advantage of the tax-free threshold.

Husbands and wives with foreign domiciles of origin

In this case gifts on death are only exempted up to £55,000. However, if your foreign spouse is given assets during your lifetime (which are tax free under the seven-year rule, see page 34), he or she can invest them abroad and they would not then be subject to Inheritance Tax on the death of either of the spouses. One way of ensuring that such a move is accepted by the Inland Revenue is to transfer your assets to an offshore company in, say, Jersey, and then give the shares of that company to your spouse – the seven-year rule would not then apply.

Estate planning

For people with assets far above the threshold for IHT, estate planning can be quite extraordinarily complex. It is therefore worth paying for the best advice you can get. Trusts may play an important part in the plan. Becoming resident in a tax haven with no death duties is desirable.

Most people are reluctant to give away large sums long before they die; inflation, the increased health expenses and lack of earning power in old age can easily get you into trouble when you are at your most helpless. One doesn't know when one is going to die, so it is foolhardy to budget at retirement age for one's own death at, say, 85, when one might hang on until the age of 93. In addition, you may well feel reluctant to give control of large sums to family members who are not mature enough to handle them. Human development being what it is, many people don't really 'grow up' until their parents die.

Deeds of variation

If the beneficiaries of a will see that there are tax advantages to be gained by changing the will, they can write a deed of variation within two years of the death. If the value of the assets in the estate increases during this period, the value can be made to 'drop out' for tax purposes by taking full advantage of the various allowances.

Trusts and IHT

Trusts separate the control over assets, the entitlement to capital and the entitlement to income. You must appoint trustees of complete integrity, as they will be responsible for the administration of the trust's assets, and you can instruct them on who will get the income and who will get the capital.

If you own a company, employee trusts can be used to avoid IHT. If you create an employee trust through your will after you have died, you can leave your shares to employees, who can be family members, provided that they each own less than 5 per cent of the company already.

If you own a company whose value you expect to increase, you could transfer up to £215,000-worth of shares into a discretionary trust; there would be no IHT to pay, and you could get a CGT benefit as well on the gain.

Reservation of benefit

GROBs, mentioned above, offer a few loopholes. For instance, although you may not reserve a benefit for yourself when you give something away, you can reserve a benefit for your spouse in the gift without it being subject to IHT. Another wrinkle is to give a lease on your house to your spouse, or to yourselves jointly, and give away the freehold, which will have a much lower value during the term of the lease, and thus reduce the amount of tax.

CGT on trusts

Trusts pay CGT, and have a lower annual exemption than people do, unless the settlor or the settlor's spouse has an interest, in which case their own exemptions come into play. Trusts pay 25 per cent CGT unless some or all of their income is liable to Income Tax, in which case CGT is charged at the higher rate. Cash held by trusts is exempt from CGT.

STARTING A COMPANY

If you are not business-minded, it may never have occurred to you that forming a limited company to hold some or all of your assets, including shares, can be a useful way of reducing taxes. Company law is complicated, and cannot be dealt with in full in this book, but here are some of the advantages.

Changing from being self-employed to having a company

If you are self-employed and your earnings are increasing, there may come a point when it becomes worth while to transfer the business into a limited company to keep profits taxed at 25 per cent, which is the 'small companies' rate' of Corporation Tax on profits up to £300,000, rather than having to pay Income Tax at the higher rate. Another advantage is that because self-employed people are taxed on a preceding year basis it is possible, with careful planning, to choose to cease trading as a self-employed person at a time when you are making large profits, and avoid paying tax on a large proportion of them due to the 'drop out' effect; get your accountant to explain how this works. You can then transfer your business to your new company.

Tax relief on borrowing

If you withdraw a large sum of money from your company and it then borrows the same amount from a bank, the company's borrowing attracts tax relief on the total interest paid, which makes it cheaper than if you borrowed it personally. You have to do this in the order described; it's no use having your company borrow the money first and then withdrawing it for your own use, as the Inland Revenue may deny you the relief.

Working abroad

If you work overseas for part of each year, and make yourself an employee of your own limited company, you can obtain a 100 per cent deduction for your foreign earnings, so long as you stagger your trips abroad carefully over a 365-day period; you need not be working for all of the time that you are abroad – holidays can be included, for instance, due to a genuine loophole in the rules. Once again, get your accountant to explain how this works.

Ex-gratia payments

Otherwise known as golden handshakes, ex-gratia payments made by a company to employees when they leave the company are tax free up to £30,000. Such a payment must be entirely separate from any contractual obligation that a company has to the employee.

3

PROSPERING AS
AN EXPATRIATE

Many people still take 'expatriate' to mean someone in a pith helmet running a plantation in the colonies, but these days expatriates are mostly employees of large companies who are sent abroad on relatively short assignments. This chapter is about the employment packages of expatriates as the better the deal is the more you can save, and once you have savings the rest of this book becomes relevant. The chapter covers:

- The benefits of expatriate employment
- Financial advisers
- No one is too poor to benefit from working overseas!
- What companies offer
- Negotiating the package
- Insurance
- Social security
- Foreign service premiums
- Hardship
- Exchange rate fluctuations

- Tax protection
- Tax equalization
- Tax pooling
- Payment net of taxes
- High inflation countries
- The balance sheet system
- Cost of living allowance
- Cost of housing
- Calculating the balance sheet
- Local salary packages
- The international salary method
- Pensions

> ' I give to get.'
>
> ARMAND HAMMER, late founder of Occidental Petroleum,
> and employer of many expats.

THE BENEFITS OF EXPATRIATE EMPLOYMENT

For most of us, a spell as an expatriate is probably the best chance we have of rapidly accumulating capital. However, many expats fail to do this successfully during their time abroad. This chapter examines the common pitfalls – many of which are to do with the deal you make with your employer before beginning the assignment – and how to avoid them. Even if you don't intend to spend much of your life overseas, your primary financial objective should be to save enough money so that you have greater financial freedom in the future. Being an expatriate offers you the chance to save much more of your income than you could expect to at home, especially if you exploit the many opportunities for avoiding tax. The principal benefits are:

- **Your salary is not subject to the overheads of living at home.**

- **In many cases you may receive your pay net of tax.**

- **You may be working in a country with a 'nil tax' regime, for example if you work in parts of the Middle East.**

- **Many expats enjoy free or subsidized housing overseas.**

- **You can receive an income by letting your house at home.**

- **Expat packages often include paid education for children, company cars, 100 per cent health cover and big expense allowances.**

- **You may receive a 'foreign service premium' and a cost of living allowance which you do not need to spend.**

- **In countries with a low cost of living, the adaptable expat can reduce living expenses massively by living and eating as the locals do.**

Suppose you are on a three-year assignment and find you can save £6,000 a month – which is not an impossible figure for many professionals. By the end of your term you should be able to accumulate around a quarter of a million pounds in safe investments, without having paid tax on the interest or any Capital Gains Tax. By getting your contract of employment right and investing wisely, you can increase your returns dramatically.

Financial advisers

The bane of the expatriate are the overseas financial advisers who form a mini-industry parasitizing expat communities. After a few months in the new job, you will probably get a friendly telephone call from one; these individuals trawl for punters in clubs, golf courses and bars where expats congregate, and get to hear about anyone who has recently arrived. Genuine Independent Financial Advisers (IFAs) can be very good indeed, but some concentrate on maximizing the commissions, retainers and bonuses they receive from the financial institutions who seek your savings without regard to your best interests. Beware the tied advisers such as insurance salespeople who basically want to sell you only one or two products out of the thousands which are available. In particular, watch out for:

● **Investments related to obscure stock markets which are not well regulated.**

● **Investments promising unusually high returns (say, above 20 per cent a year). They may be more risky than you think.**

● **Investments in companies you have never heard of.**

● **Investments involving a highly complex series of transactions which you will not be able to check yourself.**

● **Illegal activities – confidence tricksters prey on people who are tempted to break the rules, knowing that there will be no comeback because the investor has been compromised and will not complain to the authorities.**

My preference is to use IFAs on a fee-only basis, getting their agreement to rebate any commissions they receive to you, the investor. This way you know what you are letting yourself in for at the beginning. The fee may seem high, but a good IFA is probably worth it, and you can use the arrangement as a basis for comparison with other offers. In addition, it makes it easier for you to break the relationship when you want to. British expats are currently allowed to start insurance-linked offshore savings plans to which they can continue to contribute after returning home. If you set up such a plan properly you can save almost all tax on interest and capital gains. As tax-saving is the biggest advantage the expat has, you should never commit yourself to an investment without thoroughly understanding the tax implications.

No one is too poor to benefit from working overseas!

Holding investments offshore is not only for the rich, particularly if you are temporarily resident overseas and, ideally, working in a low-tax or no-tax country. Consider the effects of compounding; the higher the rate of return on your savings, the faster the money will grow and, as many secure offshore investments pay interest and dividends gross (untaxed), you can often obtain a better return while you are overseas than you would in an equivalent UK investment.

Many overseas workers are pleasantly surprised by the amount they save during a spell abroad. Even with the same salary as you earn in the UK you may well be able to save most of what you would have paid in tax at home.

Although your overseas earnings would not qualify for UK pension contributions, the trend towards short-term contracts has made the prospect of working for two or three years abroad at a higher salary increasingly attractive to many people. If you plan to return to the UK or are unsure about your future and you do not already own a home in the UK, one option to consider is the purchase of a UK property with your overseas savings. A specialist international tax solicitor at a UK law firm says;

'If you are a student, most double taxation treaties provide a clause allowing you to escape tax in the country where you are working, but anyone who works outside the UK for more than 365 days will not normally pay UK income tax, provided that any UK visits do not exceed a sixth of the period you are abroad. Thus, in any 365 days you are working abroad, you must not spend more than 62 days in the UK.'

Higher earners may need to invest money offshore during their time abroad as well; when they return to the UK they will pay tax on their offshore investment income even if it is not brought back into the country. The solicitor continues:

'I normally recommend that people dispose of such assets before they return or dispose of them and re-acquire them on their return in a bed and breakfasting operation, since you are certain then to avoid UK Capital Gains Tax on the gains you have made up to that point'.

'Even if you intend to hold investments, such as shares, offshore for the very long term and plan to retire abroad before selling them, I would still recommend that you do this for two reasons. First, because your plans may change and you may decide to retire in the UK, in which case the CGT liability could be very large and, second, because the tax laws may change in the future. Ireland and Canada have a CGT exit charge which hits people retiring abroad, and a similar rule could well be introduced here.'

Much depends on the tax rules of the country where you work. If the country has a low-tax regime, such as the United Arab Emirates, there will be few problems, but if you are working in a high-tax country, such as the USA, you may need professional advice to get the best out of the tax rules, in particular on the timing of your working periods abroad – a technique known as 'tax year arbitrage'.

Caroline Mackenzie, 28, is a typical example of the new generation of overseas workers. She has been employed in Japan for three years as an English teacher.

'I trained as a TEFL teacher, but they'll take anyone with a degree. I saw a job advertised in a UK newspaper and applied – the interview was not difficult and I went out straight away for a probationary period. I earned 250,000 yen a month after 6 per cent tax, which was then worth about £2,000, and saved about £4,000 in the first year, which I spent on three excellent foreign holidays.'

'Since then I got a better job, and have so far saved £15,000, most of which I have sent back to the UK. I'm planning to buy a house in Britain – several English people I know over here have saved enough to buy a small house outright, with no mortgage. The pound is so strong that my yen earnings aren't worth as much as they were before in sterling terms, but I'm still better off than I would be at home. Life here is good – I like the Japanese.'

The drawbacks are non-financial.

'Tokyo is very crowded and I don't like the climate. 3.5 million people pass through my train station every day, and everyone stares at me on the train because I look so different to them.'

You should make all your preparations before you take up your employment overseas and you should get advice from a specialist solicitor on your employment contract before you sign it. Read as much as you can about the country before you take the leap, and choose books with large address sections, especially if you are just starting to look for a job. Once you have found employment, make sure you can get home if everything goes wrong. For instance, you could take a credit card with a high enough spending limit to pay for flights home for the whole family in an emergency.

Unless you are an experienced investor, it may be wiser to begin saving by simply putting cash into an offshore bank account in, say, Jersey. Your UK bank may have offshore branches into which you can pay your savings by bank transfer from the country where you are working or you can open an account by letter. Anti-money laundering legislation has made offshore banks more cautious about new customers, but as long as you can prove that your earnings are legitimate, you will be able open an account.

Offshore funds vary enormously in the quality and degree of official supervision they receive, so expert independent advice is essential. London is arguably the most sophisticated world financial centre for assessing the true worth of foreign investments, so you are likely to get better investment advice in the UK than you would in most other countries.

Fluctuating exchange rates can catch out even the most sophisticated. One British employee of a Singapore bank, who asked not to be named, arranged to receive part of his salary in pounds and part in local currency when he began his job several years ago, basing his plans on the assumption that sterling would depreciate. With the increasing strength of the pound, he says that he would have been better off if he had stayed at home.

Despite the pitfalls, working abroad has become easier, and UK nationals' fears about the difficulty of establishing a new tax status are unfounded. Leaflet IR 20 from the Inland Revenue sets out the rules on residence in plain terms and, says a tax specialist, 'The calibre of Inland Revenue employees is improving. You will find them helpful in answering queries and, on the more problematical issues, they are hard but fair.'

Leaflet IR 20 is available from your local tax office or from the Inland Revenue, Somerset House, The Strand, London WC2 (0171 438 6622).

WHAT COMPANIES OFFER

At its best, life as an expat can be very good indeed. Picture this scene: you take up a five-year contract in a beautiful and exotic developing country. As a senior manager you are a member of the company's management bonus system, and you receive share options in the company each year. As an expatriate, you are getting:

- A foreign service premium (FSP).
- A hardship allowance (although you are not suffering any hardship).

- A cost of living allowance which is paid each month. Cornflakes and scotch are expensive because they are imported, but you find that you like the local food, which is very fresh and healthy, and you drink the local hooch. You tell your servant to shop in the markets, and only use Western food and drink when entertaining businesspeople.

- Your attractive house is provided free by your company.

- Your children go to a special school for foreigners – the fees are high, but the company pays them.

- In the summer term you take your family abroad on holiday; the company pays for first class air fares.

- The locals drive like maniacs, and penalties for accidents are heavy. For this reason the company insists that you have a chauffeur-driven car and that you do not drive yourself. The company pays for this, and allows the car to be freely used by your spouse. Dangers on the road are not the only reason you may be offered a company car; the difficulties of insuring a foreign driver and problems with importing and exporting your own car may also be factors. In addition, spouses may be unable to drive in some countries – for example, women are not allowed to drive in Saudi Arabia – so, far from being a perk, a chauffeur-driven car may actually be a necessity.

- Your local staff are enthusiastic and hard-working. You are amazed by the contrast between them and the demotivated individuals with whom you have had to work in your own country.

- Your office is well-appointed and a joy to work in.

- At lunchtime you go to a private club where there is a pool and a gym.

- In the evenings and at the weekends you take the family to another club with a wide range of facilities.

- The company has a boat which you can sometimes use.

Of course, it is not all paradise. You may feel that you are missing out on the jockeying for position at the company's headquarters back home – but remember that you have a clause in your contract giving you several years' salary as a lump sum if you leave the company. Meanwhile you are saving a huge portion of your salary, virtually tax free. All this may sound too good to be true, but for many expatriates it is the reality.

Negotiating the package

The time to worry about the details is at the outset when you are negotiating your terms. Companies are not all the same – not only are there several conflicting systems of remuneration in use amongst the big multinationals, but it is also a distinct possibility, especially if you are working for a small company, that your employers are not aware of issues which may severely reduce the value of your salary. The topics to look at are:

- **tax**
- **insurance**
- **social security**
- **pensions**
- **foreign exchange**
- **hardship levels**
- **foreign service premiums (FSP)**
- **cost of living allowance (COLA)**
- **home-based salary reference**
- **housing.**

Before considering these in detail, consider the main points of the contract:

- *What is your job title?*
- *What is the main location where you will be working?*
- *Is the contract for a fixed term?* Expatriate jobs are generally less stable than those at home, so make sure that there is a clause stating the expected duration of the assignment and the method of repatriation. Ideally you should get a guarantee of a job when you return home.
- *Are relocation costs covered?* Moving expenses can be high. Preferably the company should offer assistance with the practicalities, paying for costs with a lump sum. You may need to ask for initial travel costs and temporary accommodation as well.
- *Are there exchange controls in the country where you will be working?* It is not unknown for expatriates to find that they are stuck with a large amount of local currency which they are not allowed to take out of the country when they leave.

Insurance

Some companies offer schemes which give you an accidental disability policy which pays your full salary for 26 weeks followed by a further 26 weeks at 50 per cent of salary. This may require you to go home after the accident and receive a home-base salary once the illness/recovery period is known to be long term. It should give you an accidental death and disability benefit equivalent to four times your annual salary. Usually a 'home-base reference' salary is used to calculate this, which will be lower than your salary as an expatriate. The policy may have a reduced benefit for partial disability – for example, if you lose your sight or a limb – if you can get a job when you recover. It may be limited to occupational accidents, in which case you should take out extra insurance in case you have an accident on your own time. Often these policies will be equivalent to the cover you receive in your own country, but French and Dutch firms can be much more generous, offering lump sums of up to 12 times your annual salary for death resulting from occupational causes if you have children. These companies tend to have smaller pension benefits. Ask the following questions:

- *If I die how much will my family receive in addition to any widow's and orphans' pension?*
- *If I am accidentally disabled and can't work, how much will I get and for how long?*
- *Will these benefits be taxed? Is the tax avoidable?*
- *Will I be contributing to the cover? Are there compulsory or voluntary contributions to a social security scheme, or other deductions from my salary?*
- *Are these risks covered by insurance, company guarantee or by a state?*
- *If covered by insurance, is the insurance company based in my home country or in the country I will be working in?*
- *In the case of an accident or illness, is the salary my foreign service salary, or a notional home-based one?*
- *If I die, will my heirs get a lump sum or an annuity? Lump sums are often preferable as if they are properly managed they are more valuable than annuity, but it depends upon the amount offered.*
- *What is the waiting period for these payments?*

Poring over the details of the policies is essential – you must establish the potential value of the insurance. What you are offered will depend on your family status, your age, and the extent to which pension and insurance schemes that you already have, and in which you continue to participate, provide adequate 'death in service/early retirement owing to ill health' features. Another factor is the riskiness of the job itself; for example, if you are involved in dangerous construction work, the oil business or will be flying frequently in Third World countries, you should take extra care to get adequate cover.

Social security

The larger the company, the more likely it is to have a global social security programme. With smaller companies, the scheme may be local to the country where you will work. In both cases, difficulties often arise in conforming to compulsory provisions in the assignment country, especially in Western countries where state social security rules tend to be highly sophisticated. When designing their employment packages, some companies ignore the provisions of state and company sickness, insurance and workers' compensation schemes which may allow you to claim such benefits on top of what the company offers you. Other companies analyse the state benefits available in the country where you are working and build an integrated scheme for all their expats which meet a minimum global standard. If you are moving to a developed country you may find that your employer will apply the rules for local staff to you too. The main points to check are:

- **Make sure that you understand exactly what the benefits will be during your time abroad, and also if you will suffer any loss of rights in your home country because of your absence.**

- **Check whether or not you are required to make any social security contributions in the country of assignment – in the case of 'tax-equalised' packages (see page 53) this may reduce your take-home pay quite considerably.**

Foreign service premiums (FSP)

Foreign service premiums are widely used as a basic element of overseas allowances. They may be a percentage of your basic salary or simply a lump sum. If you are working for a company that only operates in developed countries this may be the only allowance you get, but multinationals, particularly those which frequently move employees from one expatriate job to another around the world, are likely to offer other allowances on top. If the FSP is a percentage of the basic salary, then it may have a ceiling – for example, the FSP may be 15 per cent of the first £2,000 of your monthly salary. There are some multinationals, however, that take the view that working abroad is a normal part of a manager's career, and offer no FSP at all.

Hardship

Every company has its own idea of the degree of hardship in a particular country. In general, the following locations are considered high on the hardship list:

- Libya
- Nigeria
- Central America
- parts of Indo-China
- parts of the ex-USSR.

These are places which are genuinely dangerous, and you can expect up to 100 per cent of your basic salary as a hardship allowance. There are many more locations which fall into a middle category, such as:

- much of Africa
- most of South America
- the Middle East
- particular cities, such as Mexico City, Beijing and Bangkok.

These are places which do cause some hardship, if only in the difficulty of adapting initially to local conditions. You can expect a hardship allowance of up to 50 per cent of your basic salary.

The criteria for hardship allowances tend to be chosen with a Western perspective, which can cause unfairness if the company employs people of many different nationalities. For example, an Egyptian expatriated to the north of England may suffer quite as much as a Yorkshireman in Cairo, if not more, but is unlikely to get a hardship allowance. A few enlightened employers appreciate this, and use the idea of 'cultural zones', categorized as:

- Europe, North America and Australasia
- South America
- Africa
- the Middle East
- Asia.

The idea is that an employee suffers less hardship when moving to a country within the same zone as the home country, and more when moving across zones. For example, the Egyptian moving to the north of England would get a hardship allowance, but would not if he or she were then moved to Morocco. Levels of hardship can be difficult to measure and disputes can arise, especially if a single manager or committee back in your own country is deciding this – perhaps making an annual review. Some companies use outside consultants to make these decisions, which has the benefit that if something goes wrong the consultants can be blamed. Consultants normally take a statistical approach, interviewing a representative sample of expatriate employees and devising a hardship or desirability rating for each country. This information can then be used to calculate a hardship weighting for each country, with security, quality of medicine and isolation all being taken into account. The climate, the food and the facilities for recreation may also be included – these are generally given less weight. Naturally this system can be used internally also – a committee of employees can be formed to set it up.

Exchange rate fluctuations

This is an interesting subject from an investment point of view, and is covered in more detail in Chapter 8. For the expat employee there is the danger of a generous salary going wrong because of it. Suppose a Briton working in Germany had agreed to be paid in sterling – over the last few years the pound has dropped against the mark by almost 30 per cent. Conversely, a Briton working in Singapore and paid in Singapore dollars would have gained by some 30 per cent over the last decade. Short-term fluctuations are less important than long-term trends, and you must take a view on your favourite currencies – mine are the Deutschemark, the Swiss franc and the Austrian schilling (and I am gloomy about sterling), but no one can predict the future, so if you guess wrongly you must accept the loss. If you have financial commitments in your home country, it may be desirable to ensure that some of your salary is paid in the home currency so that you can plan with confidence. In practice, most expatriate packages give you an element of salary protection so that you are cushioned against wild swings in currency or hyperinflation in the country of assignment. One way of doing this is the 'split salary'. This is where your salary is partly paid in your national currency and partly in the local currency. Some countries force employers to pay salaries entirely in local currency, which is highly undesirable. However, their authorities will be unlikely to be able to check your bank accounts back home, so with the co-operation of your employer it may be possible to get around this by a split salary system that is not declared in the assignment country. If you do this you must have faith in your employer's ability to help you if trouble arises. Most of the world is free of exchange controls at present, so normally your salary can be paid entirely in the home or host country. Some companies offer the expatriate the choice regarding what proportion should be paid where. The actual rate of exchange may be set once annually in the case of salary splits, which introduces a speculative element that you may be able to profit from, but a better system is to have the local currency portion adjusted more frequently – say every month or quarter – which ensures that you will not be worse off in home country terms. The deal which offers you the most freedom and profit potential is where you can choose any third currency and splits in any proportion. Well-established companies employing large numbers of expats will almost certainly have a system to protect you from exchange rate fluctuations, but smaller outfits may not appreciate the implications until it is too late. Make sure that you have currency protection in your employment contract before you take up the job.

Tax

When you are abroad you are often faced with difficulties in understanding a very different tax regime and bureaucratic ethos – and all in a foreign language. To some extent this is a lottery – the system in Dubai is entirely different to that in Finland – and the allowances and incentives will vary enormously. In your own country, your employer probably regards your tax affairs as your own business, but as an expatriate you can expect more assistance. Good companies will provide a package to suit the host country; state deductions can vary from 65 per cent to 0 per cent of the salary, and the tax thresholds, marginal rates and benefits in different countries vary just as widely. Remember that even within the EU, tax has not yet been harmonized. If you find that your employer regards tax as your responsibility, you may need professional help. If you are working in a very low-tax country this will not be too onerous, but going to a higher-tax country can cause a lot of problems. You can expect to be offered one of the following systems of dealing with tax:

- tax protection
- tax equalization
- tax pooling
- payment net of taxes.

Tax protection

This system is intended to ensure that the employee doesn't lose out when working in a high-tax country. After the tax bill is paid in the country of assignment, you show the company that you have paid more than you would have done at home, and the company refunds you the difference. If you have paid less, you can probably keep the difference.

Tax equalization

This is similar to tax protection, except that the calculations are not retrospective – everyone pays the equivalent of what they'd be paying at home. This is often used by US companies, because their own nationals are taxed in the US on worldwide income.

Tax pooling

Some companies apply a standard rate of tax to all their expatriate employees. The company pays all taxes in an assignment country and works out the average tax on all its expatriates which becomes the standard rate and is deducted from the salary. This works well for organizations which move their employees around a lot and operate in high-tax countries as well as low ones. In such cases a standard tax rate might be around 15 per cent, which is still low by Western standards.

Payment net of taxes

This system pays your salary net of tax in the assignment country, which has the benefit of removing the burden of dealing with tax from you and putting the whole issue into the hands of the company's accountants. It gives you a clear idea of what your 'take home' pay will actually be, but, like all deals which offer to solve your problems with no effort, it takes away your own opportunity for tax planning. There are many cases where the job is so demanding and the pay so good that a net of tax payment is the best deal.

High-inflation countries

You may find that you are working in a country where inflation is wildly out of control. This happened in South America in the 1980s, where it has only recently settled down, and is occuring in the ex-USSR states at present. Making an annual or quarterly adjustment will not be enough in places where inflation is 200 per cent a year or more. Your cost of living allowance (see page 55) will have to be adjusted much more frequently. Naturally, in such countries the last thing you want to have is cash savings in local currency, and there are likely to be emergency exchange controls and chaotic banking practice. Make sure that the portion of the salary which you are saving never enters the high-inflation country.

The balance sheet system

There is no real 'going rate' for most expatriate jobs; you may well find when you arrive in a country that people from other countries doing an identical job to you are being paid much more or much less. Much depends on your nationality – and this can work against you if, for example, potential employers feel that the British are poor value compared with the Indonesians and don't give you a chance to tell them how much you personally are prepared to work for (as opposed to the expectations of your compatriots). Remember that expatriates are very expensive for their companies, often costing three times what they would cost at home. There are many ways to work out the net value of an employment package, but one that is commonly used is the 'balance sheet' method. This developed after World War 2 when American companies were expanding all over the world and needed a logical system that could both be explained to their expatriate employees and be seen to be fair. The idea is to make sure that you are 'no worse off' working abroad than you would be at home. By breaking the elements of the salary down into the constituent parts described on page 56, the balance

54

sheet method enables each part to be adjusted separately as the need arises, by means of a regular review. By starting with a basic salary which fits into the salary structure in your home country, the additional elements related to working overseas can be isolated and defined. This is why rates tend to go by nationality – a Swiss will have a Swiss basic salary and a Portuguese a Portuguese one. This may be modified by offering a minimum basic salary to all nationalities, or forming nationalities into groups to prevent huge discrepancies that are hard to justify. It should be plain that much of this is management psychology rather than financial logic – people may be offered a fair deal which appears unfair to them – perhaps due to envy – and some system must be found which can be vigorously defended by the employer to all parties. The basic salary is used as a reference point for insurance and pension arrangements regardless of the other overseas allowances.

Cost of living allowance (COLA)

The balance sheet method tries to put a figure on the employee's discretionary income so that you can compare the cost of living in different countries. If costs are higher in the foreign country, a cost of living allowance (COLA) is paid. Cost comparisons are made against the 'discretionary' portion of the salary, not the whole salary, and thus many assumptions have to be made about how employees spend their money. Multinationals use tables for many nationalities against many expatriate locations, which are a huge statistical exercise to construct, so the tables are often shared between several companies. Costs are expressed in index form; those of your own country are given a base value of 100 and other locations are given a higher or lower number. Thus if your discretionary income at home is decided to be £10,000 and you are going to a country with a base of 130, the COLA would be £13,000. There are many statistical and mathematical problems with this method, and often it appears to be rough justice indeed. Single people and those who can adapt well to local habits tend to benefit more from COLA supplements because they don't actually spend them on living – they save the money instead – but families are more likely to actually need the money as their outgoings are much higher.

The cost of housing

In the balance sheet method, housing is usually excluded from the COLA element; normally the company assumes a figure – taken as a percentage of your income – which you spend on housing at home, and deducts this from the salary package. You are then provided with free housing overseas. The rent you may be getting by letting your house at home may not be taken into account, but nor will the costs of keeping it empty.

Calculating the balance sheet

Companies often calculate what your tax would have been at home and use this figure to calculate your contributions abroad, paying any extra themselves. FSPs and hardship allowances are included in the calculations net of tax. The final calculation is designed to tell you your total net salary:

	basic salary
+	FSP
+	hardship allowance
+	COLA
−	housing deduction
−	tax at home
=	net salary

The balance sheet method can be taken to extremes and is often an administrative nightmare, involving hugely complex calculations at frequent intervals as inflation, exchange rates and other factors change. For this reason many employers have substituted simpler systems on a 'take it or leave it' basis. The colonial method was different, in any case, and still survives. Because of the political need to keep up official appearances, civil servants were required to keep to a prescribed standard of living while abroad, and were given the means to do so – making it virtually impossible to save out of the cost of living allowance. The 'real' proportion of the salary was often quite low and paid at home. This explains the rather sad phenomenon of administrators who had controlled vast territories during their careers retiring to modest villas in Brighton.

Local salary packages

This is the opposite of the balance sheet method as it fits you into the system in the country of assignment, taking as your basic salary the 'going rate' for the job in that country. Clearly, this will only attract employees from countries where salaries are lower, although a high salary in a high-tax country may well be worth less than a lower salary in a low-tax country, so it is important to work out the true value. Generally this method would stick to the local country's rules on tax, social security and insurance, but give an FSP. The disadvantage is that if you move to another country to work for the same employer, your salary will change dramatically, and it can cause financial problems if you return home. This method ties you into the country where you are working, which is fine if you like the place and it is prosperous.

The international salary method

Multinationals that use this method treat all their employees as one group, with one salary structure. Salaries have to be high enough to attract people from wealthy countries. As an employee you are asked to sign an international contract which pays the same basic salary wherever you are, but with some currency protection and different additional allowances depending on the country. Pension and insurance funds will probably be operated from a tax haven. The oil industry in particular likes this system as everyone understands it, it treats everyone equally and makes employees very mobile.

Conclusion

There is no perfect system, but if you have a demanding career with a large company it is vital to fully understand your employer's method so that you know where you stand, otherwise many years of hard work could go down the drain. For those of us with less security and more freedom, these heavily bureaucratic methods are less relevant. Skilled people moving from company to company on short-term contracts can afford to be more hard-nosed about the bottom line when negotiating as the employer can hardly pretend to be offended at the lack of 'company spirit'. The goal in this case is to make sure that your savings get to a tax haven and stay there, which is easy enough if you are working in an expat paradise such as Dubai.

PENSIONS

Expatriates, especially those who spend much of their working lives abroad, have special problems with pensions. If you are only away for a year, you can probably continue with your existing plan, particularly if you are working in another EU country, even if you are compelled to participate in the host country's plan as well. For Britons, continuing Class 3 contributions to ensure the basic state pension is usually thought of as wise – but take specialist advice. Some companies have international plans that are run from tax havens; these may offer:

- **A minimum pension level based on the employee's length of service.**
- **Help with calculating the accumulated pension rights from different countries around the world where the expatriate has worked.**
- **Help with reconciling rights in different schemes from different companies which have been acquired or merged.**

The most flexible plans regard state pension rights as of little use to the mobile expat and concentrate on building a fund which will provide a pension regardless of any state. This usually involves paying a certain percentage of your salary into an offshore fund; when you retire or leave the company, the proceeds will be paid out. Be careful, though, because this money may be used by the company to fulfil a statutory requirement to redundancy pay unless your contract expressly forbids it. International plans tend to be in tax havens in order to maximize tax saving, avoid state regulation and ensure flexibility in investment. You may have some say in how these investments are handled, which is desirable. What you get out of such a scheme will vary enormously, but it will be in one of the following forms:

- **A guaranteed pension for life which is based on what you were earning when you retired and how long you worked for the company.**
- **A lump sum paid on retirement or on leaving the company.**
- **An annuity.**

Great changes are taking place in the world of pensions as the demographics of Western countries alter; as life expectancy increases, the social security guarantees of the post-war era are looking increasingly thin. At best, a pension is a way of making sure that people defer some of their income until their old age; at worst, it is an iniquitous and inequitable system which robs Peter to pay Paul. Numerous loopholes exist in pension law which allow unscrupulous businesspeople to misuse the pension funds of companies they control. The most famous example of this malpractice was the Robert Maxwell scandal; we can expect similar scandals to come to light in the future. Expatriates who work in low-tax areas have a huge advantage over their fellow wage-slaves back at home, so there is really no excuse not to save money offshore for your retirement and create your own pension fund, unencumbered by state interference.

Conclusion

Expatriates are something of a special category amongst offshore investors in that they tend to be employees of large concerns working for relatively short periods abroad; this means that they are often new to the ways of surviving financially overseas, and may not have the time to monitor their investments very closely. The majority of expatriates return to their home country eventually, which means that investments must be structured so that they can be repatriated with a minimum of tax liability. As a chance to accumulate capital rapidly, being an expatriate is highly desirable; understanding your employment package is vital. The key points to look at are:

- **tax**
- **insurance**
- **social security**
- **pensions**
- **foreign exchange**
- **hardship levels**
- **foreign service premiums (FSP)**
- **cost of living allowance (COLA)**
- **home-based salary reference**
- **housing.**

Properly negotiated, these factors can all provide the expatriate with extra funds to invest offshore.

4

THE STOCK MARKETS
OF THE WORLD

In this chapter we will look at the world's stock markets and how to use them as an offshore investor:

- Investment principles
- Where are the good brokers?
- Swiss annuities
- The London Stock Exchange
- Stock indices
- The role of the institutions
- The world's stock markets
- The US: the New York Stock Exchange (NYSE), the American Stock Exchange (AMEX) and the National Association of Securities Dealers Automated Quotations (NASDAQ)
- The Tokyo Stock Exchange (TSE)
- Continental Europe: the Paris Bourse and the German markets
- The Far East: the Stock Exchange of Hong Kong (SEHK), Korea Stock Exchange (KSE), the Stock Exchange of Singapore (SES) the Taiwan Stock Exchange and the Jakarta Stock Exchange
- The primary producing countries: the Johannesburg Stock Exchange, the New Zealand Stock Exchange, the Australian Stock Exchange and the Toronto Stock Exchange
- Beware of the lesser stock exchanges
- Buying and selling shares
- Yields and p/e ratios
- Investment strategies
- Collective investments
- Unit trusts
- Investment trusts
- The Euromarkets: the varieties of Eurodeposits and Eurobonds

'... In those days I used to work at a trading table across from an older man, a cynical Irishman whose cynicism I secretly admired. Oft was I privileged to hear him utter his favourite bit of logic to himself: "What were securities created for in the first place? They were created to be sold, so sell them."

Ever since, my tendency has been to buy stocks, all a-tremble as I do so. Then when they show a profit I sell them, exultantly. (But never within six months, of course. I'm no anarchist.) It seems to me at these moments that I have achieved life's loveliest guerdon – making some money without doing any work. Then a long time later it turns out that I should have just bought them, and thereafter I should have just sat on them like a fat, stupid peasant. A peasant, however, who is rich beyond his limited dreams of avarice.'

FRED SCHWED, JR., *Where are the Customers' Yachts?*,
Simon & Schuster 1940

'... Just in its fifth and final year,
His university career
Was blasted by the new and dread
Necessity of earning bread.
He was compelled to join a firm
Of brokers – in the summer term!
And even now, at twenty-five,
He has to work to keep alive!
Yes! All day long from 10 till 4!
For half the year or even more;
With but an hour or two to spend
At luncheon with a city friend.'

HILAIRE BELLOC, 'Peter Goole,
who ruined his father and mother by extravagance',
Selected Cautionary Verses Puffin 1950.

INVESTMENT PRINCIPLES

The underlying realities of investing offshore are the same as for investing at home in the UK; tax savings aside, the main principles must be:

- **Diversification – the process of putting one's eggs in many baskets.**
- **Correct assessment of risk – it is very difficult to do this in under-regulated jurisdictions.**
- **Deciding on the proportions of your investment money that will go into equities, pooled investments, fixed interest securities and cash.**

Much depends on your personal circumstances and the amount you have to invest; if you have more than £100,000, then you can afford good advice – the more you have, the better the advice and the more opportunities for specialized investment there are. Less than this amount and you tend to be stuck between trading on your own, using execution-only brokers, or investing in pooled investments such as unit trusts and investment trusts. A salaried expatriate in, say, the Middle East, will not find it very easy to trade actively in the world's stock markets using an execution-only broker, because of the time difference, lack of spare time in which to trade and possible difficulties in communication. For this reason many salaried expats seem to stick to pooled investments and building society deposits in the old-established tax havens. If you are not resident or ordinarily resident in the UK for a period (see page 24) and have the time to follow your investments, then using execution-only brokers is perfectly feasible from anywhere in the world, especially where you have access to good communications and are in a position to visit the country where you are investing whenever necessary.

Where are the good brokers?
'Why invest abroad?' many people ask. 'There are good brokers here in the UK.' If your portfolio is big enough to warrant the expense of a broker's advice, the London stock market certainly has brokers who are among the best in the world. So does New York. Some banks in other

jurisdictions have good advisers, but not many; Switzerland and Liechtenstein are perhaps the best places to look, although they will have close links with stockbroking firms in London and New York and will take their advice in many matters. The problem with the rest of Europe is that there is a tradition of mistrust of stock markets – bonds are preferred – hence brokers tend to be less sophisticated. They are also often less well regulated. Lack of regulation is a worldwide problem; if you think that London is bad (and it is now arguably better regulated than it has ever been), take a look at Tokyo, where the yakuza gangsters are a very real problem, and the authorities have been shown to connive at the unfair exploitation of smaller investors by some brokers. Apart from London and New York, the places to find good stockbrokers are in the more respectable tax havens, such as the Channel Islands. These can attract real talent, and are well regulated; some London firms have branches there. The London stock market is highly internationalized. Buying the shares of a multinational quoted in London is a way of automatically diversifyng abroad as they generally have big investments in many countries. Eurobonds are listed on the London Stock Exchange as well as that of Luxembourg. Many international funds, specializing in particular areas of the world or particular industries, are based in London, and offer, at their best, a safer way of investing in high-risk/high-reward markets. For British people, whether they are resident in the UK or abroad, using the London stock market as the main conduit for international investment would seem to be sensible. However, if you want to invest directly in a foreign stock market it may be better to develop a relationship wth a broker in that market as London brokers would normally use agents to make such purchases, creating an extra link in the chain.

SWISS ANNUITIES

Although there are celebrated fund managers, such as Sir John Templeton, who have based their operations offshore and have produced excellent results for their investors, the average offshore fund should be regarded with suspicion. You may be disappointed with the returns you ultimately receive, largely because the lack of regulation in offshore centres may prove too much of a temptation to immature fund managers and they may help themselves to some of the fund's profits.

Certain types of Swiss annuity may be the answer for the cautious off-shore investor who doesn't want any nasty surprises.

Unlike annuities in other countries, Swiss annuities are relatively flexible instruments which are run fairly. You can fund them by a single large deposit, which will then pay you a guaranteed income for a designated period, or by making annual deposits. The income can be paid to you anywhere in the world in the currency of your choice, annually, biannually or quarterly. If you decide to make annual deposits to fund the annuity, you can do so by opening a special interest-bearing 'premium deposit account' in Switzerland. This account is similar to a Swiss bank account, but you cannot use the money in it to buy gold, shares or other investments, but only to make payments into the annuity scheme. The interest earned on this account is free of Swiss tax.

Swiss law provides ample protection for annuity holders, on condition that the investor has designated beneficiaries and that the policy has been taken out at least six months before any bankruptcy or court order to seize assets. If, subsequently, such a disaster was shown to have been impending, an investor could make his designated beneficiaries irrevocable, and the funds would be protected from any court action. These rules are such a fundamental part of Swiss law – where insurance for the family is regarded as sacrosanct – that they provide a far more robust method of protecting assets than the many 'asset protection' structures offered by other tax havens, which may prove too easily demolished by foreign courts in a crisis.

Confidentiality is credible for these schemes; Swiss insurance companies will not divulge information to their own or foreign governments about their policy holders, and the annuity income is free of the Swiss 35 per cent witholding tax. In the event of the reintroduction of exchange controls, Swiss annuities would probably escape forced repatriation as they are generally regarded as an insurance policy which has been bought, rather than as an ongoing investment. No Swiss insurance companies have failed in more than a century.

Swiss annuities are 'no load', which means that you can cancel the investment whenever you wish without penalties, except for a small penalty in the first year. This vital feature is in strong contrast to UK annuities where, once you have signed up, you are either 'locked in' for ever or subject to swingeing penalties if you change your mind at a later date.

Types of plan vary. As with a normal annuity, the best annuity rate is given if you agree that all payments stop on your death. This is a gamble between you and the insurance company – if you live longer than they expect, you will receive an excellent return, but if you die soon, you will lose out. In either case, all payments will cease on your death and the principal goes to the company. There are, however, many variations on this basic scheme which give greater security by, for instance, refunding part of the principal to your beneficiaries on your death or by guaranteeing the income for a set number of years, even if you die beforehand.

If you are interested in finding out more about these schemes, you can contact one of the many reputable Swiss investment counsellors who speak English and accept foreign clients.

THE LONDON STOCK EXCHANGE

Since the Big Bang reform in 1986, groups of financial services have been formed, combining several kinds of business that used to be kept separate:

1. *Market making* – this means dealing in certain shares 'wholesale', guaranteeing to buy or sell these shares at all times, which ensures that investors can trade with them whenever they want to. Market makers sell shares at more than what they buy them for in order to make a profit. The difference between the price at which they will buy/('bid') and the price at which they will sell ('offer') is called the bid offer spread. On popular shares in large companies the spread is quite small, while on less popular companies the spread gets wider.
2. *Broker/dealing* – this is the business of buying shares on the behalf of investors.
3. *Investment analysis* – this is the detailed study of the performance and prospects of companies and industries.
4. *Merchant banking* – principally, this involves bringing new companies to the market, arranging rights issues and advising companies on takeover bids and defences.

These groups are called securities houses. The different parts of the organization often have access to privileged information which, in order to keep the market fair, they are not supposed to share with other parts of the group. For instance, if the merchant banking part of a securities house is privately advising a company on a planned takeover bid, it is not supposed to tell the broker/dealers or the others because they would use this inside information by buying shares in the company targeted for takeover in the hope of a quick profit. In order to prevent this kind of conflict of interest, 'Chinese Walls' exist between the various arms of the securities houses which are intended to keep sensitive information secret – often, the different arms are housed in separate buildings. A much repeated joke about Chinese Walls is that they are full of chinks; in other words, many people feel that Chinese Walls don't really work. Since the Big Bang, shares have been dealt via computer. The only places where dealers actually crowd together waving bits of paper is in the futures and options markets; everyone else sits in front of a computer screen.

Stock indices

A stock index is a mathematical measurement of the performance of a number of, say, shares, as a group. The most widely known indices are:

- The *Major Market Index*, produced by the American Stock Exchange, which follows 30 of the most important industrial shares quoted on the New York Stock Exchange.

- The *Standard and Poor's 500 Index* (S&P 500) follows 500 shares quoted on the New York Stock Exchange, American Stock Exchange and the over-the-counter market in the United States.

- The *FTSE 100* (Financial Times Stock Exchange 100 Share Index) measures 100 of the largest companies quoted in London and was introduced principally for options and futures trading.

- The *FT-30 Share Index* (also known as the Financial Times Ordinary Share Index) measures 30 blue chip companies quoted on the London Stock Market.

- The *FT Actuaries Indices* which examine the performances of different industrial sectors so you can judge the relative performance of, say, shipping and energy.

There are many more indices and they are a very helpful tool against which to compare the performance of individual companies. Anyone can run an index and you may see obscure indices advertised by private investment firms.

Stock market indices have been shown to be extremely important in the analysis and measurement of the risks of investment. They provide strong evidence that shares are a good investment over the long term, and fund managers are always trying to get their funds to 'beat' the performance of the various indexes. There are even funds and portfolios that are tied to an index, and move up and down with them, the idea being to reduce risk. Investing in funds that 'track' the indices by spreading money in the same proportions as the index uses to produce its measurements is more popular in the United States than here, possibly because the realities of the risk/reward relationship are better understood there.

The role of the institutions

In important stock markets, such as New York and London, most of the investing is done by pension funds, unit and investment trusts and insurance companies. Along with banks and building societies, they are known as the 'institutions'. Most of the money in these funds is owned indirectly by ordinary people so, in effect, the institutions are middle men. The funds are run by managers who decide how the money is invested. These managers are under enormous pressure to 'outperform' the averages of the market, as indicated by the market indices – principally because they want to do well in their personal careers, and the way to do well as a fund manager is to think short term and try to produce spectacular results. The net result is that most of these funds don't outperform the market. In fact, as they make up such a large proportion of the market's capital, one could say that they are the market, and can't outperform themselves – they are just too big.

THE WORLD'S STOCK MARKETS

There are now more than 60 countries in the world with stock exchanges. The biggest one of all is the New York Stock Exchange, where about a third of the total value of the world's shares are traded. Many of the newer stock exchanges are tiny, such as the one in Croatia, which trades only a handful of stocks and shares. Some countries, such as Germany, finance their industries more by bank lending than through shares, and their stock markets are smaller than you might expect. Then there are the highly internationalized stock markets like London and Hong Kong, where the total value of shares far exceeds the country's gross domestic product (GDP). Different countries have different rules for managing their stock exchanges. Most of the big ones now allow unrestricted foreign investment.

The US

The most important stock exchanges in the United States are based in New York:

The New York Stock Exchange (NYSE)

The NYSE is the best-known of the New York stock exchanges, trading tens of billions of shares in nearly 2,000 companies. It is well-regulated by the Securities and Exchange Commission (SEC), and individual investors get preferential treatment over institutions when buying and selling, thanks to the Individual Investor Express Delivery Service (IIEDS). The main index used is the Dow Jones Industrial Average, which is the arithmetic mean of the share price movements of 30 important companies listed on the NYSE.

The American Stock Exchange (AMEX)

Until 1921, brokers who didn't have a seat on the NYSE would trade in the street; eventually they were organized into a proper exchange, where companies which are not large enough to qualify for listing on the NYSE are listed.

National Association of Securities Dealers Automated Quotations (NASDAQ)

NASDAQ began in 1971; it has no central dealing floor, but works as an international system of trading in shares and bonds via computer screens. It has information links with the London Stock Exchange and was the first foreign exchange to be recognized by the Department of Trade and Industry in the UK.

The Tokyo Stock Exchange (TSE)

There are eight stock exchanges in Japan, but the TSE is the largest, rivalling the NYSE for the title of 'world's biggest'. Companies are listed in three sections, the first for over 1,000 of the biggest issues, the second for a few hundred smaller companies, and the third for non-Japanese companies. There is also an over-the-counter market which is separate from the TSE. The main Japanese index is the Nikkei Stock Average, which is price-weighted and includes over 200 Japanese companies from the first section of the TSE. Although there are still some limitations to foreign buying on the TSE, it is possible for a small investor to buy and sell quite freely. The TSE is volatile; its rapid rise in the 1980s is said to have been 'blue smoke and mirrors', based as it was on a stratospheric property boom in Tokyo. Japan has a particular problem with the yakuza, organized gangs, and around 3,000 listed companies hold their AGMs on the same day to minimize yakuza disruption. Although manipulating share prices is forbidden, in 1991 it was revealed that 17 of the major brokers had been improperly reimbursing favoured clients for losses, and that 'share ramping', the practice of pushing certain shares at smaller investors in order to benefit insiders, was widespread. The Japanese Finance Minister resigned after it was shown that his ministry had been aware of these practices without taking any action.

Continental Europe

Shares have been traditionally regarded with some suspicion by Europeans, and not without reason. Nevertheless markets have existed for centuries in most countries. The world trend towards liberalization has encouraged European governments to reduce taxes on dealing and to move towards standardizing their regulations. The biggest markets are in France and Germany.

The Paris Bourse
The Paris Bourse is the largest Continental exchange after Germany's. It is highly advanced in its use of technology and there is virtually no floor trading. Trading is done through the 45 members of the exchange, some of whom are foreign owned.

Germany
There are eight regional stock exchanges in Germany which together make Germany the next biggest market after New York, Tokyo and London. The biggest of these regional centres is Frankfurt. Only banks are allowed to deal in shares on behalf of investors – there are no brokers as there are elsewhere. German shares are usually issued in bearer form, meaning they

70

can be passed around almost as easily as cash. Dealing commissions are comparable to those in the UK and United States.

The Far East

Eastern Asia is the fastest growing area in the world and is likely to remain so for many decades. Japan is the most powerful economy, but the 'Tigers' (Hong Kong, Taiwan, Singapore and South Korea) are catching up. Not far behind are the 'Dragons' (Thailand, the Philippines, Malaysia and Indonesia). People in these countries tend to save a large proportion of their incomes, which is one of the reasons economists believe that their growth is sound and will continue. The Dragons are rapidly moving from being producers of commodities into heavy industries such as car and machine manufacturing.

The Stock Exchange of Hong Kong (SEHK)

Hong Kong has had a stock exchange since the last century, but it wasn't until the 1970s that the market began its rapid expansion. It suffered badly in the 1987 crash, and its regulation has been subsequently tightened. It has two main indices, the famous Hang Seng Index and the broader Hong Kong Stock Index. Hong Kong was leased from China by the British in the imperial era, and handed back in 1997; while it seems that China will try to maintain Hong Kong as a world financial centre, long-term investment in the market looks risky. At present, though, there are no restrictions on foreign investment in shares.

In the 1930s, it was Shanghai, not Hong Kong, which was the pre-eminent financial centre in Asia. However, fears that it may reassert its position are probably premature. 'With China's economy so big, you can have one or two financial centres', the Hong Kong Stock Exchange's Chairman Edgar Cheng said recently, despite Shanghai's growing strength since China began market reforms in the late 1970s. He pointed out the example of the United States, where major financial markets developed separately in New York and Chicago.

With a market capitalization of over $520 billion, the Hong Kong stock market is Asia's second largest after Tokyo, and one of the seven largest in the world. 'We are the most open market east of London, and we have the biggest international membership of any exchange,' said Cheng.

71

Cheng asserts that Hong Kong's global importance will grow. Hong Kong is a tiny enclave of 6 million people on China's south-eastern coast, but it is the world's fourth largest source of foreign investment, the fifth largest foreign exchange market and the seventh largest global trading entity.

Nevertheless, there are fears that the Chinese authorities will favour Shanghai over Hong Kong. Although it currently lacks the skills and infrastructure to compete, the features that make Hong Kong so special – in particular its English language skills, its unique position adjacent to China and its decades of experience in the global marketplace – could be lost or shared by Shanghai.

Korea Stock Exchange (KSE)
South Korea's exchange is large and modern, but foreigners' access to it is still restricted to a few funds and bonds.

Stock Exchange of Singapore (SES)
This market is almost entirely open to foreign participation – only large stakes in certain important companies are prohibited. The SES has trading links with US dealers, and many Malaysian companies are quoted on it.

Taiwan Stock Exchange
Trade in shares grew in Taiwan after a land reform in the 1950s gave owners stocks and shares in government-run companies. The market is very liquid and dominated by a few investors; foreigners are allowed to invest in some mutual funds.

Jakarta Stock Exchange
The larger of Indonesia's two exchanges, the Jakarta Stock Exchange allows foreign investment in bonds, with some restrictions on share ownership. There are two main indices, one published by PT Jardine Fleming Nusantra Finance, and the other by BT Brokerage.

Primary producing countries

These are Australia, New Zealand, Canada and South Africa. They have highly developed industries and infrastructures, unlike the 'developing' countries, but are heavily reliant on the export of 'primary' commodities and raw materials. Mining companies and commodity producers dominate their stock exchanges, whose fortunes are thus closely linked to world commodity prices.

Johannesburg Stock Exchange
Established in 1886, the market was difficult for foreigners to get into because of exchange controls and trade embargoes during the apartheid period. It is now opening up, but it remains to be seen whether the new government is capable of maintaining the controls needed to make it of interest to smaller investors.

New Zealand Stock Exchange
About 130 companies are listed on the market, which is self-regulating. Most companies are also listed on the Australian stock exchange. The main index is the NZSE-40, introduced in 1991.

Australian Stock Exchange
The regulation of the market has often been called into question, especially during the 1980s which saw the rapid rise and fall of colourful tycoons such as Alan Bond who financed their activities with huge borrowings. The rules have been tightened up, and foreign investment is being encouraged. The main index is the All Ordinaries Index, which includes 250 companies.

Toronto Stock Exchange
Toronto is the oldest and largest of Canada's stock markets; the main index is the TSE Composite which includes around 300 companies. There are no exchange controls and foreign investment is encouraged. Canadian markets are active in developing derivatives products. Markets in Winnipeg and Vancouver have suffered a number of scandals over recent years.

Beware of the lesser stock exchanges

It cannot be said too often that stock exchanges are not all the same. Unless you are experienced and sophisticated, you should stay well away from direct investment in companies which are not quoted on the large, well-regulated exchanges such as London and New York. The recent Bre-X mining scandal, allegedly involving the 'salting' of gold mines in Indonesia, illustrates the need for caution – the company was listed on the Toronto and Alberta stock exchanges, whose regulators have suffered heavy criticism.

Another Canadian market, the Vancouver Stock Exchange (VSE), has also had its critics. The VSE routinely destroys its public company file material (including filing statements, corporate financials, press releases, statements of material facts, prospectuses, etc.) after it passes five to seven years of age, making it difficult for analysts to identify fraudulent practices in VSE-quoted companies.

An offical enquiry, the Matkin Report (1994), called for sweeping changes to the regulation of the VSE, which it criticized as being too 'passive' and 'reactive' an agency. It recommended the removal of the VSE's self-regulatory status, long recognized as a central reason for the market's problems. As yet, no substantial reforms have been implemented.

Buying and selling shares

Except for new issues, you must usually buy shares through a broker. Since the Big Bang, brokers have found that increased costs have made it difficult to offer an ideal service to everyone, so, unless you have £50,000 or more to invest, the best deal available is the 'execution-only' service which means that the broker just does what you ask, without offering any advice. Not all brokers offer this service, so you will have to shop around.

Yields and p/e ratios

These are the two main ways that investors judge shares, both of which are published in the financial pages. The yield tells you the rate of income, as dividends, that you will get at the current share price. The p/e, or price to earnings, ratio is the market price of the share divided by the company's earnings per share. It is a measure of how much the market is prepared to pay for the company, given the profits that it makes. It is often said that the actual number of a p/e ratio is irrelevant, and that it is whether that number is right that is important.

Investment strategies

Try this exercise when considering which shares to invest in. Obtain the prospectuses of a number of very successful investments and unit trusts that look for long-term growth and see which shares they hold. Make a list of these companies, and organize them into their various industries.

Now obtain annual reports for all these companies, and try to get to know them a little better. Look for companies that have good growth rates, a strong position in their own market and who sell something for which you believe there will be a continuing and growing demand.

Now get in-depth studies for each of the companies on this shorter list – you may have to pay for these, and do some detective work to find them, but they do exist. Try to understand these studies as fully as possible. Now list all the pros and cons for each of these companies, and narrow down your list of companies. Pretend to invest in each of the companies in your short list and watch what happens for a year.

By the end of this process you will not only be well-acquainted with some of the best companies available, you will also have learned a great deal about the interface between the stock market and business in general – you will be much better qualified to make your investment decisions.

Here are some strategies you may want to consider:

- **If you have invested in a share that has increased dramatically, sell off enough to get back the original investment, and hold on to the rest. This helps you to stay calm – losing a profit is not as bad as losing your capital.**

- **Look for companies that are worth a lot more than their share price. You can find this out by looking at their accounts and reading studies on them.**

- **Look for companies that have good growth potential, but a share price that is still low.**

- **Look for companies that are likely to be taken over.**

- **If the market crashes in a big way, buy good-value shares – they will probably go up again.**

Here are my pet 'don'ts':

- **Don't** believe in technical analysis, which is the prediction of future prices on the basis of past patterns. It is supposed to work because of the 'psychology' of investors, but it has a rather less rational basis than astrology or the study of UFOs.

- **Don't** spread yourself too thin. Specialize in certain areas, and get to know them well.

- **Don't** be forever jumping in and out of shares in the hope of a quick buck. This will cost you money. Have the guts to hold on to companies which you believe in, having done the hard work of studying them before you bought.

COLLECTIVE INVESTMENTS

The principle of collective investments is sound; small investors pool their money in a fund which is professionally managed, giving, in theory, better diversification than could be had otherwise and the benefit of the manager's experience and access to information. Studies have shown, however, that most funds do not outperform the markets; this may not matter for the cautious investor who simply wants to do better than he or she could with a bank deposit. There is a growing number of offshore funds, based in tax havens, some of which have performed well. The idea is that offshore funds should grow faster, all things being equal, than onshore funds, because they pay less tax; thus, although participants who are residents of high-tax countries will still pay tax on their profits, the fund itself should have grown more than a similar fund onshore. However, tax is only one consideration – more important are the talent and ability of the fund manager, and the nature of the investments that the fund makes. In general, investment trusts would seem to be better value than unit trusts, in the UK, at least; the latter's charges seem to be increasing.

UNIT TRUSTS

Before we look at what unit trusts are, you should be aware of these points:

- Unit trusts which are closely linked to stock market indices are one of the safest ways to invest in shares.
- I believe that investment trusts generally offer better value than unit trusts.
- Unit trusts are heavily marketed financial products aimed at the general public. Their literature and sales approach is designed to put fearful savers at their ease and is generally bland; the image projected is paternalistic and reassuring. You pay for all this 'service' in the charges.
- You hear a lot about how advantageous it is for you to put your money into the hands of the professional unit trust manager who will invest it so much better than you can. There is considerable evidence that this is not really the case.

Unit trusts, introduced into the UK in the 1930s, came from America, where they are known as 'mutual funds'. The idea is that a large number of investors put their money into a fund, for which they receive 'units'. The fund is then professionally managed and spread across a range of investments, including shares and bonds in the UK and in foreign markets. Each investor can buy and sell units in the trust, and the value of the units fluctuates with the value of the investments of the funds. As you pay charges to buy and hold units, they are medium- to long-term investments. In other words, you should expect to hold them for at least three years. Traditionally, the main advantages of unit trusts are considered to be:

- Good diversification for the small investor – possibly better than you could do on your own.
- Less worry, and less work, than holding your own portfolio.
- At times it has been difficult for small investors to find brokers to handle their business; in such conditions, which do not exist currently, unit trusts were virtually the only way a small investor could get into the stock market.
- Unit trusts have been well-regulated and far freer from scandal than other investments.

The money is held by a trustee, such as a bank or an insurance company, not by the unit trust company itself, and is regulated with reference to a trust deed, which lays down all the rules of how the money is to be handled.

Types of unit trust

There are different categories of unit trusts, specializing in different kinds of investments. Here are the main ones:

- **UK general trusts.**
- **UK growth trusts.**
- **UK equity income trusts.**
- **Gilt and fixed interest trusts** – these trusts invest in bonds, not shares, and are intended to provide safety, a higher income and low growth.
- **Growth trusts spread across shares in particular countries or areas of the world,** such as the Far East, Europe, Japan and the US. They are

designed to increase the capital value, and are thus more risky than income-oriented funds.

- **Financial trusts** – these specialize in buying the shares of banks and insurance companies.

Offshore unit trusts

This is a British definition, meaning a trust which is not an 'authorized unit trust' in the UK. Many of them are run from places like the Channel Islands, Bermuda and the Cayman Islands, and are run on the same lines as 'onshore' unit trusts. They are harder to buy and sell in the UK, and are, in some cases, less well regulated, so you should check the companies out very carefully before investing. Their charges tend to be higher, and there are no direct tax advantages for UK taxpayers.

Savings schemes

Many trusts allow you to pay in a monthly sum, and you can miss a few months, or reduce or increase your payment without any penalties. Such schemes should outperform financial products such as endowment and unit-linked insurance policies.

Managed funds

The difference between an ordinary unit trust and a managed fund is that the latter uses an independent professional to decide how the money should be invested. The idea is that as the manager is independent and can be dismissed easily, he or she will have no motive to 'churn' (needlessly buy and sell) the investments held by the trust.

Umbrella funds

These are offshore trusts which have separate funds in different parts of the world, allowing you to switch from one fund to another at low cost.

Buying and selling unit trusts

There are many ways to buy unit trusts; you can buy through a newspaper advertisement, a bank, a solicitor, an accountant, a stockbroker or an insurance broker. If you buy through an intermediary, you will be expected to hand over a cheque once the units have been bought and then you will receive a contract note recording your purchase. Some weeks later you should receive a unit trust certificate which is your proof of ownership. As with all business documents, you should always check both the contract note and the certificate to see that the right type of unit trust is recorded, that the number of units are the same on the contract note and the certificate, and that your name and address appear correctly. If all is well, you should then store the documents somewhere safe where they will not be lost or destroyed.

When you come to sell, contact the organization you bought the units from and send them the certificate, having signed it first. Normally you should get the money within ten days. If you lose the certificate, you must apply for a new one, which will take several weeks. You can still sell units in the meantime, but you won't receive the money until you have surrendered the duplicate certificate.

Check newspapers for the bid and offer prices; remember that the higher one, the offer, is the one you must pay when buying, and the lower one, or bid, is the one you get when selling. Check the difference between the bid and offer prices; normally they are around 6 per cent, but they can be more than double this. The majority of unit trusts quote prices every day, but some may do so once a week, or even once a month. You may find that the trust has rounded up a buying price or rounded down a selling price by 1.25p or 1 per cent, whichever is the smaller; they are allowed to do this.

The charges

The two main charges are the 'front-end load' or fee that you pay when you buy, and an annual management fee. The front-end load is included in the published offer price. If you buy into a unit trust and sell soon after, you will probably lose 5 per cent or so; the idea is to hang on until the units grow enough to cover the front-end load. These charges are in addition to the bid/offer spread discussed above.

Check the annual management fee before you buy. It is usually 1 per cent or less, but VAT is added. This fee is usually taken from investment income automatically by the management.

Exchanges

If you have good-quality shares, you can exchange them for units in many unit trusts. The cost of doing this is usually lower than if you sold the shares in the normal way and then bought units, because the trusts want you to join their scheme. You can do such swaps if your shares are worth more than around £500.

Tax

Income Tax is deducted from your dividends at the basic rate, and you will have to pay Capital Gains Tax (CGT) on profits over your annual exemption. However, there is no CGT on gains made within the fund, if, for instance, the manager switches investments.

Unit trust advisory services (UTAS)

There are over 1,000 unit trusts available in the UK, managed by nearly 200 groups, and the trusts are in many categories. In order to expedite the process of picking the ones you want, there are unit trust advisory services (UTAS) available that monitor most or all of the trusts in the marketplace and will give detailed reports on them. Often the first report is free, after which, if you invest through a UTAS, you will continue to get advice for an annual fee of 0.75 per cent. If you like paying people to hold your hand, then this scheme may have some value; personally, I'd get the free report, then save the money and do my own research.

INVESTMENT TRUSTS

Investment trusts are similar to unit trusts in that they are pooled funds which are professionally invested into a wide range of shares. They are not trusts, however, but companies whose shares are quoted on the stock market; you buy shares, rather than units, in an investment trust. They are taxed in much the same way, and offer a similar variety of categories, including monthly savings schemes. Generally, they are better value than unit trusts, because the buying costs are often lower and the shares can often be bought at a discount to the value of the fund. The bid/offer spread is around 2 per cent, as opposed to 5 per cent in unit trusts, annual management fees are about half, and the initial charges are lower too. Another feature is that, unlike unit trusts, they are allowed to borrow money to invest; this makes them slightly riskier and more volatile than unit trusts. All this helps to boost their performance, and you can expect investment trusts to do better than unit trusts in the future.

THE EUROMARKETS

For historical reasons large amounts of the major currencies are held outside the jurisdiction of their home country. The prefix 'Euro' does not mean that they are all European currencies or that they are held in Europe.

The Eurodeposit market

Companies and private individuals are able to hold foreign Eurocurrencies on deposit in British banks, each currency earning interest at a rate related to those prevailing in its home country. Originally looked down upon by traditionalists, the relaxation of exchange controls has caused this market to mushroom, and it has become so respectable that even countries borrow in the market.

The Eurobond market

Despite its name, the market for Eurobonds is truly international; both issuers of the bonds and investors can come from any country, and while most of the banks involved in the market base their Eurobond offices in London, they too are from all over the world. Some $7 billions' worth of Eurobonds are traded every day over the telephone across the world. Eurobonds can be denominated in any currency, and are issued outside the country of the borrower (issuer); an important feature is that they are issued in 'bearer form'. This means that whoever is holding the bond owns it, giving a great degree of discretion and anonymity to the investor. If Eurobonds ever lose their bearer status, the market is likely to shrink dramatically.

How Eurobonds started
In the 1960s, United States legislation made it increasingly difficult for American lenders to provide dollars for foreign borrowers. The

Eurodollar pool of capital, which was outside US control, then became the obvious place to go to borrow dollars. Banks in London jumped at the chance of earning fees, and had a more sophisticated infrastructure than elsewhere in Europe at the time. Thus, London became the focus of the Eurobond market. The market has now grown to include all currencies, not just dollars. Eurobonds can even be denominated in ECUs, the EU's currency unit based on its member countries' currencies.

The Eurobond market really came into its own in the late 1960s, with the introduction of a clearing system. In fact, there are two: Euroclear in Belgium and Cedel in Luxembourg. Euroclear is the bigger system, having an annual turnover of trillions of dollars' worth of bonds, and holding hundreds of billions of dollars' worth of bonds for their owners.

Who issues Eurobonds?

Banks, large companies, governments, quasi-governmental bodies and organizations such as the EU all issue Eurobonds. Banks are the most active issuers.

Who invests in Eurobonds?

Banks, insurance companies, pension funds, government organizations and large companies all invest in Eurobonds, as can private investors. Unsurprisingly, most investment is done by institutions.

Interest and the credit rating of Eurobonds

Interest is paid gross, with no withholding tax deducted. Common maturity dates are five, seven, ten and twelve years. Like other bonds, most Eurobonds are rated by Moody's and Standard and Poor's, the best quality being rated as 'triple A'. Curiously, corporate bond issuers with household names are often more popular with investors, and can thus offer a lower rate of interest than obscure companies with higher credit ratings.

Fixed rate bonds

This is the most common kind of Eurobond, having a final maturity date and paying a fixed rate of interest. As with other kinds of bonds, if interest rates elsewhere rise above the fixed rate of the bond at some time during its life, the resale value of the bond goes down, and if rates fall, the bond's value will rise.

Floating rate bonds

This variety ties the rate of interest to LIBOR or some other short-term interest rate by means of a stated formula.

Convertible bonds

An investor can exchange a convertible bond for shares in the issuing company at a predetermined price.

The Eurobond market is dynamic and innovative, offering a great variety of bonds which are beyond the scope of this book; examples include 'tap stock', 'dual currency bonds' and 'zero coupon bonds'.

Interest rate and currency swaps

It is possible for two Eurobond issuers to 'swap' (exchange) interest rates on their bonds, or even to swap the principal from one currency to another. The exchange is usually between a fixed rate bond and a floating rate bond, and gives both issuers an 'arbitrage' benefit. Local authorities in the UK got into this in a big way in the 1980s, and some began to speculate wildly on interest rates. Hammersmith and Fulham were the worst culprits, Hammersmith swapping interest on some £7 billion which it didn't have. When interest rates doubled it was in serious trouble, but after courts ruled that local authorities were not allowed to make swaps and that the deals were invalid, the financial institutions who had dealt with Hammersmith had to take the losses.

Conclusion

In this age of globalization and free exchange, offshore investors operate in a similar way to onshore investors. The problems for offshore investors are mainly to do with the difficulties of finding good brokers and getting good advice in the smaller markets; but using the New York, London and Hong Kong stock exchanges should enable investors to diversify adequately in equities all around the world. Equity investments may benefit from tax exemptions if held offshore, but methodical analysis and the minimizing of trading must be the primary concerns of the investor, rather than tax saving. Collective investment funds of good quality are available in some offshore centres, and many UK expatriates use these as savings vehicles for their overseas earnings. Despite the popularity of unit trusts they have high charges, and investment trusts often represent better value, whether onshore or offshore.

5

OFFSHORE COMPANIES –
STRUCTURE AND
TAXATION

As we have seen in Chapter 2, high-tax countries discriminate against tax havens; havens don't have much bargaining power when it comes to trying to negotiate double-taxation treaties as they can't usually offer a reduction in their own taxes. In this chapter we will look at how 'real' businesses use offshore centres; in general, this is more expensive and complex than one might expect, but it is necessary when you are doing most of your business, and generating most of your profits 'onshore', or wish to repatriate them to an onshore country. The topics covered are:

- Starting in business
- Gough's rules for business beginners
- Bankruptcy
- Treaty shopping
- Transfer pricing
- The 'arm's length' rule
- How transfers are valued
- Interest
- On-line information services
- FT Profile
- Offshore companies in the Caribbean
- Bermuda
- The Caymans
- The Bahamas
- Turks and Caicos

- Jamaica and the British Virgin Islands
- How to use offshore centres
- Big-time exploiters of offshore companies
- The 'Winebox' Inquiry
- Holland
- Advance rulings from the Dutch tax authorities
- Licensing companies
- Finance companies
- Uses of holding companies
- The participation exemption
- Foreign branches of Dutch companies
- The Dutch Antilles

'Socialism is capitalism with a human face. Socialism stands for maximizing the freedom of the individual, protection from monopoly, protection from employers, encouraging freedom of the press and providing basic services for all people. I do not discharge workers lightly. Before I let them go I will try every method of keeping them. In the case of the (New York Daily) News, past management and unions conspired to create an entity that was sinking itself. Before we can go forward, we have to reach a reasonable level. But I certainly remember what it felt like when my father was out of work. To me, human beings are worth more than things; I'm not attached to property.'

ROBERT MAXWELL, 1991

'Do you honestly believe I would put my hand in the pension fund and steal it?'

ROBERT MAXWELL, 1985

STARTING IN BUSINESS

Experienced businesspeople can skip this section as they will already know how to survive (the first priority) and how to prosper (the second priority) in business. The vast majority of us, however, know very little about business; you may have worked as an employed manager all your life and still be in this position. The horrific fact is that the vast majority of enterprises go out of business within two or three years of starting up. Here are the factors that I believe are the cause of these failures:

1. *Running your own business is very hard work.* Much harder, in fact, than being an employee; the pressures and responsibilities are simply much greater, especially in the early years.

2. *Many business start-ups use money borrowed from banks.* It is easier to borrow than to pay back, the costs are high and, to an extent, unpredictable, and it is very difficult, especially if you are inexperienced, to estimate accurately your level and rate of sales.

3. *You cannot trust anyone in business.* This doesn't mean that everyone is crooked, just that if you do not constantly take steps to ensure that you are not vulnerable to having money taken from you, someone will notice your exposure and take advantage of you. This can be in a myriad of forms: overcharging, under-delivering, failure to keep agreements, theft, deliberate misinformation and slow payments, to name a few, are all part of your daily life in business, and if you do not know how to fight your corner they will push your business under.

4. *Businesses are vulnerable to red tape and bureaucracy.* What's more, you can't plan for it. Suppose you start up a small food factory; you know how to make the food, you borrow the money secured on your own house and you take a few people on as employees. Unless you are highly experienced, you will immediately become bogged down in a mass of accounting work to do with employment regulations and VAT. Isn't the solution simply to get a good accountant? Not really – accountants do their best, but they can't save you from yourself, and the more work that they do, the more they charge. You must have a good accountant, but if you don't understand how your country's system works and have a basic

grasp of accounting, you will soon get into a mess. Let's assume, though, that you get past these hurdles; the next thing you know a series of officials from the fire and health departments will be demanding that you spend a fortune on changes to your factory that you had never considered; it's no use protesting that you checked the rules before you started – Brussels, or some other mysterious power, will have changed the rules without your knowing. To survive these trials you need good judgement and experience.

5. *Most businesses have a negative cash flow for five or six years*, but most business beginners only produce cash flows for two or three years at most. Nobody likes producing cash flows anyway, and often one only does it in order to obtain a loan. Unless you have a grounding in accountancy you will not appreciate how long it takes to get established and into profit – which means that you are likely to run out of money before your cash flow turns positive.

Gough's rules for business beginners

Here are my rules for success:

1 **Use your own money.** Borrowing is fine if you really understand how to make money by borrowing, but for most beginners it is fatal. This means that you will probably have to save a good deal before you start your company – all very boring, perhaps, but it will make you a far tougher customer, and give you a better chance of success when you do start.

2 **Don't lie and cheat to get out of trouble.** Some tycoons do, of course, but beginners aren't in that league. Often what happens is that the business owner gets into cash flow difficulties, can't pay the bills and then tries to find the easy way out. If you do this your business is likely to fail. Nobody worth while will respect you and if you don't have any business friends (not quite the same as personal friends, admittedly) then you will have no one to turn to when things get worse.

3 **Fill a need.** There is no point in trying to build a better mousetrap for a market where there are no mice. This may be obvious, but people are always doing it. Your job is to sell things that people want, not what they don't want. One is so isolated as a business owner that it is easy to start thinking that the customers are the problem, and they are fools not to buy your product. Be realistic, and avoid justifying a failure – if people aren't buying, you are almost certainly selling the wrong thing, assuming that your delivery, marketing and packaging are right.

4 **Be frugal.** Just because you make a profit doesn't mean you have to eat out every night, employ a butler or buy a Rolls-Royce. Nor does it mean that you should move into more expensive premises. You are in business to make a profit, not to show off.

5 **Seek a patron.** There are wealthy, wise, successful people in every field of business who are older than you. Let them give you the benefit of their experience, and listen to them.

6 **Have the guts to cut your losses.** If some particular enterprise isn't working out, close it down and take the loss. If you press on regardless, you may drive yourself into insolvency.

7 **Minimize lawsuits.** Sometimes they are inevitable; but they are also extremely expensive, time-wasting and uncertain. Remember the gypsy curse: 'May you have a lawsuit and be in the right.' Don't expect justice in the courts.

8 **Don't try to get something for nothing.** It rarely works out, and you'll be a happier budding tycoon if you get on with providing goods and services for money.

9 **Don't confuse giving credit with getting paid.** Some beginners try to increase sales by extending credit to all and sundry. Unscrupulous types will see you coming, and you will have great difficulty in extracting the agreed price from them.

Naturally there are many other laws that could be included in this list, but those listed are most frequently violated by beginners, to their detriment. A lot of people in business are going nowhere – be aware of this and avoid them. Good relationships that are beneficial for both parties over many years are a great, perhaps *the* great, way to make money.

Bankruptcy

In past times bankruptcy had an appalling social stigma. These days, in the UK at any rate, bankrupts are almost fashionable. While the mitigation of the laws of bankruptcy is laudable in so far as it prevents people from being ruined for the rest of their days, it does make life hard for small businesspeople who find that their invoices aren't paid because their customers are bankrupt. For many people, bankruptcy has become a soft option – be aware of this and be cautious about who you extend credit to. Learn something about the laws of insolvency for limited companies and about personal bankruptcy, and protect yourself.

Buying a business

If you have the money, it is better to buy an established business with a good cash flow than to start from scratch. Everyone seems to learn this one the hard way. You can graft any new schemes and deals on to the business that you buy, so this doesn't mean that you can't be 'creative'.

TREATY SHOPPING

For over 40 years many high-tax countries have tried to take action against companies who indulge in 'treaty shopping', which means incorporating a subsidiary or holding company in another country which has better double-taxation treaties than its own. Switzerland, for example, denies the full benefit of its tax treaties to treaty shoppers. The UK tries to limit tax refunds available under treaties to treaty shoppers.

TRANSFER PRICING

It is sometimes said that profits can be moved into low-tax regions by using a group of companies based in different jurisdictions in order to, for example, undercharge a member company for goods and services. If only life were so simple! This practice is known as transfer pricing, and is often the subject of disputes between companies and revenue authorities. Even when companies are not under common ownership or control, transfers of profit in order to avoid tax can be attacked. Profits on currency speculation are taxable.

The 'arm's length' rule

In the UK, transactions between members of a group of companies are assessed for tax under the 'arm's length' rule, which means that prices must be the same as they would be if the companies were completely separate from one another. The Inland Revenue does not like to lose tax from such transactions when they are not made principally for commercial reasons. Some companies are able to exploit the fact that the title to goods can be transferred without physical delivery; get advice from an expert. To decide whether or not particular companies are in fact part of a group, the following rules are applied:

- **For transfer pricing rules to apply, the companies must either be under common control, or one must control the other.**

- **A company that does not own more than 50 per cent of another is not regarded as controlling it.**

- **Interlocking share ownership can sometimes be used to avoid the rule on control.**

Different countries take different approaches to transfer pricing, and double taxation can arise. Appeals are long and involved, and tax authorities may agree to settle a dispute on more favourable terms if the company threatens to appeal under the provisions of a double-taxation treaty.

How transfers are valued

The principles used to value a transfer include:

- **What the market value of the transaction would have been. This is not always possible to define.**

- **Assessing the price on the basis of production costs plus a normal percentage of profit.**

- **Comparing prices with those of other companies in the same business.**

- **Costing out individual components.**

Companies are able to use pre-agreed terms and conditions to alter prices to some extent. Setting special prices for delivery, assembly, insurance, management charges and after-sales service may be allowable.

Interest
Some interest payments may be chargeable to tax under the transfer pricing rules. Loans made between a group are not normally taxable. The Inland Revenue sometimes assesses the transfer of royalty-earning property and licences for tax.

On-line information services

Many readers will be aware of the increasing importance of online information services in the process of 'globalization' of businesses and financial markets. Despite the hype, no one can be certain of the future, and it remains to be seen just whether information technology (IT) will really be a great democratizer or just another way of excluding the majority from

---

functioning as fully as they might. What is certain, though, is that rapid access to information is both more possible and more necessary than ever before, and that IT offers many new opportunities to investors who are working overseas. 'E-mail', messages transmitted via the Internet, is a cheap and quick way of keeping in touch with your brokers and professional advisers when you are abroad, and even the patchy financial information services available free on the Internet allow investors to check changes in share prices with a great deal more frequency than ever before.

International businesspeople and professionals need more than this, however. On-line information services are available, at a price, which reduce the time taken on research very dramatically. One of these is FT Profile, provided by Financial Times Information.

FT Profile
The FT Profile is an easy-to-use database containing a vast amount of business and professional information provided by some 5,000 sources, and is constantly updated. To access it, all you need is a PC, modem and a telephone line. Here is a brief selection of some of the information available:

- Company profiles, reports and accounts for most quoted companies across the world.

- More than 100,000 broker research reports on thousands of companies worldwide, provided by Merrill Lynch, Morgan Stanley and others.

- Massive international news coverage from many sources, including the *Financial Times*, *Washington Post*, *American Banker* and *Agence France-Presse*.

- Business news from providers such as *Forbes*, *Money Management*, *Asia Week*, *The Economist* and *Business Week*. Country reports from the Economist Intelligence Unit.

- Possibly the most comprehensive database for detailed business information on Asia, via 'Asia Intelligence Wire'.

- Detailed market research reports on a wide range of industries, including electronics, food, healthcare, household products, building engineering and chemicals across the world.

Dedicated international investors will also be able to use the database to monitor political and regulatory changes affecting their passport and residency plans.

Commercial rates for using FT Profile are on a 'pay as you go' basis, plus a one-off registration charge, currently (1997) £250. Costs depend on the time you spend on the system (there is a connection charge of 40p a minute) and which sources you access (news files cost 4p per line, while some market research costs 40p per line). Internet users, however, will be pleasantly surprised at the rapidity with which large amounts of data can be downloaded onto their PC for subsequent perusal using this service – there is no nonsense with 'spam' or endless useless pages to be scrolled through, as is the case with the Internet.

OFFSHORE COMPANIES IN THE CARIBBEAN

More than 45,000 offshore companies are formed each year in the Caribbean, Bermuda and Panama. Many of the tax havens in this area are dependencies of the UK or former British colonies, the main ones being Bermuda, the Bahamas and the Cayman Islands. All use English common law and language, and Bermuda is the oldest self-governing British colony in the world.

Bermuda

Bermuda began as an offshore centre in the late 1930s when it first allowed offshore companies to be formed. Bermuda authorities check applicants out very carefully, and the island has great professional expertise which attracts large financial institutions. Many companies from Hong Kong have their holding companies on the island. About 40 per cent of companies quoted on the Hong Kong stock exchange are domiciled in Bermuda.

The Cayman Islands

The Cayman Islands are said to have been 'invented' as a tax haven by a British lawyer on holiday there in the early 1960s. It broadened the rules on exempt companies so that:

- The company name can be in any language.
- Anonymity of the shareholders is allowed.
- Bearer shares are allowed.
- Companies are not subject to tax.

The Cayman Islands have grown rapidly into a major financial centre with over 500 licensed banks and 400 licensed insurance companies.

Bahamas

The Bahamas are also a major corporate domicile because of their proximity to the United States. There are over 400 licensed banks and trust companies.

The Turks and Caicos Islands

The Turks and Caicos Islands have introduced a very flexible and cheap exempted company:

- It does not have to file details of debtors or shareholders with the Registrar.
- It can have bearer or registered shareholders.
- Audited accounts are not required.

Jamaica and the British Virgin Islands

Jamaica invented a new type of offshore company, the International Business Company (IBC), which has been adopted by many other tax havens. The British Virgin Islands, which offer IBCs, have become a major offshore incorporation centre after companies moved there from Panama following the collapse of Noriega (see page 139). IBCs enjoy:

- low government incorporation and annual fees
- no corporate tax or stamp duty
- no public disclosure of directors or shareholders
- bearer shares are permitted
- one-person companies are possible
- no residence requirements for directors and shareholders
- annually audited accounts are not necessary.

How to use offshore centres

UK companies must be very careful about how they use offshore finance centres. The UK has introduced laws on 'controlled foreign companies' (CFCs) to limit their use to avoid tax, as have many other countries. Offshore companies must have a commercial justification. Tax breaks must not be the sole means of maximizing investment in a given country. The CFC legislation states that companies with offshore interests must pass one of three tests:

1. *The acceptable distribution of income test* – some profits have to go back to the UK within a given time period.

2. *The exempt activities test* – a company has to show it has genuine business interests in that country.

3. *The motive test* – a company's main motive must be to do business, not just to avoid tax. Evidence includes the number of people the offshore company employs and the size of its offices.

These laws mean that many 'onshore' companies have given up using zero tax-rate havens such as Bermuda, the Cayman Islands and the Netherlands Antilles in favour of other countries with low rates of tax where it is easier to justify a true commercial interest.

Big-time exploiters of offshore companies

During the boom of the 1980s, several Australian tycoons are known to have taken advantage of tax anomalies in offshore centres. In 1988, for example, the Bond Corporation company accounts showed that more than 90 per cent of its profits had been channelled through the Cook Islands. Another corporate hero, John Spalvins, paid less than a cent in the dollar in 1987 and 1988 on the profits of his Adelaide Steamship Company.

In 1990, Rupert Murdoch's News Corporation paid tax at just 1.76 cents in the dollar at a time when the statutory rate was 39 per cent. More than half the media empire's profits were channelled through Caribbean tax havens in 1990. The Bermuda-based News Publishers Ltd, the most active of News Corporation's 24 tax-haven companies, made more than 277 million Australian dollars. Murdoch's inventive use of tax schemes by his highly profitable Hong Kong newspaper, the *South China Morning Post*, caused him to be styled 'Citizen Cayman' by the respected *Far Eastern Economic Review*. While News Corporation still uses offshore vehicles, particularly in the Netherlands, where all its newspaper mastheads are owned, tax experts say that this is legitimate for such a large multinational.

The 'Winebox' Inquiry

A Royal Commission inquiry in New Zealand examined a large number of deals done in the Cook Islands by the European Pacific Banking Group. More than 1 billion US dollars were channelled through Euro Pacific tax schemes by some of New Zealand's biggest companies. A 1,500-page bundle known as the 'Winebox Documents' is alleged to have been stolen from Euro Pacific, owned in the late 1980s by Brierley Investments Ltd, the Bank of New Zealand and Fay Richwhite. The documents are incomplete and in some cases refer to proposed deals which never took place, but include schemes which hid 200 million NZ dollars in losses in the Bank of New Zealand balance sheet, helped the Bond Corporation fund its own profits and that allowed Alan Bond to move 119 million Australian dollars from Weeks Petroleum and J. N. Taylor to his group via back-to-back loans. This structure allowed him to move funds between companies without disclosure, despite a pledge to his bankers which restricted direct loans.

HOLLAND

Holland is an important domicile for 'onshore' businesses because of its unusual tax advantages combined with its large network of double- taxation treaties. It is not a tax haven as companies are taxed at between 35 per cent and 40 per cent on profits, while individuals are subject to income tax and wealth tax. This has enabled Holland to make double-taxation treaties with most high-tax countries, but these treaties are quite favourable to certain companies. It is possible to arrange the structure of a company or a group of companies so that income into Holland gets favourable tax treatment, avoids withholding tax in the country from which it comes, and then can be paid out to companies or individuals in other countries which are either tax havens or have a double-taxation treaty with Holland. The country's policy towards trade aims at 'neutrality' between taxing local and foreign income. Many multinationals from the US, Britain and elsewhere have holding companies in Holland to mitigate taxes. Holland's tax system has the following useful features:

1. Advance rulings from the tax authorities. This enables a company to make sure that a particular transaction or kind of transaction will not be taxed unfavourably in Holland before it takes action. In many

other countries, including the UK, one is often in the position of not knowing how transactions will be taxed until it is too late to alter arrangements. The advance ruling is also a guarantee that the tax authorities will not change their minds, as they do elsewhere.

2. No withholding tax on royalty payments; many groups have a Dutch licensing company and an offshore company based in a tax haven to take advantage of this. Royalties are paid into the Dutch company, subject to a reduced or even nil rate of withholding tax under double-taxation treaties, and do not suffer Dutch withholding tax when the royalties are paid out to the offshore company.

3. No withholding tax on interest payments – this works in a similar way to royalty payments.

4. Companies with a branch in Holland may get exemption from tax on genuine profits made by the branch.

5. The 'participation exemption'. This rule enables many companies to avoid Dutch tax on the dividends they receive.

Advance rulings from the Dutch tax authorities

Advance rulings can be obtained for all kinds of knotty problems, including questions to do with transfer pricing and the 'arm's length' rule. The Inspector of Taxes decides the minimum profit which will be subject to Dutch tax and gives the advance ruling which lasts for three years and can be extended. The minimum taxable profit will never be less than 10,000 Dutch guilders a year and claims for other tax reliefs on this sum will not be allowed.

Licensing companies

Almost all of Holland's double-taxation agreements have a clause which reduces foreign withholding tax on any royalties which a Dutch company receives. To ensure that royalties will not suffer tax in Holland, you can get an advance ruling. If a licensing company has a minimum profit on the royalties of 7 per cent, or 10,000 Dutch guilders if the profit share is less, then Holland says that it is dealing at arm's length. If royalties are more than 2 million guilders, the licensing company's taxable percentage is reduced; over 10 million guilders it is only 2 per cent, except for film companies where the taxable profit is always 6 per cent.

Finance companies

A group can create a Dutch subsidiary which borrows money and passes it on to members of the group, reducing or avoiding income tax on interest payments. Gains made on currency exchange are taxable, though. Finance companies can get advance rulings, and in general pay tax on 0.25 per cent of the average annual borrowings between a group, and as little as 1/32 of average annual borrowings from unrelated lenders.

Uses of holding companies

Dutch holding companies have many uses. Capital Gains Tax at home can be deferred indefinitely if it is made by a subsidiary in a country which does not tax capital gains; this is done by keeping the capital gain in the Dutch holding company.

UK companies are often doubly taxed in situations where they have investments in other high-tax countries. A Dutch holding company is allowed to average the underlying rates of tax in the different locations of its subsidiaries so that investments in low-tax areas can be used to offset unrelieved tax in high-tax countries. In addition, Dutch double-taxation treaties are often more favourable than those of the UK and other countries, which means that withholding taxes can be lower. Home country tax on dividends can be deferred by using a Dutch holding company, which is helpful to cash flow, especially if a group is expanding overseas. This is done by the holding company reinvesting dividends using the participation exemption. Beware the UK's Controlled Foreign Company laws, however.

The participation exemption

The participation exemption was introduced in 1893 as a way of avoiding double taxation of dividends moving between companies. Dividends are exempt from tax to the receiving company, whether or not the company paying the dividends is resident in Holland. The exemption can also be used to avoid Capital Gains Tax on the sale of shares. To get a participation exemption, the rules are:

1. The receiving company must usually own a minimum of 5 per cent of the company paying the dividend. There are exceptions, but get an advance ruling in any case. Dealing in shares is usually not allowed.

2. The ultimate holding company and the investments must not be 'passive'. The overseas subsidiaries must be actual operating companies. This rule does not apply to companies in other EU countries, but the minimum ownership is increased to 25 per cent.

3. Non-resident companies in which the Dutch company invests must pay some tax to some authority – but if it is enjoying a tax holiday it may still be possible to get participation exemption. Investments in tax havens which allow you to choose the rate of tax you pay may still qualify.

4. Interest, losses on currency exchange and professional fees connected with the investments are not usually tax deductible.

Foreign branches of Dutch companies

If you create a branch of a Dutch company in a low-tax area, it is possible to retain profits within the Dutch company but pay a low rate of tax. The branch must be a real operation, and you should get an advance ruling.

Summary

Holland is an ultra-respectable country whose tax breaks have been used by large businesses for many years. Nevertheless, it does suffer pressure; the US courts have begun to use the idea of tax treaty 'overrides' to disallow some of the Dutch tax advantages, and this has created some uncertainty. If you are doing a lot of business in Europe, though, Holland is hard to beat as a domicile.

THE DUTCH ANTILLES

The Dutch Antilles and the breakaway island of Aruba are in the Caribbean, off the coast of Venezuela (see pages 256). They are separate countries, but are still part of the Kingdom of the Netherlands, and together with Holland form three 'kingdom partners'. Aruba is a tax haven on Caribbean lines, with the advantages and disadvantages that that entails, but the Dutch Antilles do impose some taxes. The islands offer tax breaks to companies involved in licensing, financing and holding investments, and such companies pay 3 per cent tax or less. Companies incorporated in any of the kingdom partners can switch their domicile to another partner easily by drawing up a deed in advance – this facility was much used in the lead up to World War 2 to escape the German invasion of Holland. The Antilles also allows its companies to switch to any other jurisdiction which allows such moves; this means that a company's domicile can be moved right out of the kingdom very rapidly indeed. Another way of avoiding political problems is to have 20 per cent of a company's shares in non-cumulative preferred form, and the rest in ordinary shares. The capital representing the ordinary shares can be paid out easily in an emergency.

Companies which are resident in the Antilles and own a minimum of 25 per cent of the shares of a Dutch company enjoy reduced withholding tax in Holland. Normally withholding tax is 25 per cent, but if the money goes to an Antilles parent company this is reduced to 7.5 per cent or less. The Dutch 7.5 per cent withholding tax on dividends paid to Antilles companies was introduced 10 years ago (previously there had been no withholding tax at all) partly in response to international pressure. The advantages of Holland and the Antilles are often combined by having an intermediate holding company in Holland which receives, amongst other tax breaks, the participation exemption, and having the ultimate holding company in the Antilles.

Conclusion

Multinationals use offshore companies extensively as part of their groups to mitigate tax, particularly in the areas of employee pensions and insurance, and also by using holding companies in favourable jurisdictions. Smaller companies in high-tax areas can do the same, but with relatively greater expense and fewer advantages. Creating an anonymous offshore company can be useful for individuals as an investment vehicle, but if it does business with high-tax regions it is likely to come under close scrutiny. Transfer pricing and treaty shopping are restricted onshore, and expert advice is needed to ensure schemes will have a chance of success – this is costly. Holland and the Antilles provide interesting loopholes for minimizing the taxation of groups, but are under pressure to reduce these; the ability to obtain an advance ruling on many issues from the Dutch tax authorities make the Dutch tax regime much easier to work with than those of many other countries, including the UK.

6
TRUSTS

In this chapter we will look at the basics of trusts:

- What is a trust?
- Which countries accept trusts?
- How long can a trust last?
- Accumulation periods
- The trust instrument
- The many uses of trusts
- Offshore trusts
- Asset Protection Trusts
- Some other uses of offshore trusts
- Flight clauses in an offshore trust deed
- Choosing a jurisdiction
- How trusts work
- The history of trusts
- Types of trust
- Discretionary trusts
- Accumulation and maintenance trusts
- Bare trusts
- Fixed interest trusts
- Secret trusts
- Trading trusts
- The settlor
- The protector
- Using protectors
- The beneficiaries
- Trustees
- Other duties of trustees
- Trusts and civil law states
- Difficulties with trusts in civil law countries
- The Hague Trusts Convention

'Thus from settlement of the greatest of wars down to the simplest inheritance on death, from the most audacious Wall Street scheme down to the protection of grandchildren, the trust can see marching before it the motley procession of the whole of human endeavour: dreams of peace, commercial imperialism, attempts to strangle competition or to reach paradise, hatred or philanthropy, love of one's family or the desire to strip it of everything after one's death, all those in the procession being dressed either in robes or in rags, and either crowned with a halo or walking with a grin. The trust is the guardian angel of the Anglo-Saxon, accompanying him everywhere, from the cradle to the grave.'

PIERRE LEPAULLE, a renowned French lawyer, in *Traite theorique et pratique des trusts en droit interne, en droit fiscal et en droit international*, Paris p.113, 1932

'If we were asked what is the greatest and most distinctive achievement performed by Englishmen in the field of jurisprudence I cannot think that we should have any better answer to give than this, namely the development from century to century of the trust idea.'

MAITLAND, famous legal historian, in *Selected Essays*, p.129, 1936

The idea of the trust is an extraordinarily subtle and flexible legal concept invented by English lawyers that developed over the centuries as a way of protecting assets. As we will see below, the uses of a trust, both internationally and in the UK, are enormously varied, and while their validity is accepted to some degree in many countries, and is likely to gain wider acceptance in the future, the fact that they are based on English law does cause problems abroad. The cost of maintaining a trust is high; £1,000 per annum would be normal. Professional trustees who have a long-standing relationship with you may be willing to take on smaller business or charge lower fees, but forming an offshore trust does not really become economic unless you have half a million pounds or so which you want to protect in this way.

The main players in a trust are the settlor, who is the person transferring the assets into the trust, the trustees, who administer the trust, and SEE ALSO P. 116 the beneficiaries, who receive the benefits of the assets. Trusts are normally set up to run for about 100 years. It is extremely unwise to attempt to set up a trust on a do-it-yourself basis; this is one activity where you have no choice but to use lawyers. Nefarious acts by trustees and other interested parties in a trust have been the stuff of pulp fiction and melodrama since the last century, and not without reason. Although the duties and responsibilities of trustees are extremely heavy, there are obvious temptations, especially when the settlor has become too old to think clearly, or the beneficiaries are at war with one another. This makes it vital for anyone considering setting up a trust to learn as much about them as possible; at the very least, it will help to cut the costs of having expensive advisers explaining the basics to you in person.

WHAT IS A TRUST?

A trust is not a person in law in the way that a company or an individual is. Thus it can't 'own' anything itself – the assets of the trust are 'vested' in the trustees, who can be companies or individuals. One way of thinking of a trust is to say that it is a kind of slow-motion gift from the settlor to the beneficiaries (the settlor may, in many cases, be a beneficiary as well). The trustees are the people who look after the gift in the meantime, and are usually paid to do this. A typical British trust would be where a wealthy settlor wanted to leave money to young children and 'remoter issue', such as grandchildren, some of whom might not yet be born, and wanted both to mitigate the effects of inheritance and other taxes and also to protect immature individuals against themselves. If you were in this position, you might specify, for example, that the beneficiaries only gained access to the trust fund when they reached a particular age (say 18 or 25) or when they married. Meanwhile the trust fund, which can be in any form under UK law, so it could be a mixture of cash, property, investments and insurance policies, is under the control of the trustees who act as caretakers with specific duties and responsibilities.

Which countries accept trusts?

English law is based on 'common law', which is a body of judgments rather than a codified set of rules. In many countries which were formerly governed or colonized by Britain, trusts are a familiar part of financial life. These are some of the important ones:

- Australia
- Canada
- New Zealand
- the US (however, some states, such as Louisiana and California, are based on the civil law codes derived from Spain and France)
- Ireland
- Gibraltar
- the Cayman Islands
- Bermuda
- the Bahamas.

Some of the above are tax havens, while others have harsh tax regimes. How a trust is taxed depends entirely upon the legal jurisdiction of the trust, the countries in which the funds are held and the domiciles of the settlor, the trustees and the beneficiaries. Various countries try to tax the assets of a trust by special rules dealing with the parties involved. Almost all of the tax havens, whether common law countries or not, have accommodated trusts into their systems. The position with countries that do not have a common law system is more complex (see page 120); essentially, many of these other countries do now recognize trusts. These may be Muslim law countries, the ex-communist countries, and 'civil law' countries which base their system on Napoleonic or Roman law, such as France and Spain.

How long can a trust last?

Except in certain jurisdictions (for example, in Manitoba, a province of Canada) a trust cannot last forever, unless it is a charitable trust. In England the life of a trust is linked to the 'royal lives' period; at present this means 21 years after the death of the last survivor of all the descendants of Queen Elizabeth II who were alive when the trust was created. You can choose to make the trust last a maximum of 80 years instead of using 'royal lives'. Jersey and Guernsey allow a maximum of 100 years. If there were no limitation on the length of time a trust could last, theoretically it might be possible to amass a vast proportion of the world's wealth in one fund over the centuries. Normally, a trust is wound up and the funds are distributed once the beneficiaries are grown up and ready for the money. Settlors who are using trusts for their own benefit may terminate them after only a few years.

Accumulation periods

In most jurisdictions the length of time that the income can be saved up within the trust (the accumulation period) is also limited. In England trusts have a maximum accumulation period of either the settlor's life or 21 years. Jersey and Guernsey allow 100 years for perpetuity, while Ireland allows the royal lives period, with no lower limit for the accumulation period. Once the accumulation period is over, the income has to be distributed to the beneficiaries. Clever management of investments can make good use of the accumulation period but trusts that last the full term have not always been very successful at getting good returns. The nineteenth-century English trust often had its money in 'consols', a type of bond; after two world wars, inflation, the massive increase in taxes and the loss of an empire, its assets were often sadly depleted by the time the trust was terminated.

The trust instrument

A trust can be created by various documents; it is not in itself a holding company, a contract or a will, but it can be created by these, as well as by a gift from the settlor during his or her lifetime. The document creating the trust may be called:

- the trust deed
- the trust agreement
- the trust instrument
- the settlement
- the declaration of trust.

A settlor can become a trustee, or can disguise his identity by informally telling the trustees to set up the trust and having them formally declare it. An illegal practice is to create trusts and transfer documents of property and keep them in a drawer – if the need arises, the settlor produces them, and if circumstances change the settlor can tear them up without anyone being the wiser.

The many uses of trusts

As well as the well-known, and possibly unambitious, use of trusts as a way of passing on money to one's own family and friends, trusts can be used for grander and more arcane purposes. There are no reliable estimates of the amount of trust funds that exist worldwide. These are some of the ways that trusts are used:

- Charities' money is held on trust. In the UK, charitable trust funds and funds of charitable corporations are said to have a turnover of more than £17 billion a year, giving them tax and similar savings of some £3 billion a year.
- Life policies are held on trust; you can take out such a policy to be held on trust for your spouse and children.
- Land in England and Wales that is owned by more than one person is held on trust for sale for the co-owners.
- Clubs and societies which are not incorporated often have funds which are held on trust for their members.
- Unit trusts (mutual funds in the US) are collective investments which are held on trust for the benefit of their investors (investment

trusts, however, are not technically trusts). Over five million people in the UK invest in unit trusts.

- The enormous funds of trade unions are held in trust for the members and are used to support the political and economic aims of these organizations.

- Pension funds are held in trust. In the UK these are worth some £300 billion.

- Many companies who issue debentures offer property as security for the loans; this is held on trust for the debenture holders who have lent a company money by purchasing its debenture stock. If the company defaults, the trust's assets would be used to recompense the debenture holders.

- Eurobonds are issued under a 'trust deed'. If the issuer defaults, the trustees collect the money owed and hold it on trust for the purchasers of the bonds.

- Countries can set up trusts to help newly autonomous or remote regions. For example, the UK, Australia and New Zealand set up a trust fund for the Tuvalu islanders in 1987, worth £12 million, following the demise of the British Phosphate Commission on the islands.

- At the end of World War 1, the Allies imposed heavy war reparations on Germany, and set up a trust which was managed by the Bank of International Settlements as trustee. Germany made payments to the trust, and the trustees distributed it to the victorious nations.

- In the United States in the last century laws prohibited companies from owning shares in other companies, the intention being to prevent large-scale monopolies. To get around this, tycoons began to use trusts as a way of retaining control over their vast business interests; their trustees could hold controlling shares in many companies on behalf of a trust, in effect becoming the tycoon's holding company. Eventually the Sherman Anti-trust Act was passed to prevent this, and the word 'anti-trust' survives to this day to mean 'against monopolies', particularly in the US, but also in the UK. For example, the EU's policies against monopolies are sometimes described as 'anti-trust', even though they have nothing to do with trusts.

Clearly, trusts are not used just to save some tax. Consider the following problems:

1. You are a success in business, but one of your children was born mentally and physically handicapped. The strain of coping has resulted in divorce, and you have remarried; your handicapped child is expected to outlive you by decades, but you are worried that there will be no one to protect him if you die.

2. Your daughter has left university, got her first job and is living in London. You bought her a smart flat so that she didn't have to live in a slum, but you have noticed that her social life is getting wilder and she is surrounded by indigent hangers-on. Blaming yourself for being overprotective in the past, you nevertheless have reason to fear that she is liable to fall for a good-looking villain with a drug problem who is out for all he can get. How can you pass more funds on to her without risking them falling into his clutches?

3. Your children are grown up and have children of their own. You want to pass on large sums of money to your grandchildren, but you don't want them to get it until they are mature enough to handle it. Others may say that 25 is a reasonable age to inherit, but your belief is that they won't be ready for it until they are 40.

4. You've had many marriages in your colourful life, and now in your fifties you have married a man in his thirties. You are both happy, but you know that when you die he will marry again; in fact, you want him to for the sake of his happiness. How do you provide for your children by previous marriages, give your husband something as well, making sure that the money goes where you want it without the risk of an interloper grabbing it after you're dead?

All these problems can be dealt with using trusts. As the settlor, you design the trust to fit your purposes, and instruct the trustees accordingly. Social mores change all the time. Marriage is on the wane and equality of the sexes on the increase, but whatever the circumstances the chances are that there will be vulnerable people in your life who you will want to help financially after your death. However, to prevent the dead ruling the living forever, trusts have a limited life in most jurisdictions (see page 105), except for charities.

OFFSHORE TRUSTS

Offshore trusts present special problems for settlors. Essentially people set them up in order to circumvent the laws of other countries in some way; this may be legal or illegal, and in the latter case there may be strong moral grounds for breaking the law – for example if you are severely persecuted in your own country. It has to be said, though, that offshore trusts, like offshore companies, have their attractions to 'genuine' criminals, and thus some tax havens have more than their fair share of danger and corruption, as well as plenty of unwelcome attention from the authorities in other countries. These factors are the reason for the wall of silence that surrounds offshore trusts, and which this book can only begin to penetrate. You will find, though, that lawyers and trustees will be more optimistic and helpful in private consultation than any published literature can hope to be.

Offshore trustees are not likely ever to have a shortage of business as there will always be people who are looking for ways of making their money safe from confiscatory regimes, revolutions, wars, and revenue collectors. It is said that the interest in offshore trusts goes up and down with the level of mayhem and catastrophe around the world.

Currently, much of the new trust business is coming from these parts of the world:

- Hong Kong, which was leased to Britain in the last century, was handed back to China in 1997. Many Hong Kong residents are keen to protect their assets from China by getting them offshore.

- South Africa has just undergone a radical political change. Many wealthy whites are getting their money out for fear of future disturbances.

- South and Central America have unstable regimes and great differences between the rich and the poor. Wealthy Latin Americans like to get money offshore whenever there is an opportunity to do so.

- There is some interest in trusts amongst the wealthy in continental Europe; the concept of a trust is, however, alien there, and many individuals are nervous about handing their money over to a trustee.

Few offshore trusts are being formed by American and British nationals at present, largely because it is virtually impossible for UK and US nationals who are resident, ordinarily resident and domiciled in their own countries to use offshore trusts to avoid much tax legally (see page 23). In 1991 Britain introduced rules taxing settlors of such trusts, irrespective of whether they were getting any benefit from them. The Society of Trust and Estate Practitioners (STEP) was launched in 1991 and has over 900 members spread across the world; membership of this body is regarded as giving a degree of respectability to an offshore trustee.

Asset Protection Trusts

Currently there is a great deal of activity in the field of 'asset protection'. This is a relatively new way of structuring a trust which is designed to protect assets against litigation from creditors and angry spouses. Asset Protection Trusts (APTs) are most popular in the US, but there are drawbacks; trusts are not supposed to be used to defraud genuine creditors, so if, for example, you are a bankrupt or have been served with writs, it may not be legal for you to set up a trust, and if you do so you may find that it is set aside by the courts. Some offshore havens are rather more sympathetic to APTs than others, and it may be that people who are trying to protect their assets from litigation by using an APT can form one so quickly, and design it with such complexity, that the APT becomes worthy of its name. Naturally, professional trustees in all jurisdictions are keen to emphasize that they do not knowingly form APTs in such circumstances, and that they make every effort to investigate their clients and satisfy themselves about their solvency and the source of their funds. It is said that most applications for APTs are refused immediately by reputable trustees.

Jersey has the 'Bankruptcy-Desastre Jersey Law' against the unscrupulous use of APTs. For example, there is a five-year 'look-back' clause at any transaction at an undervalue but transactions conducted more than two years ago will be upheld if it can be proved the settlor was solvent at that point. The main APT providers are exceptionally cautious about the people that they do business with.

Some other uses of offshore trusts

Insider trading is not illegal in many stock markets, and it is thought that offshore trusts are sometimes used for this purpose. Many perfectly legitimate entrepreneurs have good reasons for disguising their financial activities, and maintaining a web of entities internationally is almost *de rigueur* for the powerful businessperson. If you use nominees for business activities, you are, in fact, using a 'bare trust' (see page 115) where the nominee is the trustee and holds the assets on your behalf.

The pitfalls and traps of using offshore trusts are discussed on page 117, but first we should look at the technicalities in more detail.

Flight clauses in an offshore trust deed

A flight clause copes with political upheaval in the trustees' jurisdiction. If, for example, you had a trust in the Cayman Islands, you would want to be sure that if they were ever invaded or were subject to a revolution – however unlikely that scenario might be – that you could move the trust to another jurisdiction with the stroke of a pen. This does not affect where the assets are held, but simply under what jurisdiction the trust is administered; moving jurisdictions would stop a government in the old jurisdiction being able to bring trust assets back to its country and confiscate them. The events which would cause the automatic trigger to take place must be carefully specified to prevent misunderstandings, and this usually means that the new trustees are given the right to decide if the 'triggering events' have actually occurred. Another way is to retain the power to decide this as a settlor, or to give that power to a protector (see page 116).

Choosing a jurisdiction

Many offshore centres allow you to choose which country's laws will govern a trust – you can change this if you wish, and you don't have to use the laws of the tax haven itself. This is recognized in international law by the Hague Trusts Convention and the Recognition of Trusts Act 1987 (see page 122). Under these international agreements, a settlor can choose the law to govern all aspects of a trust or choose different laws to govern different aspects of it. For example, you can separate the jurisdictions governing:

- **the trust deed itself**
- **the validity of the trust**
- **how the trust is administered**
- **trust assets located in different countries.**

Furthermore, you can write into the trust deed, clauses allowing the settlor or the protector (see pages 116–7) to replace the law governing validity or the law governing administration by another law. However, there must be a court that can decide and guide the trustees and beneficiaries on how the trust is administered or the trust could be invalidated. This guidance must cover matters such as:

- **how the trustees can invest the trust's money**
- **what happens when a trustee retires**
- **how the trustees can delegate**
- **how new trustees can be appointed**
- **how the trustees can be paid and claim expenses**
- **the indemnity of trustees**
- **whether the court itself has the power to authorize particular acts or change the terms of the trust deed. This may seem circular, but it goes with the territory!**

HOW TRUSTS WORK

If you decide to put some assets into a trust you must do everything possible to ensure that your intentions regarding those assets are successful. It would clearly be disastrous if after you had set up the trust it was set aside by a court, or you were the victim of fraud or sequestration. In order to understand how the law views trusts, we should first look at their early history.

THE HISTORY OF TRUSTS

In the Middle Ages all land in England was owned by the Crown; in fact, it still is. In those far off days when life was more violent and barbarous than it is now, people were often in danger of losing what they had to an aggressor. Most of us think of the world as being a safer place today, but nevertheless there are still individuals and organizations who will take what they can by fair means or foul from those who are weaker than they are. Thus an understanding of the problems of mediaeval property owners may be more relevant to you than it may appear at first.

English common law never dealt directly with the ownership of land because it all belonged to the Crown. The King parcelled out land by granting estates to his major followers and supporters under various terms – sometimes for life, or at best, forever. In turn, these estate holders granted smaller estates to their followers, and they in their turn did the same. This process, known as 'subinfeudation', was abolished in the late thirteenth century. Gradually the importance of the terms of a person's tenure of their land reduced, while the rights of a person became more important. Originally there were three main kinds of estate:

- The estate for life, in which a man could have the land for life.
- The estate in fee tail, where a man kept the estate and could pass it on to his descendants for as long as he had direct descendants.
- The estate in fee simple, where a man could leave his estate to people who were not direct descendants, and it would only revert to an overlord or to the Crown if there were no heirs.

When it became possible to leave estates in a will, possessing an estate in fee simple effectively meant owning it forever. During the Crusades, a problem arose for land-owning knights who were setting off for the East, perhaps never to return. While the knight was away, there was the very real danger that someone would try to grab all or part of his land, and his wife and children would not be able to take legal action to prevent this. This was because litigation could only be started by an adult male who had good grounds for claiming that he had a better title to the land than the person who was trying to steal it. Thus the trust was born; in its first incarnation, it simply meant that the crusading knight would give his land to a trusted male friend to hold 'for the use of' the knight's family while he was away, the understanding being that the friend would take legal action to protect the estate. If the friend turned out to be a crook and refused to give the land back when the knight returned, the only thing the knight could do was petition the king directly for the return of the property; he could not go to a common law court because they regarded such an arrangement as meaning that the friend had legal ownership of the land. Other groups also used this system; for example, some religious orders had taken vows not to own any kind of property, but nevertheless wanted somewhere to live. In this case the religious group would arrange for a knight to purchase the land (with money given to the order), and he would own it on their behalf, holding it for their use. If the knight decided to keep the land for himself, the religious order would have to go to the king to ask for permission to have the property transferred to someone else to hold it for them.

By the middle of the sixteenth century this unsatisfactory state of affairs had been improved upon, and holding an estate 'for the use of' someone else came to be called a trust. The legal owner, or trustee, was compelled by law to use the assets he was holding on trust for the benefit of the beneficiaries, and not for himself or anyone else. This is the principle underlying modern trusts; trustees are not allowed to use the trust's assets for their own benefit, but only for the beneficiaries; nor can a trustee use the trust's assets for the benefit of a settlor, unless the settlor is a beneficiary under the trust deed.

TYPES OF TRUST

Tailoring a trust to your own particular purposes and circumstances is essential, and clearly it may be that you should change your circumstances – for example, where you are ordinarily resident – to gain the most benefit. There are two main types of trust:

- Interest in Possession Trusts.
- No Interest in Possession Trusts.

Interest in Possession simply means that at least one beneficiary of the trust has the right to receive income, such as interest, from the trust fund as it arises. For example, if you have a life policy to benefit your dependants, you could arrange for an Interest in Possession Trust where your family would receive income from the trust fund on your death until the children had grown up, when the capital would be divided. This would avoid the need for probate, avoid Inheritance Tax and enable you to make sure that the money was provided in a measured fashion. The beneficiaries would be said to have an 'interest in possession', and you could, in the case of a 'flexible trust' be able to give the trustees a 'power of appointment' which means that they have the power to switch part or all of the money from one beneficiary to others, under conditions set by you, the settlor.

No Interest in Possession Trusts are where the beneficiaries are not entitled to income from the trust fund as it arises; the trustees have the power to choose whether to distribute such income or to let it build up until later.

Discretionary trusts

This is a type of No Interest in Possession Trust where the trustee has the power to decide the amount of money a beneficiary can receive, and which beneficiary to give it to. The trust's income is taxed at 35 per cent in the UK, but a beneficiary who is a lower-rate taxpayer can get part of this back from the Inland Revenue. This high tax rate is the main disadvantage for this type of trust in the UK, another disadvantage being that Inheritance Tax is charged at a low rate once every decade and when the money finally leaves the trust.

Accumulation and maintenance trusts

This is for beneficiaries up to the age of 25, and has special advantages for Inheritance Tax. The funds in the trust must either be accumulated, or else used for the education and maintenance of beneficiaries. In the UK it is taxed in the same way as discretionary trusts, except that there is no Inheritance Tax charge each decade or at the end of the trust.

Bare trusts

With bare trusts, the trustees act as nominees who hold assets for someone else, who still legally possesses them. They can be useful to higher-rate taxpayers who want to accumulate money for their children; a child can possess the assets, held by the trustee who reinvests the income. Because this income belongs to the child but is not paid to the child, it is tax free in the UK up to £3,525.

Fixed interest trusts

In this kind of trust, the beneficiaries receive income from the trust, which is liable for Income Tax. If the trust deed allows it, the settlor or trustees can cancel this if the beneficiaries behave in a way that they don't like.

Secret trusts

Suppose you are a married man with a mistress who has borne you an illegitimate child. In order to prevent your wife finding out that you have settled money on trust for the mistress and her child, you can create a secret trust; this is a difficult area of law, and you must take precautions such as giving the secret beneficiaries a document enabling them to prove that they are indeed the beneficiaries.

Trading trusts

These are where the trustees carry on a business for the benefit of the beneficiaries. In the UK they are unattractive because of taxation rates, but overseas they may have their uses. Professional trustees are unlikely to be willing to take on the additional responsibilities and risks of running a business.

THE SETTLOR

The settlor is the person who has established the trust. It is possible, though, for other people to put assets into ('settle') a trust as well, and they too are described as settlors. The settlor can retain some powers over what happens through the trust deed; the main thing to remember, though, is that it is the trustees who legally own the assets of the trust. The settlor may retain the power to appoint new trustees, or require approval before the trustees take important actions. Usually a settlor creates a trust by transferring assets to two or more trustees and declaring a trust, but it is possible for settlors to keep the assets and that they themselves are the trustees of specified assets. Another way that a settlor can safeguard the trust assets is by appointing a protector to monitor the activities of the trustees. The protector might well be a lawyer who is a trusted associate of the settlor.

THE PROTECTOR

Using protectors is becoming more and more common, especially when setting up offshore trusts which may be thousands of miles from where you live. You can give a protector powers to:

- approve the fees and expenses charged by the trustees
- change the trustees
- change the jurisdiction under which the trust is governed
- monitor the way the trust is being run
- stop a proposed investment
- stop a proposed distribution of money from the trust to a beneficiary

- stop an addition of a beneficiary, or the removal of one
- decide whether the powers over the trust which the settlor kept back can be temporarily set aside because he is under duress (for example if the settlor were being held by an oppressive regime who wanted to influence the trust), or if the settlor has gone mad.

Protectors will be keen to limit their liabilities, so they may insist that the trust instrument specifies that their powers are purely personal and that they simply have to act in good faith in order to be safe from negligence claims.

Using protectors

While protectors are not statutorily defined in most jurisdictions, they are used widely. Many countries insist that the ownership connection between the settlor and the trust is entirely severed if the trust is to get any tax benefit; this makes settlors nervous, particularly if the trust is in a remote country, and appointing a protector is a way of still keeping tabs on the settlement. Often the protector will be the settlor's family solicitor in the home country. Trust companies can be faceless organizations – their staff may move on and the company may be part of an international group. A professional protector is better able to resist any detrimental moves on the part of a trust company than a settlor can. Protectors should be given enough powers to become intimately involved with the trust when the need arises, and should receive full information on trustees' activities on behalf of the trust. It is generally better to use a professional protector for these reasons, particularly if the settlor is old, as he or she can enforce the settlor's wishes after death. Trust companies may be under pressure to invest money in funds managed by a sister company, and protectors can prevent this if necessary.

THE BENEFICIARIES

The beneficiaries are the people who are named in the trust instrument as the people for whom the trustees are holding the assets. They can be named individuals, or a particular class of people (for example, the descendants of the settlor, including unborn grandchildren), and the trust deed can specify situations where beneficiaries can be removed or added.

They have the right to sue the trustees and to trace where the trust's assets have gone. Often, though, beneficiaries are unaware of their rights, or even that they are beneficiaries. There are many trust funds sitting quietly around the world where the beneficiaries have not been found.

TRUSTEES

The ideal trustee is, as the word suggests, someone you can trust absolutely. Experienced cynics say that while British, American and Channel Island trustees are 'reasonably honest', some trustees in other jurisdictions may be less so. The law has heavy penalties for trustees who act wrongly, but as a settlor you must consider what remedies you (or your beneficiaries after your death) may have if they do misbehave. Technically it is the beneficiaries, not the settlor, who can take legal action against trustees, but in practice a settlor can retain some control by retaining some rights specified in the trust deed, for example by keeping the right to change trustees at will.

You will want to make sure that you have the funds available to pursue them through the courts in such an event, and also that the jurisdiction under which the trust is governed will allow you to do so. However, outright theft is rare, and generally occurs where the settlor has died and the beneficiaries do not have the capacity to assert their rights – obviously a situation which could tempt a trustee.

More common is simple overcharging; in addition to the agreed remuneration, you may find that the fund is billed for various 'expenses' which, if allowed to go unchallenged, can make quite a dent in the trust's assets over time. As with other professions, the principle would appear to be that the unscrupulous trustee tries to take what will go unnoticed because the amount is not that much relative to the size of the fund, can be justified and can be given back if the settlor or the beneficiaries demand it fiercely enough, without the trustee losing too much face.

Nor can one be entirely confident with the Trust Department of a bank, given that, like any large bureaucracy, it is liable to make silly mistakes. Let's assume, though, that you are careful and fortunate enough to have trustees worthy of the name. Professional trustees are worth paying for:

- They must understand international tax law and standards of regulation, which is no easy task.

- While they are the legal owners of the trust fund, they hold it for the benefit of the beneficiaries and can only do things with the trust fund which the trust deed says that they can.

- They are obliged to use the utmost diligence in carrying out their duties. This means, for example, that they must avoid making financial losses with the trust fund.

- They must keep proper accounts.

- They must obey the laws relating to trusts in the jurisdiction the trust comes under and the obligations imposed by the trust deed.

- They may have to enter into contracts on trust business whereby they become personally liable.

- They have a legal duty to act in the best interests of the beneficiaries.

- As trusts are not 'legal persons', it is the trustees who can sue or be sued.

- As is the case for sole traders and most business partnerships, trustees are jointly and severally liable for losses. This means that if the trust fund made a loss, say on an unwise investment, any of the trustees could be made to make good the entire loss out of their personal wealth. The trustee would then have to pursue other trustees for a contribution, but this would be nothing to do with the trust fund. Saying that you were a 'sleeping' trustee with no active involvement would be no defence, and you would still be liable for the whole of the loss. In fact, all trustees are supposed to take an active part in managing a trust, and cannot delegate their functions unless they are authorized by the trust instrument or under a one-year power of attorney. In the latter case the trustee would still be liable for the whole loss.

- If a trustee did not have enough personal wealth to make good a loss, he or she would be made bankrupt.

Clearly these last two points would not be of much value if the trustees had no money of their own. In different jurisdictions there may be variations of these rules. In Jersey and Guernsey, for instance, different rules apply with regard to trustees' liabilities if they act in breach of trust, or for their acts and omissions over contracts (see page 198). In addition, you are likely to find that trustees will insist on clauses in a trust deed which exonerate them from any losses to the trust fund that have occurred so long as they have acted in good faith. Proving that they have not acted in good faith can be exceedingly difficult.

A trustee must not put himself in a position where there is a possibility of a conflict between his personal self-interest and his altruistic fiduciary duty. For instance, trustees cannot sell their own property to the trust or buy trust property for themselves. They must account for any profit made by using trust property and profits made by virtue of their position as a trustee. However, this may be varied by the trust deed or by the agreement of the beneficiaries; such an agreement would only stand up in court if the beneficiaries were fully informed about the issue and were sane and of responsible age.

When trouble arises, trustees can go to court to get guidance on how to act. However, any expenses incurred by doing this would be charged to the trust fund – and this could be very expensive.

Other duties of trustees

Trustees must:

- usually keep the trust's assets separately from their private assets. The trust deed may authorize them to keep it in the name of one trustee or a nominee
- get professional advice for any investments which they make with the trust's assets
- administer the trust assets honestly and impartially for all beneficiaries
- keep a fair balance between beneficiaries interested in income and those interested in capital
- not use the assets of the trust as part of their own property. If a trustee dies, goes bankrupt or gets divorced, the trust fund remains an independent fund which is only available for the beneficiaries
- act unanimously unless the trust is a charitable trust or the trust deed authorizes them to act by a majority
- decide for themselves what to do with the trust. If they simply do as the settlor tells them they are in breach of trust.

TRUSTS AND CIVIL LAW STATES

In the civil law, which is based on Roman law, ownership is an abstract concept. Unlike common law where land ultimately belongs to the

Crown, in civil law ownership of property means that the owner has all ownership rights, such as:

- the right to dispose of property as desired
- the right to manage the property freely
- the right to 'enjoy' the property freely.

In civil law two or more people cannot be owners of an asset. Where there are co-owners, each co-owner is the absolute owner of his or her share of the whole property. People who are not the owner can have rights over the owner's property, or rights against the owner as a person. Rights against an owner's property have to be officially registered, and include such things as:

- restrictive covenants on land
- mortgages
- rights to the use of property
- rights to income from property – this can be for life or for a shorter period.

Another important feature of civil law is that the power of a person to choose the people who will inherit his or her estate is more limited than in common law countries. Widows and blood relatives, for instance, tend to have rights to inherit a portion of an estate whether the owner likes it or not – these are known as 'forced heirship' rights. Forced heirship laws are often circumvented by making prenuptial agreements, which are acceptable to courts in many civil law countries.

The civil law's idea of contract is much wider than in common law, where, for example, in English law only someone who is a 'party' to a contract can sue over it, and only then if the person has given something as 'consideration' as his or her part of the bargain. In civil law, a contract can have a clause related to a third party, who can sue to have it enforced. This means that a trust is, in a way, covered by civil law contract, but, unlike in common law, the beneficiaries would not be able to enforce their rights against the creditors of a trustee or people who had received assets from the trust fund wrongfully, unless such transferees knew that the trustees were acting wrongfully.

Difficulties with trusts in civil law countries

Civil law countries, which include all the countries in the EU except the UK and Ireland, do not recognize equitable interests in property, such as where two or more people own a house under a joint tenancy in the UK. In a joint tenancy if one person dies, the whole equity in the property belongs to the other person, and does not have to go through probate.

All this means that if the assets of a trust are located in a civil law country which has not enacted laws that implement the Hague Trusts Convention the trust will not be recognized. Thus, if you had several houses in such a country which was held on trust for some members of your family but not others, you could find that the properties went to the wrong people! Trustees have to be very careful not to transfer assets to such jurisdictions or make sure that such assets are not traceable to them.

The Hague Trusts Convention

The good news is that civil law states that have ratified the Hague Convention on the Law Applicable to Trusts and passed laws implementing it will deal more kindly with trusts, and also that because of the existence of the Hague Convention, courts in countries which have not ratified the convention are likely to take it into account when passing judgement. For instance, they may use the convention as a basis for resolving issues involving trusts.

The convention describes trusts as follows (Article 2):

> For the purposes of this Convention, the term 'trust' refers to the legal relationships created – *inter vivos* or on death – by a person, the settlor, when assets have been placed under the control of a trustee for the benefit of a beneficiary or for a specified purpose. A trust has the following characteristics:
> (a) the assets constitute a separate fund and are not a part of the trustee's own estate;
> (b) title to the trust assets stand in the name of the trustee or in the name of another person on behalf of the trustee;
> (c) the trustee has the power and the duty, in respect of which he is accountable, to manage, employ or dispose of the assets in accordance with the terms of the trust and the special duties imposed upon him by law.
> The reservation by the settlor of certain rights and powers, and the fact that the trustee may himself have rights as a beneficiary, are not necessarily inconsistent with the existence of a trust.

Article 11 says that a trust created in accordance with the applicable law 'shall be recognized as a trust', and goes on to say that:

Such recognition shall imply, as a minimum, that the trust property constitutes a separate fund, that the trustee may sue and be sued in his capacity as trustee, and that he may appear or act in this capacity before a notary or any person acting in an official capacity. In so far as the law applicable to the trust requires or provides, such recognition shall imply, in particular:

(a) that personal creditors of the trustee shall have no recourse against the trust assets;

(b) that the trust assets shall not form part of the trustee's estate upon his insolvency or bankruptcy;

(c) that the trust assets shall not form part of the matrimonial property of the trustee or his spouse nor part of the trustee's estate upon his death;

(d) that the trust assets may be recovered when the trustee, in breach of trust, has mingled trust assets with his own property or has alienated trust assets. However, the rights and obligations of any third party holder of the assets shall remain subject to the law determined by the choice of law rules of the forum.

The Convention only came into force in 1987, and the process of ratification and implementation is still continuing. Countries and regions jurisdictions which have signed the Convention include:

- Australia
- Bermuda
- Canada (some provinces only)
- France
- Gibraltar
- Holland
- Hong Kong
- Isle of Man
- Italy
- Jersey
- the UK
- the US.

The Convention does not try to introduce the idea of the trust into civil law countries, but establishes international law rules to decide which laws will apply when deciding how a particular trust is administered, or if it is valid. It recognizes all the characteristics of a trust except that beneficiaries are not given the right to trace the assets of a trust in a non-trust country.

Conclusion

It should be clear by now that setting up a trust is a deadly serious undertaking. More than one tax lawyer has told me privately that they don't believe that any of their clients really understand all the legal implications. One has to rely on the professionals, and while this may be entirely sensible if you have close, long-standing relationships with a lawyer – and a professional trustee – it would not be wise to set up a trust by walking into the first solicitor's office you see on the high street. It would be a sensible precaution not to put all your eggs in one basket; having at least as great a proportion of disposable assets outside a trust fund as you have in it will enable you to fight your corner with more chance of success. Given that the bare minimum that is economic to put into a trust is about £250,000, and more realistically £500,000, a settlor probably needs to have £1 million in free assets before setting up a trust.

7
BANKING OVERSEAS

Banks are not all the same, especially when they are in foreign jurisdictions, and great care should be taken in choosing the right bank. In this chapter we will look at:

- Dealing with banks
- The BCCI story
- Choosing a bank
- Opening an offshore account
- Class A and Class B banks
- Buying your own bank
- Banking strategies
- Bearer instruments
- Bearer instruments as an investment
- The US bond-rating system
- Which bonds to buy?
- Hawalah and chop banking
- Money laundering
- Drug trafficking – the background
- The narco-economics of the Americas
- Political aspects of the trade
- Robert Vesco – an offshore outlaw
- Dangers for the innocent investor
- New technology

'Banks have done more injury to the religion, morality, tranquility, prosperity and even wealth of the nation than they have done or ever will do good.'

US PRESIDENT JOHN ADAMS, 1819

'The process by which banks create money is so simple that the mind is repelled.'

J. K. GALBRAITH

DEALING WITH BANKS

Any claims by tax havens or banks to offer 'total banking secrecy' should be taken with a pinch of salt. Austria, Switzerland and Liechtenstein have strong traditions of banking secrecy, and while banks based there are unlikely to protect a known drug dealer who is wanted by international law enforcers, they are known for their robust defence of foreign clients' privacy. The same cannot be said for other banks, especially those with branches in the United States; a powerful government finds it easy to bully most banks into telling them what it wants to know, these days. While legitimate offshore investors may not immediately see the desirability of total secrecy, consider the following:

(a) Many countries regularly freeze the accounts of foreign nationals in case of hostilities. For example, if you were a Kuwaiti with a US bank account at the beginning of the Gulf War, you had your bank account frozen. Pleading that it was your country that had been invaded and that you were an injured party would have been to no avail in the short term, although the accounts were eventually unfrozen. If a bank doesn't know your nationality, or does not have to reveal it to anyone, your account is safe in such cases.

(b) In a bitter divorce, your ex-spouse employs dirty tactics, accusing you of some crime such as child abuse with the intention of acquiring more than a fair share of the marital assets. Keeping money where it can't be found is desirable.

(c) A fellow director of a company commits fraud and your business collapses. You are under suspicion and creditors are obtaining orders to seize all your assets. You know that you will be exonerated in the long term, but in the meantime you fend them off by moving some assets abroad to play for time.

If you have never experienced events like these they may sound far-fetched, but the reality is that they are happening all the time.

Banks are businesses which offer services; you, the customer, need to be sure that your bank is trustworthy. Much depends on the jurisdiction of the bank – the branches of a bank have to obey the laws of the country where they are located – but it is not enough to assume that a bank with a branch in a country known for its sound banking will be OK. Where there is money, there is fraud, and the banking community has its fair share of villains. What many people do not realize is that banks are, by their nature, involved in the grey world that lies between politics and commerce. To give an example, when Iraq invaded Kuwait its forces seized a vast amount of Kuwaiti dinars held in cash by Kuwaiti banks. After the liberation of Kuwait, its government changed the currency in order to prevent the looted currency being spent; anyone holding the old currency legitimately could apply to change it for the new money. To my personal knowledge, at least one London branch of a foreign-owned bank assisted in the changing of old money captured by Iraqis, using Kuwaiti middlemen as a cover. Was a crime committed? Presumably some Kuwaiti laws were broken, though perhaps British ones weren't. This kind of thing goes on all the time, but is very rarely reported.

The BCCI story

The collapse of BCCI, the Bank of Credit and Commerce International, brought to light examples of fraud and what might be called 'political crime'. BCCI had allegedly operated accounts for terrorist organizations, laundered drug money on a large scale, and, it was claimed, assisted the CIA, also Britain's secret services, and those of several Islamic countries in covert operations. It has even been suggested that civil servants working for the regulatory bodies were actually afraid to do anything about BCCI because of its intelligence connections.

The bank was started in the late 1960s by Pakistani bankers using oil money from the Gulf. Its operational headquarters was in London, though it was legally based in Luxembourg and the Cayman Islands, and it had branches all over the world. In the early 1970s it opened more than 40 retail branches in the UK, mainly serving Asian customers who had recently immigrated to Britain. By the late 1970s, the Bank of America, which had increased its shareholding in BCCI from 25 per cent to almost 50 per cent in 1973, was eager to sell out, which it managed to do in 1980. In 1979, the Banking Act in the UK tightened the rules on what kinds of bodies could call themselves banks, and BCCI found itself awarded the status of 'licensed deposit taker'. Because it had overseas branches, it could still use the word 'bank' in its name, but it had to display a sign reading 'licensed deposit taker' at its branches to warn customers that it was not as safe as a bank – in fact, ill-informed customers were told that this meant that BCCI was a more stable and important bank than the others with high street branches.

Major losses followed, and BCCI began to pay out old depositors with the new ones' money. In 1985 the Bank of England forced BCCI to move its money market operations to Abu Dhabi, and soon afterwards the authorities in Luxembourg asked the Bank of England to take over the supervision of the bank, which it refused to do. In 1987 a compromise was reached in which the central banks of several countries, including the Bank of England, formed a 'College of Regulators' to supervise BCCI. The following year several senior BCCI employees were arrested for drug money laundering in Florida. While banks acted to reduce their exposure to BCCI, customers kept on coming, in the touching belief that an international bank of its size (it had assets of $20billion) would be properly controlled by the governments in whose countries it operated.

In 1991 the Bank of England finally made its move, leading some 69 regulators across the world in closing down BCCI. Unhappy customers mobbed its branches, and a succession of court cases followed. The Sheikh of Abu Dhabi, as the majority shareholder of the bank, has promised to give compensation, but the row trundles on. Perhaps the whole story of what happened, and why the regulatory authorities took so long to act, will never emerge.

The BCCI story does have a moral for bank customers; one wouldn't have had to be particularly well-informed to have realized in Britain what BCCI's 'licensed deposit taker' status meant (no Bank of England guarantee on deposits), nor could one have failed to notice that the BCCI style was rather different from other banks. Several years of adverse press reports should have alerted depositors to possible problems so, when in doubt, move to another bank.

Choosing a bank

It should be plain by now that banks are not all the same! They vary from ultra-rich, ultra-conservative organizations with reputations to protect, to out-and-out crooks, with every shade and variety imaginable in between. Appearances are everything in banking; to paraphrase the famous remarks made by Keynes, bankers have a herd instinct and all rush together into disasters. It is perfectly respectable to be a banker who has lost money as long as all the other bankers have lost too. At present the world of derivatives is almost out of control – all the banks, and many of the large companies are actively trading in derivatives markets on their own account. Of course, they all say they are not speculating but hedging, but perhaps the recent collapse of that hugely respectable and centuries-old merchant bank, Barings, is a taste of things to come.

In terms of stability and security, the biggest US, UK, German and Swiss banks are probably the best, followed by certain banks in other German-speaking countries (Austria, Liechtenstein); recent trends in legislation (see page 141), however, mean that one cannot expect much confidentiality from a US bank or a bank which has a US branch – this is because of the current money laundering hysteria. British nationals investing overseas may prefer not to use a British bank for similar reasons. Switzerland is not the paragon of secrecy it used to be, largely due to American pressure.

Opening an offshore account

Write to a number of banks which are of interest to you, keeping the letter short and to the point. A professional approach helps, particularly if the amounts concerned are not large (under £1 million is chicken feed to some banks) as they may decline your business as unprofitable. You may wish to use a pseudonym and a different address when making the first approach; this way you have retained your anonymity while obtaining the information you require. The bank will ask for information from you too; specimen signatures, and references will usually be required.

Numbered accounts and other methods of ensuring anonymity do exist but the bottom line is that they are almost all for very rich people only, and anyone else will simply be told that they do not exist. If you are a very rich person, you will know who to ask. If you are not, and want to protect yourself with layers of secrecy, investigate all the possible types of savings accounts in banks and building society equivalents in respectable countries. You will find one or two that can be opened without references and can then be used as references themselves to open offshore accounts.

Class A and Class B banks

Many tax havens have two classes of bank. Class A banks have offices and counter staff, and are as fully regulated as the haven demands.

130

These are the ones to use in most cases. Class **B** banks may or may not be allowed to open an account for you and provide you with banking services, but unless you are closely connected with the principals and understand the exact nature of their particular business, you should not attempt to deal with one.

Buying your own bank

It's an attractive idea; an offshore banking licence can be had for only a few thousand pounds in some jurisdictions, and one may only have to show a net worth of £150,000 or so. Once your bank is formed, you can:

- deal in the money markets
- take deposits
- borrow at inter-bank lending rates
- enjoy cheaper banking transactions
- obtain discounts and credit on monetary instruments
- lend money.

Sounds wonderful? Forget it! Unless you are a banker already or have a much greater net worth than £150,000, this is not for you. Leave it to the professionals.

Banking strategies

Make a plan, on paper, of your banking needs. Here are some hints:

- Spread your assets across different banks in different countries with, say, a maximum of 15 per cent in each bank, and keep the money in different currencies. Countries such as Liechtenstein and Switzerland are attractive, but banking is expensive.

- Tend towards old established banks, but research them as thoroughly as you can – they may have been bought by less stable organizations. Size isn't everything, as the BCCI case amply demonstrates.

- Check where all a bank's branches are, and avoid banks with US branches.

- Find out the location of the head office, and read up on banking regulations in that country.

- Read the banking regulations of the country in which your account will be held.

- Read the financial press; news of a bank's difficulties regularly precede its collapse. At the first sign of trouble, switch to another bank.

- Watch out for hints of nationalization.

- Check out guarantee schemes in the case of a bank's failure.

- Avoid keeping long-term deposits in countries with a track record of seizure or instability.

- Where legal, use 'noms de guerre' to open accounts as a confidentiality measure. If you are a child pornographer or a drug dealer this will not protect you, but it may help you protect yourself against creditors, spouses and tax collectors.

BEARER INSTRUMENTS

Transporting large sums of cash internationally can often be difficult, but there are other options, in particular bearer shares and bearer bonds. Bearer shares and bonds can be freely bought, sold, traded and given away in most countries without much documentation or the need for them to pass through the banking system. 'Bearer' instruments are legally owned by the person who has them in their possession (and is thus the 'bearer'). Generally they are not registered.

Many large and stable companies quoted on one of the major stock markets issue bearer instruments, but only in countries where it is legal to do so. If one has an offshore company in an appropriate jurisdiction, one can issue one's own bearer instruments. These could be used, for example, to sell property owned by the company simply by handing over all its shares in bearer form in return for payment which could also be in bearer form.

Even governments issue bearer bonds, as do banks, insurance companies, local authorities and quasi-governmental bodies. Eurobonds are issued in bearer form. Compared with cash or gold, bearer instruments are very light and small; a million pounds' worth of gold is difficult to take on an aeroplane, and suitcases stuffed with bank notes can attract unwelcome attention, but a bearer instrument can be kept with a sheaf of papers on one's own person.

Bearer instruments can be bought through stockbrokers, normally in the currency denomination of your choice. Good stockbrokers can arrange for anonymity when purchasing. They can then be sold at banks and stockbrokers in other countries.

Like cash, these instruments are not safe for long-term holding; if they are destroyed, stolen or lost, you have lost the money they represent. As with cash, they can be insured, but the cost is high – some 12 per cent of their value – and replacement takes time. Fraud is another danger as bearer instruments can be forged and cancelled ones may be passed off as valid. Cancelled bonds may only have tiny holes or perforations to indicate that they have been cancelled. For this reason, one should only deal with the old-fashioned brokers and banks who have the highest reputations. They will give you a receipt and guarantee that the instrument is bona fide.

Bearer instruments as an investment

Unlike cash, bearer bonds pay interest, and bearer shares may pay dividends. As with registered shares and bonds their value fluctuates, so they should be regarded as an investment, and purchased accordingly; even a few days could wreak havoc on their value if you buy when the market is going the wrong way.

Bearer bonds may have coupons attached to them and are known as coupon bonds. The coupons are detached from the bond at specified intervals and can be redeemed at financial institutions for cash, as an interest payment. The bond itself can be held until it matures and then redeemed for its face value, or can be sold on at current market value beforehand. The current market value of a bond largely depends on interest rate fluctuations.

Non-coupon bonds simply pay the interest in full when the bond is redeemed.

The US bond-rating system

Not all bonds are the same – it all depends on the quality of the issuer. Bonds are rated by Moody's and Standard and Poor's. They are as follows:

	Standard and Poor's	*Moody's*
Top-quality bonds	AAA	Aaa
High-quality bonds	AA	Aa

	Standard and Poor's	*Moody's*
Good bonds	A	A
Medium-quality bonds which may be insecure in the long term	BBB	Baa
Bonds with only moderate security	BB	Ba

The following categories are for bonds which are generally considered to be bad investments for small investors:

Standard and Poor's	*Moody's*
B	B

The 'C' categories are for bonds which have sometimes defaulted or are in danger of doing so:

Standard and Poor's	*Moody's*
CCC	Caa
CC	Ca
C	C
In default D	–

Which bonds to buy?

If you buy a bond just before market interest rates take a dive, you can make a substantial tax-free capital gain, as the market value of the bond will rise. Buying bonds outside your own country in other currencies can be a good bet if you think the value of your own currency is falling. For those who don't want to become specialists in the field, bonds are basically safe and boring. If you live in the UK or another country where the government perpetually fiddles with interest rates, you will have to keep a weather eye on the economy at all times if you hold long bonds unless you hold them to redemption, and even then you may find that inflation has taken a bite out of them. Eurobonds are more attractive because they are outside the jurisdiction of any government. Personally, I find speculation on interest rates unappealing – it is so easy to get it wrong. Choose 'Triple A' (AAA)-rated bonds for moving money around – they are easy to sell. The days of the bearer bond are numbered; it is only a matter of time before they are abolished as the cashless society approaches.

HAWALAH AND CHOP BANKING

Banking developed centuries ago from the practice of depositing money with trusted individuals (often goldsmiths) for a fee; these people would then re-lend the money to make additional profits. There are a number of survivors of this system, which is used to transfer money internationally, notably the Indian 'hawalah' and the Chinese 'chop' banking methods. 'Hawalah' banking works thus: a deposit is made with the banker and the money is rapidly transferred to a hawalah banker in another country where it can be withdrawn, less a commission, which can be as high as 15 per cent. 'Chop' banking is well-known in Hong Kong and other centres with large Chinese communities – a deposit is made, and a token is given as a receipt. The token can then be used to withdraw the money from a chop banker in another country. These practices are illegal in many countries and are generally unregulated.

It is estimated that there are thousands of full-time hawalah dealers throughout the world; the majority are Indian and are based either in the Gulf or in South East Asia. While some are big-time dealers, many cater for the impoverished Indian migrants who wish to send money home without suffering from regulatory burdens and high charges in conventional Indian banks. For example, a worker in the Gulf might have to wait a month for his money to be received in India if he sent it by a legitimate route, but could do it in three days by going to a hawalah dealer. Unfortunately hawalah dealing is associated with other criminal activities and many clients find themselves blackmailed into becoming 'mules' in smuggling operations. One disturbing aspect of hawalah deals is their relation to illegal organ operations – not long ago a party of Turkish kidney patients was apprehended in Bombay, where they had arrived for transplants, having paid the medical fees to hawalah dealers in Istanbul. More conventional deals include the regular undervaluing of goods leaving India and over-invoicing of foreign importers, the balance being paid abroad via the hawalah system.

135

MONEY LAUNDERING

The expression 'money laundering' seems to have first appeared in the 1970s in connection with the Watergate scandal. Richard Nixon's Committee to Re-elect the President raised large sums of money from big businesses who were keen to keep their donations anonymous. This was achieved through a variety of means involving false accounting and the channelling of funds through third parties in foreign countries in order to make the original donors more difficult to trace. These days, however, 'money laundering' generally refers to the attempts by illegal drug traffickers to legitimize their ill-gotten gains. The amounts of money involved are so vast that drug money laundering has become a significant part of the world's economy, and in recent years a considerable amount of anti-money laundering legislation has been passed all over the world. Unfortunately, 'catch-all' anti-drug laws are affecting the innocent as well as the guilty, and for this reason it is important for offshore investors to be aware of what is going on. While this book is not intended for 'true crime' aficionados, I am firmly of the opinion that offshore investors are putting their heads in the sand if they do not keep themselves informed about this ugly aspect of international finance.

Drug trafficking – the background

Drug abuse is as old as human history. There have always been individuals who have chosen to dose themselves with medicines for non-medical reasons, and there always will be. Different eras and cultures have taken widely different attitudes towards this vice, ranging from complete tolerance to draconian attempts to stamp it out. To see how rapidly attitudes to drug abuse have changed in the 'civilized' Western countries, consider the following, written by Rudyard Kipling in 1900 (*From Sea to Sea*, Vol 2, Macmillan):

> On the banks of the Ganges, forty miles below Benares as the crow flies, stands the Ghazipur Factory, an opium mint as it were, whence issue the precious cakes that are to replenish the coffers of the Indian Government. The busy season is setting in, for with April the opium comes up from the districts after having run the gauntlet of the district officers of the Opium Department, who will pass it as fit for use . . . The district officer submits forms – never was

such a place for forms as the Ghazipur Factory – showing the quality and weight of each pot . . . if any pots are broken or tampered with, an unfortunate individual called the import-officer, appointed to work like a horse from dawn to dewy eve, must examine the man in charge of the challan and reduce his statement to writing. Fancy getting any native to explain how a jar has been smashed! But the Perfect Flower is about as valuable as silver.'

Kipling is describing the state opium industry in British India. Throughout the nineteenth century Western traders had sought to open up markets for opium, and in China they hit paydirt. Despite China's determination not to legalize what was plainly a social evil, the industry was hugely successful, resulting in two Opium Wars being fought between China and Britain (with various Western allies). By 1917, however, China had virtually stamped out the trade, and the twentieth century has seen concerted attempts on the part of many nations to eliminate drug trafficking for non-medical purposes. In Western countries drug abuse was virtually limited to a minority of sailors, soldiers on overseas postings and beatniks until the 1960s, when the spontaneous appearance of the mass youth movement, known by many names, of which the most appropriate is perhaps the 'Flower Power Era', brought the non-medical use of drugs to millions of young Westerners from all backgrounds and levels of education. Increasingly severe legislation followed. At first, legislators failed to distinguish between 'soft' and 'hard' drugs, and many individuals received harsh punishments for the possession of small quantities of drugs which, at present, would be dealt with far less severely in the UK and many other jurisdictions.

From the point of view of the drug trafficker, the really big money is in 'hard drugs', particularly heroin and cocaine, for two main reasons: heroin and cocaine addiction is so severe that addicts are prepared to pay high prices for small quantities; and it is far more profitable and economic to smuggle small quantites of heroin and cocaine than it is to smuggle large quantities of, say, cannabis, a 'soft drug'.

In the 1970s heroin addiction was regarded as the principle drug menace. A derivative of opium, grown widely in the Far East, it was only a matter of time before organized crime, terrorists and political groups had established factories in the growing countries and found ever more sophisticated ways of getting it to the lucrative markets of the West. Pressure on countries such as Turkey, Thailand, Pakistan, Malaysia and Indonesia to crack down on the trade caused them to introduce extremely severe penalties for drug smuggling, which remain in place to this day. A major change occurred in the early 1980s; suddenly cocaine use was all the rage in America amongst the well-to-do young. Lawyers, accountants, actors and businesspeople began to spend thousands of dollars on cocaine for 'recreational' use. These were not the degraded and bankrupted individuals who had been the market for heroin, but educated, upwardly mobile yuppies. Cocaine is derived from the coca plant, which grows in South America, and a new force in international crime developed.

The narco-economics of the Americas

Most cocaine comes from Bolivia and Peru, but it was in Colombia that the export trade became properly organized. The towns of Cali and Medellin are the headquarters of 'drug cartels' which have become the only really big foreign exchange earners of the region. Official estimates are probably exaggerated, but their assets are said to exceed $400 billion across the world, with some $100 billion annual turnover.

Leading Colombian drug barons are said to be among the top ten richest people in the world. One such individual was the late Señor Pablo Escobar, finally gunned down in 1993. Born in 1949, Escobar typifies the cocaine dealer of the 1980s; establishing a large number of smuggling routes via Mexico, Central America and the Caribbean, to the United States, Escobar was able to corrupt politicians and the judiciary in many countries. Cultivating a Robin Hood image amongst the Colombian poor, Escobar controlled factories, fleets of aeroplanes and an army of gangsters, many of whom were reportedly trained in the arts of war by British and Israeli mercenaries. He became such a public figure that the Colombian government was forced to act against him. He retaliated by waging a terrorist campaign against government officials and the judiciary, blowing up an Avianca aeroplane with 107 people on board and conducting a bombing campaign throughout the country. In all he is said to have been responsible for thousands of successful assassinations. Although Escobar is dead, other cartel leaders are still very much in business today. Their money-laundering activities are spread across the world, and tax havens are a natural focus for their attentions.

Political aspects of the trade

Many politicians in the countries through which cocaine passes on its route to the US are deeply involved in the trade, as is well documented.

A striking example is General Manuel Noriega, the ruler of Panama for five years. Heavily dominated by the US, Panama subsists on the trade passing through the Colon Free Zone on the Panama canal, the second largest duty-free trading zone in the world after Hong Kong. In the early 1980s, Noriega is alleged to have been earning $10 million a month in commissions by providing facilities for drug smugglers. Playing a double game, Noriega assisted the US Drug Enforcement Agency (DEA) in capturing several big-time dealers, and for a time it appeared that he was very much on the side of law and order.

Meanwhile, he was jockeying for position with the rival Colombian cartels, and busily laundering money through banks such as BCCI (see page 128). As late as 1986, a senior DEA official wrote to Noriega thus:

> Many millions of dollars and many thousands of pounds of drugs have been taken from the drug traffickers and international money launderers. Your personal commitment to Operation Pisces and the competent, professional and tireless efforts of other officials in the Republic of Panama were essential to the final outcome of this investigation. Drug traffickers around the world are on notice that the proceeds and profits of illegal ventures are not welcome in Panama.

Three years later US troops invaded Panama and took Noriega by force back to the US to stand trial. In 1992 he was convicted for drug trafficking and sentenced to 40 years in prison.

Robert Vesco – an offshore outlaw

The remarkable career of Robert Vesco illustrates how a determined individual can exploit offshore anomalies for decades in an extreme and criminal way with apparent impunity. His recent come-uppance may also serve as a warning to those tempted to follow in his footsteps.

International financier, banker, fraudster, legitimate entrepreneur, outlaw, double agent, drug dealer, bribe-giver and political manipulator, 'El Americano' has had an extraordinary career since his blue-collar beginnings in Detroit some 62 years ago. It is impossible to encapsulate the variety and scope of his activities in a few lines, but here are some of the important facts that are known about the course of this secretive man's life:

Leaving school at 15, Vesco began his working life in an automobile repair shop, studying engineering at night school. Before he was 20, he had designed the first aluminium grille for the Oldsmobile, but within a few years he had abandoned practical engineering for his real vocation: finance.

By his mid-thirties, Vesco was a freelance financial finder, and had put together a group of small engineering and electrical businesses under the grand title of 'International Controls Corporation (ICC).

In 1968, Vesco raised a 25 million Eurodollar loan by means of debentures, arranged by Butler's Bank of the Bahamas. In 1970, Vesco successfully restructured the debt by issuing new paper, requiring the holders of the original debentures to accept losses. With his new financial strength, Vesco lent $15 million to IOS, the soon-to-be-doomed investment fund controlled by the notorious Bernie Cornfeld; in return he received warrants to buy IOS shares.

By 1972, the SEC had a warrant out for his arrest, charging him with looting some $220 million (about $800 million in today's money) from IOS, and Vesco went on the run, fleeing to Costa Rica.

Meanwhile, Vesco had become closely associated with Richard Nixon, allegedly becoming Nixon's 'bag man', funnelling money for the corrupt administration's Watergate misdeeds. Vesco is said to have held financial proxies for secret Caribbean bank accounts owned by Nixon.

In 1973, Vesco was indicted for making illegal contributions to CREEP, Nixon's re-election campaign group.

Vesco spent most of the 1970s in Costa Rica, protected by President Jose 'Don Pepe' Figueres, who passed a notorious 'Vesco Law' to prevent his extradition.

In 1975, Vesco used Panamanian officials, provided by his business partner General Manuel Noriega, to recapture his yacht which had been confiscated by the US government. (In 1989, US troops invaded Panama and took Noriega by force back to the US to stand trial for drug trafficking. In 1992 he was convicted and sentenced to 40 years in prison.)

In the late 1970s, Vesco was forced out of Costa Rica, and had to move from country to country in the Caribbean and Central America.

In 1980, a US congressional committee investigated allegations that Vesco had tried to bribe Carter administration officials to get authorization for the shipment of military aircraft previously bought by Libya. When that failed, the committee concluded, he sought to embarrass President Carter by arranging a $220,000 'loan' to his brother, Billy Carter, from Libya.

In 1981, he was forced to leave the Bahamas after the failure of his Bahamas Commonwealth Bank. In 1987, the son of Lyndon Pyndling, then prime minister, accused Vesco of bribing both his father and other officials to conceal a drugs trans-shipment centre in the islands.

In 1982, Vesco was seen in Nicaragua where he is believed to have developed close ties with the Medellin cocaine cartel from Colombia.

Later in 1982, Vesco moved to Cuba where Castro allowed him to operate multifarious sanction-busting business activities. Thus began the most curious period of his career. Fidel Castro, hero of the revolution, dictator and ideologue, has been the USA's *bête noire* for decades; Vesco became a pawn in his complicated political manouvres against the US. Living under an assumed name in Havana, Vesco was protected by the Cuban regime in much the same way as it is said to protect other renegade US citizens such as Frank Terpil, a CIA agent turned gun-runner.

In May 1995, Vesco, by now a sick man, was arrested by the Cuban authorities, along with business partner 'Don-Don' Nixon, Richard Nixon's nephew. At his trial, Vesco denied guilt for alleged 'economic crimes' against Cuba, in particular trying to market a new cancer drug without the Cuban government's permission.

The Cuban court convicted him in 1996 of economic crimes against the state and sentenced him to 13 years in prison. Lidia Alfonsa Llauger, Vesco's Cuban wife, was convicted of lesser charges in the case and sentenced to nine years. Vesco's lawyer presented only a few witnesses during the trial, and argued that the evidence was weak, saying that Vesco had always acted in good faith in the hope of aiding Cuba's desperately ailing economy, ruined since the cessation of aid from the USSR. There is much speculation that Vesco's conviction was motivated by Castro's need to improve relations with the USA. In this sense, Vesco's very existence on Cuban soil might be said to be damaging to the island's economy. He is known to have had close personal contact with Castro and the great dictator is reported to have played with his children.

Dangers for the innocent investor

It should be plain by now that against such a background of violence and easy money the legitimate offshore investor can accidentally come under suspicion. Various international agreements, including the Vienna Convention and the Council of Europe Convention, have led to many countries introducing tough legislation against banking secrecy. In the UK, laws such as the Criminal Justice Act 1993, the Drug Trafficking Offences Act 1976, the Prevention of Terrorism Act 1989, the Bank of England's money laundering regulations of 1993 and dozens of other statutory instruments and informal agreements between financial institutions and the authorities, have effectively abolished banking confidentiality, let alone banking secrecy. Until recently a court order was required before bankers' books could be inspected, but now bankers are obliged to disclose information on demand to various authorities, not just the police or the courts.

Bankers are timid souls, and in most cases it is not necessary to use these laws as it is easier for a banker to give in to any request for information, especially in light of the penalties for failing to report a suspicious transaction. In such cases it is for the defendant to prove that he or she had no reason to suspect that the transaction was suspicious. It is not necessary to prove 'mens rea' (guilty intent), and the court is required to 'look at the objective circumstances of the transaction', a disturbingly vague phrase. UK banks must now employ a money laundering officer who must maintain contact with the authorities. This has led to such absurd events as a Spanish waiter being handed back the thousand pounds or so of legitimate savings which he was attempting to deposit in a branch of the Halifax Building Society (see *The Times*, 18 June 1994). These laws affect solicitors, estate agents, auctioneers, antique dealers, casino managers and shopkeepers – in short, anyone who is likely to be dealing in quantities of cash – and have the effect of turning a large section of the population into part-time, unpaid policemen.

A disturbing aspect of this phenomenon is that it is becoming increasingly easy for public-sector workers of all kinds to gain access to bank information; scenarios such as where a hospital administrator, eager to find an excuse to refuse an operation, could use this regime to access a patient's bank accounts to prove he or she was a smoker, and thus not appropriate to be operated upon, are becoming increasingly likely. This catch-all system of rules is in place in many Western countries; the pressure is on to reduce the number of cash transactions to an absolute minimum, and no tax haven or bank can afford not to support the anti-money laundering rhetoric, even if they are more reasonable in private. Pressure groups abound that wish to reduce privacy one way or another in furtherance of their worthy cause, and big business, while it will always resist restrictions to its own freedoms, gets a payoff in the form of guaranteed market share when it goes along with this legislation. For example, large banks, being financially able to conform to the heavy reporting duties, benefit from this legislation because it is becoming increasingly difficult for newer, smaller banks to get into the tightly controlled Western markets.

New technology

The motor behind this creeping abolition of cash transactions is information technology. The silicon chip is revolutionizing the financial world, and together with the globalization of markets and the collapse of exchange controls, smart cards and credit cards can be used to monitor how any individual spends their money – information which is extremely useful for marketing, as well as for the authorities. In many ways, though, information technology balances the conflict; for every step towards Big Brother and totalitarianism, there is an opposite step towards freedom and decentralization. Currently there is huge interest in the Internet, a system of cheap communications between computers, large and small, worldwide, which is at present virtually unregulated. Regulation will come, no doubt, but it would appear that as ever-more sophisticated encryption methods become available the Internet could become a secure method of transferring funds in total privacy.

Conclusion

As with any service, getting the most out of banks takes experience and a wide understanding of the context in which they work:

- **Remember that secrecy can never be absolutely assured, and avoid banks in countries with a track record of interference or the freezing of foreign assets.**

- **BCCI's collapse is evidence that bad banks can grow very big indeed before they are closed down. Don't be impressed by size alone.**

- **Approach offshore banks by letter, stating your intentions; this will make them more likely to accept your business. Investigate a short list of banks methodically, and aim to develop relationships with them over time.**

- **Occasionally the virtues of forming your own bank are promoted to businesspeople; unless you are a banker, or have a high net worth, this is probably inadvisable.**

- **Spread your assets across different banks in different countries. Avoid banks with US branches.**

- **Follow the press for reports of banking difficulties – if your bank seems to be heading for trouble, switch to another bank.**

- **Avoid keeping long-term deposits in countries with a track record of seizure or instability.**

- Bearer instruments are useful as a means of transporting money across borders anonymously, and also as an investment.

- Money laundering is a hot issue at present, and is being used as an excuse to develop a 'cashless' world and to reduce banking confidentiality. 'Know your customer' rules mean that new customers can have difficulty in opening offshore accounts, and must be able to prove the source of their funds.

8
FOREIGN EXCHANGE

The world has recently undergone a revolution; currencies can now be exchanged with one another more freely than ever before. This offers a great deal of scope to investors who wish to take advantage of investment opportunities in currencies other than their own. In this chapter we will look at the origins and mechanisms of foreign exchange. The areas covered are:

- The Bretton Woods system – why it was set up after World War 2, how it worked and why it has ended
- The floating rate system – how it emerged and why it is good news for private investors
- The Euromarkets
- The foreign exchange market. How currencies are traded

- Exchange rates – how to calculate them, and how to hedge in currencies. Arbitrage and speculation, and how to predict exchange rates
- The Special Drawing Right (SDR)
- The European Monetary System (EMS)

'In Manus' transactions with Balowan, where sago is scarce, one package of sago offered by Manus will bring ten mud hen's eggs from Balowan; but the equivalent of a package of sago offered by Manus to Balowan in shell money commands only three mud hen's eggs. (Clearly if the Manus anywhere can convert these several items, they make a killing.)'

MARSHALL SAHLINS, *Stone Age Economics* p. 285 Routledge 1988

THE BRETTON WOODS SYSTEM

As World War 2 drew to a close, the Allied nations and their support-ers met in the United States at Bretton Woods in New Hampshire to plan an international monetary system for the post-war era. They cre-ated the International Monetary Fund (IMF) and the World Bank, and set up a system which was intended to provide stability to exchange rates. As the US had become by far the most powerful country in the world, the system was tied to the US dollar at $33 to an ounce of gold. All other currencies were defined in terms of dollars. If a country wanted to change its rate of exchange against the dollar, it had to make a formal announcement that it was revaluing, or devaluing, its currency. In 1949, 28 countries devalued their currencies.

Bretton Woods set the stage for the rise of socialism. Countries were able to pay for the huge cost of creating welfare states by issuing bonds, which in turn encouraged inflation. As world trade mushroomed and the economic balance between countries began to change, vast funds grew up which were highly mobile, and could be switched from one country to another without the permission of governments. The demand for gold was high, and the official price of $33 to an ounce was undermined by the creation of secondary markets, where gold was traded at much higher prices. As its economic strength diminished, the United States decided unilaterally to abandon the Bretton Woods system when, in 1971, it suspended the right to convert dollars for gold at $33 to the ounce, and devalued the dollar.

THE FLOATING EXCHANGE RATE SYSTEM

Bretton Woods was supplanted by the floating exchange rate system, where no currency is formally linked to any other, or to gold. The rate at which you can exchange one currency for another is simply the best rate that someone will give you, so exchange rates are highly volatile (this is why they are called 'floating'). During the oil crises of 1973 and 1979, when OPEC dramatically increased the price of oil, the floating

147

system helped to minimize the chaos, as the strain was taken by an adjustment in exchange rates (the OPEC countries currencies suddenly became much more valuable), rather than by curtailing real economic activity, as would have happened if the Bretton Woods system had still been operating.

The floating system does have disadvantages; the principal ones are that it encourages countries to act 'selfishly' rather than co-operatively and that it greatly exaggerates the extremes in the cycle of exchange rates. Countries are tempted to manipulate their exchange rates for short-term advantage. For instance, Japan managed to keep the yen artificially low for some years in order to encourage exports, as did Britain, with less success. This kind of manipulation can only work for a few years before it becomes impossible to sustain.

The United States, too, tries to use the floating system for its own advantage. Its massive trade deficit will eventually have to be paid for with higher taxes, more unemployment and lower living standards, but the US government has staved off the evil day for some time by allowing the dollar to depreciate against other currencies. State banks throughout the world have attempted to counteract this by buying dollars to raise its rate.

THE BALANCE OF PAYMENTS AND THE BLACK HOLE

Countries are like companies in that they have accounts; money flows in and out of them, and one can take a 'snapshot' of a country's accounts which purports to show its debts and assets, just as a balance sheet does for a company. Balance of payments accounts are produced each year, identifying the state's net earnings from abroad (the 'current account'), its savings or debts (the 'capital account'), and the borrowings the government may have to make to balance the books.

When a government has to borrow in order to balance its accounts, it usually goes to banks or other governments for a short-term loan. If all else fails, it must go to an international organization such as the International Monetary Fund (IMF) which will insist on rigid economic controls. For this reason, governments tend to regard this last course of action as highly undesirable.

If a country's current account is negative, meaning that it has spent more than it has earned when trading abroad, it usually means that the country's currency is weakening. Conversely, if the current account is in surplus year after year, it usually means that the currency is getting stronger.

Much is made of balance of payments by politicians, economists and commentators. However, they are unreliable, just as the accounts of many companies are. If you reconcile the annual balance of payments figures for every country in the world, they should all add up. They don't – there is a 'black hole' of many tens of billions that cannot be accounted for. This black hole makes it impossible to know the true picture, and thus there can be no description of the world's economy that is entirely accurate.

THE EUROMARKETS

The Euromarkets are a banking system which is truly international and operates beyond the control of governments. It handles huge amounts of cash belonging to companies, institutional funds, countries and wealthy individuals. The amount of money in the Euromarkets is so large that it can significantly affect exchange rates, the money supply and inflation as it moves around the world. The ease with which money can be borrowed through the Euromarkets makes them attractive as sources of finance for large projects. Because of its international character, there is no central organization controlling it, and no complete figures on its size or movements. The City of London has benefited from the growth of Euromarkets because its physical location, halfway between Tokyo and New York, has enabled it to exploit its 'middle position' in the time zones.

THE FOREIGN EXCHANGE MARKET

The important difference between doing business with a company in your own country and doing business with one abroad is that the two currencies of the respective countries will usually be involved. A German importer will usually pay a Japanese exporter in yen, a French exporter in francs, an American exporter in dollars and so on. The importer will have to buy the required currency on the foreign exchange market.

The foreign exchange market is international, and consists of banks, brokers and others buying and selling currencies from most of the countries in the world. Rates change very fast, so they communicate by fax, computer, telephone and telex continuously.

The main centres for foreign exchange trading are New York, London, Tokyo, Zurich and Frankfurt, which turn over hundreds of billions of dollars a day. The US dollar is by far the most frequently traded, and is called a 'vehicle currency'. This means that commodities such as coffee, gold and oil are normally priced in dollars. It is often cheaper for, say, a Japanese dealer who wants to buy Italian lire to buy dollars first and then use the dollars to buy lire, rather than buying them directly with yen.

The central banks in each country often try to influence the exchange rate of their currency by buying and selling in large amounts. For example, when there is an agreed target exchange rate, the central banks have to buy and sell their own currencies according to the fluctuation in supply and demand, to try to drive their currencies towards the desired rate.

The merchant banks, or commercial banks, trade in currencies for themselves, and also on behalf of clients such as companies and large investors who want foreign currency. They trade with other banks, and also use brokers.

The brokers are used by banks because they can get the best price quicker and more cheaply than the bank itself. There are just a few authorized brokers in each financial centre.

What is an exchange rate?

An exchange rate is simply the ratio at which one currency can be exchanged for another at a given time. It can be given in two ways; either as the amount of currency A that will buy one unit of currency B, or the amount of currency B that will buy currency A. It doesn't matter which way round the ratio is expressed, as long as it is made clear which currency is being taken as one unit, though there is usually a convention for any given pair of currencies.

If the rate for marks per dollar has changed from DM2:$1 to DM2.01:$1, you will have to pay more in marks for a dollar, so the mark has 'depreciated' and the dollar has 'appreciated'. If the dollars per mark rate has changed from $0.50:DM1 to $0.51:DM1, you will have to pay more in dollars for a mark, so marks have appreciated and dollars have depreciated. This is why it can be confusing if someone says that the exchange rate has risen – which way round do they mean?

The nominal exchange rate

The nominal exchange rate is the prevailing rate of exchange between two currencies on a given day. In other words, it is simply the price of buying one currency with another. It is sometimes given as an index relative to some base time.

If the base dollar/Deutschemark rate is, say, $0.50:DM1, and some time later the rate is $0.55:DM1, the nominal index of the mark will then be 110 – the mark has appreciated against the dollar by 10 per cent.

The nominal rate doesn't tell you anything about how price levels in the respective countries, however, so a formula is used to convert it into the 'real exchange rate', which does.

The real exchange rate

The real exchange rate takes the price levels of the two countries into account. The formula for calculating it is:

$$E_r = (E \times P) \div P^*$$

where E_r is the real exchange rate, E is the nominal exchange rate given as the amount of foreign currency for one unit of domestic currency, P is the local price index and P^* is the foreign price index.

Suppose that the nominal exchange rate of dollars to marks is $0.50:DM1. If both the German and the US price indices are 100, then the real exchange rate is

$$E_r = (0.50 \times 100) \div 100 = 0.50$$

which is the same as the nominal rate. Now suppose that at a later date the nominal exchange rate is still the same, but the US price index has risen to 110. The real exchange rate is now

$$E_r = (0.50 \times 100) \div 110 = 0.4545$$

The real exchange rate is telling you what the nominal exchange rate doesn't, namely that the mark will buy fewer goods in America than it could have previously. One problem though, is what price index is used; for instance, some indices include the prices of fast food, which are hardly a good guide to value.

The effective exchange rate

Have you ever heard a news report about your local currency going up or down against 'a basket of currencies'? What is happening is that the local, or domestic, currency is being compared with the currencies of several countries with which your country trades. The result is called the 'effective exchange rate'.

To understand the principle, suppose Japan does 60 per cent of its foreign business with the United States and 40 per cent with Germany. The exchange rate index is weighted by 0.6 times the exchange rate with the dollar and 0.4 times the exchange rate with the mark.

At the base period the indices are all set to 100 and will look like this:

Nominal index	Nominal index	Effective index
DM:Y1	$:Y1	Y
100	100	100

If the yen subsequently appreciated against the mark by 20 per cent and depreciated against the dollar by 20 per cent the indices would look like this:

Nominal index	Nominal index	Effective index
DM:Y1	$:Y1	Y
80	120	104

The effective exchange rate index has been calculated by multiplying the nominal indices by their respective weights, thus:

$$80 \times 0.4 = 32$$
$$120 \times 0.6 = 72$$

Adding them together we get 32 + 72 = 104, which is the effective rate index given above.

Spot rates

The 'spot rate' is the rate between two currencies for delivery at once. Once a deal has been done, it usually takes two days before the currencies are actually exchanged because of the paperwork involved – it is a 'paper transaction' where bank notes are not physically exchanged.

The forward exchange market

If you know you want to buy yen in 90 days' time to settle a bill, but you want to be sure exactly how much it is going to cost you, you can buy currency at the forward exchange rate, which will be different from the spot rate.

Suppose you are a German company which owes $100,000 to an American company, due on 31 June. You may decide to buy $100,000 on 1 April at the three-month forward rate, and the money will be delivered to you on the day you must pay the American company.

To see why companies do this, let's look at the participants in the foreign exchange market.

Hedging

The German company doesn't want the uncertainty of not knowing how much its American debt will cost in three month's time on 31 June. Perhaps it suspects that the dollar will cost more in Deutschemarks at that time than it does now. Suppose the spot exchange rate on 1 April is $0.50:DM1 and the three-month forward exchange rate is $0.52:DM1. If it buys at the spot rate, $100,000 will cost DM200,000, and if it buys at the three-month forward rate it will cost DM192,307 now. Suppose that when three months have elapsed, the spot rate has changed to $0.53:DM1. The company could have kept its money in Deutschmarks until the last moment and paid DM188,679 for its dollars instead of DM192,307, saving DM3,628. The company is more interested in being sure what its liability will be in three months' time than in speculating, so no sleep is lost over the gamble. It has protected itself against nasty surprises by making a 'forward contract'. This is known as 'hedging'.

You may wonder why companies don't simply buy the necessary currency at the spot rate far in advance of the time that they need it. This is because companies often don't want to spend the cash in advance – the money is needed for other things.

Arbitrage

'Arbitrage' means being able to buy something and then sell it immediately at a higher price, thus guaranteeing a profit. The communications in the foreign exchange market are so good that arbitrage opportunites only occur very briefly and require rapid trading if advantage is to be taken of them.

There are two kinds of basic arbitrage:

- *Financial centre arbitrage* has the effect of keeping the exchange rates in different financial centres the same. If you can get $0.50 for DM1 in Tokyo, but $0.52 for DM1 in Frankfurt, you would frantically buy as many dollars as you could in Frankfurt and sell them immediately in Tokyo, making a no-risk 4 per cent profit. Every time a chance like this comes up, people take advantage of it, which brings the rates in different places back into line.

- *Cross-rate arbitrage* works in the same way to keep exchange rates in different currencies compatible with each other. If you are in France wanting to buy Deutschmarks and you see that the rate for yen to the mark is Y100:DM1, the rate for yen to the franc is Y40:FF1 and that the rate for francs to the mark is FF3:DM1, you could buy DM100 for FF300, then buy Y12,000 for FF300, and then buy DM120 with the yen for a no-risk profit. As with financial centre arbitrage, the constant exploitation of such opportunities keeps bringing the rates into line with each other.

'Arbitrageurs' are people who engage in arbitrage, the process of looking for opportunities to make profits without risk by buying and selling currencies. They are usually banks. Another kind of arbitrage opportunity they can sometimes exploit is in the difference between interest rates in different countries combined with the difference between forward and spot rates. It is also possible to find arbitrage opportunities in mispriced futures contracts.

So why isn't everyone an arbitrageur? The reasons are that they need very sophisticated equipment, and also that the more arbitrageurs there are, the fewer opportunities there are for arbitrage.

Forward discounts and premiums

If the spot rate is less than the forward rate for a currency (in other words, if you get more of the foreign currency for your money by buying at the forward rate), the currency is at a 'forward premium', as it was for our German company on 1 April. If the forward rate is less than the spot rate, the currency is at a 'forward discount'.

The discount or premium of the forward rate is most often given as a percentage of the spot rate. The formula is:

$$\text{Forward premium/discount} = (F - S) \div S \times 100$$

where F is the forward rate and S is the spot rate. Thus, if the forward rate is \$0.52:DM1 and the spot rate is \$0.50:DM1, the premium is:

$$\text{Forward premium} = (0.52 - 0.50) \div 0.50 \times 100$$
$$= (0.02 \div 0.50) \times 100$$
$$= 4\%$$

Speculation

Speculators are different from arbitrageurs because they are taking a risk; they try to make money on the basis of predictions about the way the markets are moving, rather than looking for momentary mismatches between exchange rates as arbitrageurs do. Speculators who think a currency is going to cost more in the future than it does now are called 'bullish' (optimistic) about the currency, and ones who think it will cost less are called 'bearish' (pessimistic).

Suppose a speculator in, say Hong Kong (it could be anywhere), bought \$100,000 in Deutschmarks at the forward rate of \$0.52:DM1 on 1 April, at the same time as the German company in our example, hoping to sell the dollars back into Deutschmarks at the end of June for a quick profit. This is called 'going long' on the dollar. At the end of June the spot rate is \$0.53:DM1. The speculator agreed to pay DM192,307 for the dollars; changing the dollars back into marks would produce DM188,679, so the speculator has lost DM3,628 if the dollars are exchanged.

To make the principles of foreign exchange easier to understand, we haven't taken the dealing costs into account. These are small, however (fractions of 1 per cent of a unit of currency), so they do not prevent banks and large investors from making a profit. All this is a very different business from the 'tourist rates', where paper money actually has to be moved around physically.

The frenetic activity in foreign exchange is possible due to most of the world's countries allowing free trade in currency; this has not always been the case in the past, and if free trade in currency were to be slowed by governments at some time in the future, the markets would slow down with it.

PREDICTING EXCHANGE RATES

As we saw on page 148, it is the trading profits or losses of countries which are the main force affecting exchange rates in the long term. However, when trying to predict exchange rates, many other factors are considered:

- *Inflation*. Countries with high inflation relative to other countries find that the prices of the goods and services that they export rise also. This leads to fewer customers for their goods, a higher amount of imports, consequent trading losses and a weakening currency.

- *Monthly and quarterly trade figures*. These tend to be far less reliable than the annual balance of payment accounts, which, as we have seen, are not very reliable themselves. Nevertheless, the foreign exchange market grasps eagerly for such interim figures as they are published, in the hope of finding clues about the future.

- *Flows of capital*. If, for example, a country is trading at a loss but is enjoying a large amount of investment from abroad, its currency may not weaken as it otherwise would.

- *Interest rates*. A country which offers a higher rate of interest than others do will often attract money from abroad in the short term. However, if investors believe that the currency is likely to become worthless, they will switch their money to a safer currency.

- *Investment abroad*. Countries whose companies are purchasing or setting up businesses overseas are generally thought to have currencies which will get stronger for a decade or more, since it will take that length of time for the companies to make their profits.

- *Money flowing into a country's stock markets* is usually a sign that the currency will be strong, at least for three years or so.

- *Productivity*. A country with a high rate of productivity and economic growth is often thought to have a strengthening currency.

- *Savings*. Populations who spend everything they earn make their currencies weaker by increasing trading losses. It is notable that economically strong countries, such as Japan and Germany, have a high rate of saving per head of population.

- *Bank intervention*. A country's central bank may buy its own currency to make it stronger, or sell it to make it weaker.

- *Confidence in policies*. Investors from outside a country will look at its political situation to assess the risks of investing there. Not many people will buy bonds, for example, from a government which looks as if it is collapsing.

- *Bull and bear markets*. As with shares, if investors think that a currency is increasing or decreasing, they will invest accordingly, creating a self-fulfilling prophecy in the short term.

156

- *Singular events*. Wars, commodity price hikes and other one-off occurrences will have short-term effects on exchange rates.

THE EFFECTS OF EXCHANGE RATES ON SHARES

It doesn't occur to most people to invest outside their own countries because they have a feeling that it is risky. In fact, the reverse may be true. If you invest in the well-regulated stock markets of nations with strong currencies, you are helping to reduce the risk by spreading it across several currencies. This is of great importance to British investors, since the natural tendency to keep their money at home will almost certainly produce lower returns, as Britain lumbers onwards towards a future of lowered international status and industrial uncertainty. Holding high-quality shares in several countries does complicate matters, certainly, but not necessarily to such a degree that it is not worth a private investor's while to do so. The main factor affecting an international portfolio is that exchange rates will affect real profits and losses.

If you are British and make, say, a 50 per cent profit investing in a Japanese company, the profits that you will actually receive if you sell and convert the money into sterling will depend on what has happened to the sterling/yen rate in the interim.

To make the sums easy, suppose that when you invested, the yen/sterling rate was 1:1, and that in the meantime the yen has depreciated by 50 per cent against the pound; if you had invested £10,000 (e.g. Y10,000), you would now have Y15,000, but since the sterling/yen rate is now 1:2, you would only get £7,500 back. However, since the future for yen is bright, it is more likely that the yen would actually appreciate against the pound; if the sterling/yen rate were now 1:0.5, you would receive £30,000 for your Y15,000. Thus, the ability to correctly assess currency trends over periods of more than five years can add value to your returns.

This kind of bet is nowhere near as risky as the short-term gambling on quarterly or annual exchange rates that the professionals go in for. If you take a global view of investment, you should be able to develop a framework for yourself by identifying the industries in different countries which are likely to prosper, which currencies are likely to become stronger and the political outlook in those regions. Once you have done this, you can then select individual stocks in the normal way, by assessing their p/e ratios and fundamentals.

THE EFFECTS OF EXCHANGE RATES ON BONDS

When the interest rates of a country fall, the value of its bonds goes up. As rates are currently low throughout the world, bond markets are active. When investing in bonds from other countries, care should be taken to check credit ratings and to assess the country's record on previous defaults. It is also possible to invest in foreign bonds through managed funds. Bonds in strong currencies usually offer lower interest rates than those in weaker currencies, 2.5 per cent being, by convention, the lowest acceptable 'real' rate of interest. When the average yield of interest of international bonds is higher than this figure, bonds are thought of as being good value.

Interest rates on British gilts have been high on average over the past few decades due to the weakness of the pound and high inflation. When investing in bonds internationally, you must try to choose countries where the long-term exchange rates and inflation figures are improving and buy bonds there before yield rates have adjusted to the new conditions.

THE EFFECTS OF EXCHANGE RATES ON CASH

When stock markets around the world are falling, many investors sell shares and increase their bond and cash holdings. Since World War 2, the value of sterling has dropped dramatically against other currencies. If you had overcome exchange controls and had invested in a spread of currencies during this period, as some have been able to do, you would have done far better than if you had stayed in sterling exclusively.

There are now a number of managed currency funds which change the proportions of the various currencies they hold according to movements in exchange rates; ideally, such a fund should produce a greater return than holding the strongest currency throughout a particular period. Look for a fund that is not committed to basing itself around one particular currency, such as that of its home country, as this may result in poor results if the fund does not respond to a weakening trend. Usually, though, a fund will produce its final accounts in one currency, but this does not necessarily indicate a bias. Whether you are investing in a fund or on your own, you should stick to major countries or currencies which are closely tied to them.

THE SPECIAL DRAWING RIGHT (SDR) OF THE IMF

The International Monetary Fund's role during the Bretton Woods era was to be the lender of last resort to its member countries, which numbered about 150. Each member pays an annual subscription to the IMF which is a fixed proportion of its GDP, and this money is used to assist countries in difficulty. The amount a country pays governs the amount it can borrow, and affects its voting rights. A country can borrow foreign currency for between three and five years from the IMF up to its subscription quota. Switzerland is not a member of the IMF, but does participate in the 'Paris Club' or 'Group of Ten' countries which provide further monies for countries in trouble.

The special drawing right (SDR) was invented as a way of accounting between the IMF and central state banks. It is tied to a 'basket' of several strong currencies, and the proportions of each in the basket are fixed for five years. Member countries of the IMF can pay each other in SDRs, but they are not directly convertible into any currency, and countries may only hold limited SDR reserves. It is now possible to buy bonds denominated in SDRs. As a kind of benchmark of the strong currencies, the SDR is probably the fairest of those available.

THE EUROPEAN MONETARY SYSTEM (EMS)

The aim of the European Union (EU) is to create a truly united federation of Europe. This is an immensely difficult task and may well not succeed, owing to the natural rivalry between its member countries. Thus we have an EU divided into competing factions, with strong currency countries such as Germany, Holland and Luxembourg desiring low inflation and conservative economies, and weaker currency countries such as Ireland, Italy and Denmark seeking relaxed rules. The European Monetary System (EMS) is a compromise designed to stabilize exchange rates between its members' currencies as a step towards the EU's ideal of a single common currency for Europe. It has already created a currency unit called the ECU, which is a basket of various proportions of EU members' currencies, similar in principle to the SDR. As yet, the ECU is not very widely used. It is possible to buy bonds denominated in ECUs, and to borrow ECUs from some banks and state organizations.

Conclusion

Whatever the merits and demerits of the floating rate system may be for nations, private investors can certainly benefit from the freedom and opportunities that it offers. Take advantage of it while you can – like all previous systems, it is unlikely to last forever. What will replace it is moot. There have been proposals for a world monetary system which would allow currencies, or linked currency blocks, to move against one another within fixed ranges; such a system might reintroduce sweeping currency controls.

9
EMIGRANTS AND PERPETUAL TRAVELLERS

In this chapter we will look at some little-known aspects of international life:

- The perpetual traveller
- Investment as a perpetual traveller
- Running a business as a perpetual traveller
- Dual nationality
- Why get dual nationality?
- The 'Zapato Unico' syndrome
- How to apply for nationality
- Emigration
- Ancestry
- Marriage
- Investment

- Passports for sale
- Religion
- Becoming a parent
- Quasi-diplomatic status
- Ethnicity
- The United States – a special case
- Passports and the EU
- Camouflage passports
- Pitfalls
- Gough's three dual nationality rules
- Conclusion

'. . . [Periander] sent a representative to the court of this despot (Thrasybulus), to ask his opinion on the best and safest form of political constitution, and Thrasybulus invited the man to walk with him from the city to a field where corn was growing. As he passed through this cornfield, continually asking questions about why the messenger had come to him from Corinth, he kept cutting off all of the tallest ears of wheat that he could see, and throwing them away, until the finest and best grown part of the crop was ruined. In this way he went right through the field, and then sent the messenger away without a word.

On his return to Corinth, Periander was eager to hear what advice Thrasybulus had given, and the man replied that he had not given any at all, adding that he was surprised to have been sent to visit such a person, who was evidently mad and a wanton destroyer of his own property – and then he described what he had seen Thrasybulus do. Periander seized the point at once; it was perfectly plain to him that Thrasybulus recommended the murder of all the people in the city who were outstanding in influence or ability.'

HERODOTUS (born *circa* 490 *BC*), *The Histories*, Book 5

Some people get tired of their own country, and, if they have enough money, contemplate leaving permanently for sunnier, less regulated climes. Britons tend to choose the Iberian peninsula or English-speaking countries such as the United States and Australia, which is a shame because the opportunities are far wider than these. Fear of the unknown and lack of experience keeps many people from even considering the wider possibilities. Americans are just the same – the vast majority never leave their own country, and are terrified of really 'foreign' places. It's a matter of taste, perhaps, but as an antidote to the 'don't leave home' brigade, who will always be in the majority, this chapter will look at some of the strategies open to those who do leave their home country for good. A word of warning, though – the methods outlined here are for self-reliant individuals only.

THE PERPETUAL TRAVELLER

If you have a net worth of £250,000 or more, you can adopt a radical strategy; rather than simply moving from one burdensome, over-regulated country to another (which may turn out to be equally burdensome), you don't settle anywhere, but only stay in a country for a few months before moving on to the next. Properly arranged, this way of life is neither hugely expensive nor rootless – but it does not work if you have a permanent 9 to 5 job where you must be present at a particular office every day. You can avoid rootlessness by moving between three or four countries on a rota, using rented accommodation but cultivating friendships and connections in those places. The idea is to separate those elements of one's social identity which are used by states to control their populations; here's how it works:

- *Nationality* – acquire dual or triple nationality (see pages 166–76) to give yourself much greater freedom to travel, confidentiality and business opportunities which would otherwise be closed to you.

- *Domicile and 'ordinary residence'* (see page 24) – move these to an offshore centre. Ideally you shouldn't actually have to live there or even go there, unless you want to.

163

- *Location of assets* – these should be mainly liquid, and legally located and controlled in a country with no exchange controls and great expertise in investment and banking.

- *Location of business* – if you are still working and earning money, do this in a separate, different country. Consultancies, journalism and many service businesses can be operated easily in this way.

- *Temporary residence* – these are the countries where you actually live for a few months at a time on a rota basis. You choose them for their charm and convenience, and your status there is always 'tourist'.

This idea is not new – rich people have been practising versions of it for centuries – but it is radical in most people's eyes. The reason for separating the elements is to obtain all the advantages of settling in a tax haven without their disadvantages. Sadly, life in your average tax haven is not too thrilling, especially in the well-run, stable ones, where there are a lot of well-to-do retired people living quiet lives, but not much else. Perpetual travelling may have more appeal to the younger person, or to those for whom the smugness of, say, Guernsey or the Isle of Man does not appeal. It's a matter of taste, but countries that are joyful and full of life tend also to be ones where permanent residence is undesirable for the wealthy foreigner; for example:

- Turkey – delightful people, good weather and food, but politically fraught.

- Brazil – tropical, hot-blooded and exciting, but crime is out of control, especially in Rio. Kidnapping rich people is a national sport.

- Thailand – perhaps the most fashionable exotic holiday location, but very difficult to obtain residence (see page 173).

INVESTMENT AS A PERPETUAL TRAVELLER

Much of this book has been about using offshore companies and trusts to maximize opportunities and minimize tax. If you are actively in business or cannot move from your own country, then these vehicles are necessary, but they are not usually cheap and they take up a lot of time. If you can realize £250,000 and invest it through an offshore centre in a respectable, low-risk portfolio of, say, shares listed on the major stock markets, good bonds and bank deposits, you should be able to obtain capital growth and some income – not enough to live in luxury, perhaps, but certainly a useful supplement to your earnings. As an experienced businessperson or professional, you will be able to find a way to earn money as a traveller; it may be less than you earn at home, but you won't be paying any tax and you will be able to stay for long periods in pleasant, inexpensive countries. If quality of life is more important to you than status, this strategy is definitely realistic.

RUNNING A BUSINESS AS A PERPETUAL TRAVELLER

A famous film producer, Sam Spiegel, lived for years on a yacht in the Mediterranean to minimize taxes, but was able to run his operations internationally. In effect he had a mobile office which could be taken to many of the important international film markets (Cannes, Venice) when necessary. If you have a large and well-established international business of this kind, you may well be able to arrange your work to suit your desired lifestyle, in which case perpetual travelling will not present many problems. Retired and semi-retired people with pensions and investment income are similarly free to move about. People owning and managing smaller businesses in their own country face bigger challenges; unless you can realize your assets and retire, you will have to take a step back from the day-to-day running of the company.

Becoming a consultant is a possibility. You can do the bulk of consultancy work from almost anywhere if you have good communications, a portable fax and personal computer, and access to libraries and computer databases. For example, a three-month commission from a client in one country should normally enable you to spend two months of the period writing up your reports in another country.

Fees can be paid to an offshore centre, thus minimizing or avoiding tax altogether. Normally licences and official registration are not necessary to set up in business and you can choose your clients, your working hours and the amount of work you do. The main problem is how to get your clients.

- **Be good at what you do, and your reputation will spread.**
- **Publish articles and handbooks about your area of expertise.**
- **Have an office arrangement where you can receive your post and messages; there are many bureaux which offer these services.**

- **Print brochures and literature advertising your services.**
- **Advertise in the international press and niche market magazines.**
- **Identify and approach potential clients.**
- **Run seminars in your field of expertise.**
- **Attend conferences and cultivate contacts.**
- **Approach international organizations for short-term contracts.**

Anyone with experience of marketing should be able to get a business going within 12 months or so. If you don't have the experience or know-how, consider getting some training, and perhaps a few clients, before making the move. Doctors and lawyers, for example, may offer services in a specialist area such as medical journalism or offshore finance which are related but not identical to the work they have done in the past.

DUAL NATIONALITY

The information in this section is liable to change at short notice – please check with the authorities of the relevant country for up-to-date naturalization requirements.

It is possible to become a national of more than one country; many countries do not forbid it, while others turn a blind eye or have no means of discovering the fact. Forged and stolen passports are for the criminal classes – it is perfectly possible to get a second and third passport legally. A second nationality is normally obtained by one of the following methods:

- *Emigration* – moving to the country and living there for several years often entitles you to apply for citizenship; this is the only method that most people are aware of.
- *Ancestry* – this is where the country concerned gives citizenship to the descendants of their nationals.
- *Marriage* – you can often obtain the nationality of the person you marry.
- *Investment* – many countries effectively sell citizenship and passports.
- *Religion* – some countries give passports to members of certain faiths.

- *Becoming a parent* – having a child in a country can entitle you to citizenship.
- *Quasi-diplomatic status* – honorary consulships and similar posts can sometimes be obtained and used to acquire a passport.
- *Ethnicity* – some countries give citizenship to nationals of other countries who have close historical and blood links.

The bottom line about nationality is that despite the pious rhetoric emanating from organizations such as the United Nations, there is no effective international system of rules that governs nationality.

Why get dual nationality?

Holding dual nationality with two passports, one from each country, follows the wise investor's golden rule to diversify. A second nationality simply gives you more choice and more opportunity. It is often quite legal to have a different name on your second passport, which extends the opportunities for confidentiality. People from impoverished, politically unstable or tyrannical countries have no difficulties in seeing that dual nationality is desirable, but, for sceptical readers, here are some of the reasons people have used second passports in the last 50 years.

1. In the lead up to World War 2, many Europeans used legally acquired second passports to escape the Nazis. It is a feature of impending crises that travel becomes more difficult, and even 'good guy' countries take steps to prevent their own people from leaving and refugees from entering.

2. Being a refugee is no fun at all; being a national of the country you are entering, or of a neutral third country, helps you to avoid getting refugee status.

3. At the higher levels of business there are many grey areas of activity; what is legal today may become a crime tomorrow, and businesspeople sometimes find it necessary to leave a country quickly.

4. Even in peacetime, some countries have the less than charming habit of revoking, confiscating or suspending the passports of some of their citizens to prevent them leaving – a second passport will get you out.

5. US and British nationals, for example, are very unpopular in some parts of the world; when travelling in such places it is preferable to be 'something else'.

6. Some countries are international pariahs; if you are, for example, a Libyan who wants to travel in Europe, you will find it very difficult indeed. Nor do CIS citizens find life easy abroad.

7. Terrorists pick on Americans in particular, but also on the nationals of other Western countries. When you're on a hijacked airliner, it is better to produce, say, a Belizean passport than a British one.

8. Some countries have heavy military service requirements. Second passports can be used to evade these.

9. When your country is facing political uncertainty it is advisable to make sure you can leave. The wealthier inhabitants of Hong Kong did their best to acquire second passports as the 1997 Chinese takeover approached. Naturally, this became harder and harder to do as the deadline approached – the smart money got theirs years ago.

Some Westerners think that dreadful crises only happen to others who are unfortunate enough to have been born in the Third World or in tyrannous countries. Let's hope they are right (they aren't). Second passports stop you becoming a Vietnamese boat person, a Rwandan refugee or a besieged Bosnian; they can save your life and your assets, and they can also help you make money by circumventing restrictions.

The 'Zapato Unico' syndrome

This is described amusingly by John Train, a well-known American investment writer, to demonstrate the evils of price controls. The scenario goes like this:

1. A businessman sets up a shoe factory in a small Latin American country selling a variety of products at different prices.

2. A new government comes to power – whether it is to the right or to the left is irrelevant – and orders pay increases for the workforce.

3. Inflation goes up and prices increase.

4. The government blames business for the inflation and introduces price controls.

5. The shoe manufacturer discontinues the top of the range products and sells the lower quality shoes at the expensive shoe prices.

6. The government introduces quality controls to prevent this.

7. The controls don't work – no one knows what a good local shoe is anymore.

8. The government announces a single standard for many products – for the shoe manufacturer this means he may only make '*zapato unico*' (one shoe type).

9. The shoe manufacturer sees the writing on the wall. He decides to leave the country. At the border he is arrested and imprisoned, pending an investigation.

10. The government puts in a civil servant to manage the factory. The company loses money more quickly.

11. The government blames the factory owner and makes him liable for the new losses. His assets are seized.

12. The factory owner is convicted for economic sabotage and remains in jail, penniless. It is very hard to buy shoes in the country. The multinationals pull out or retrench. Life is miserable for everyone.

Investors cannot afford to have ideologies; survival must be the prime goal, followed by prosperity. In the case of the shoe manufacturer these aims might have been achieved by:

1. Having a second or third passport that the authorities knew nothing about, making it easier to cross the border.

2. Having a large part of his assets overseas.

3. Getting out early.

These days governments all over the world are tending towards the free market, and exchange controls and state-run economies are becoming a thing of the past. It could be said that '*zapato unico*' situations are unlikely to occur; if this is so, then international investors are in for an era of peace and plenty, but there is no harm in taking out dual nationality as a precaution in any case.

How to apply for nationality

A second nationality of any country is preferable to none at all, but some are much more desirable than others because of the freedom of movement which they give. The application process may be swift and cheap – a matter of weeks in some cases – or it may take years and cost a fortune; it all depends on your circumstances and original nationality. If you can obtain a passport on your own, do so – lawyers and agencies are expensive and not always honest. One important point to bear in mind is the possibility of obtaining a chain of nationalities which ultimately enable you to get the one you want; for example, you could convert to Judaism, get an Israeli passport and use it to obtain a German or a Spanish passport (see page 174).

Emigration

Not every country will give you citizenship, even if you have lived there legally for decades, but most do. Those that don't are often countries with small populations, including some tax havens (Andorra, for instance) for whom an influx of naturalized foreigners would present very serious problems. The Gulf States are another example. In the rest of the world, there is a general principle that a long period of legal residence entitles you to apply for citizenship and a passport, but the goal posts are often moved; the UK's immigration policies, for example, are currently iniquitous. The period of residency ranges widely, from two years in Argentina and Ecuador to 10 years in Luxembourg and Spain and 12 years in Switzerland. The average time is about five years.

The strictness with which residency is defined and enforced varies greatly between countries. In some, you may only need to have a postal address and make an occasional visit during the residency period, while in others you are barely allowed out for a holiday (e.g. the UK). The first hurdle may be acquiring residence in the first place; a good, specialist job in the country or having private wealth almost always helps, and you will usually have to convince the authorities you are not a criminal or some other undesirable. Marriage to a national usually speeds up the process (see below).

Ancestry

Many countries will give citizenship and a passport to people who have a parent who was a national. If you are in this fortunate position, you will normally be able to get a passport rapidly at low cost. Some countries widen the net by giving passports to the grandchildren of nationals. Two of the more desirable countries in this category are: Ireland and Italy.

Marriage

Many countries give the right to citizenship to spouses of their nationals. The UK is not one of them. Often there is a distinction between the sexes; for example, a foreign woman, but not a foreign man, can obtain nationality by marriage in Liechtenstein, Saudi Arabia and the Gulf States. Some countries give the right to nationality to spouses of both sexes, but make it quicker or immediate for women. These include:

- Argentina (immediate for women)
- Barbados (immediate for women)
- Cyprus (one year for women, four years for men)
- Liechtenstein (6 years for resident women, 12 years for non-resident women, almost never for men)
- Malta (immediate for women)
- Monaco (immediate for women)
- Switzerland (immediate for women).

France, not otherwise famous for liberal tendencies, used to allow foreign spouses of either sex to apply for citizenship after only six months, but the system is being tightened up. Countries which give spouses immediate rights to apply for a passport include:

- Lebanon
- New Zealand
- Panama
- Portugal
- St Kitts
- Turkey.

Enlightened, liberal Holland extends this by allowing individuals who have a 'serious relationship' with a Dutch national to apply. Such relationships include gay couples and informal adoptions, but must last for three years before application.

There are even countries which favour men as foreign spouses, such as:

- Andorra – a foreigner marrying a woman who is an only child can immediately apply for citizenship.
- The Dominican Republic – a foreigner marrying a Dominican woman can immediately apply for citizenship.

Residency requirements vary for foreign spouses – a surprisingly large number of countries allow foreign spouses to apply after a certain period even if they have never visited the country. Marriages of convenience are definitely possible, but you have to trust your partner and know what you are doing – the consulates of the world are filled with unfortunate people trying to convince jaded officials that their sham marriage is a genuine love-match.

Investment

As a rule, countries want rich people to come, but don't want poor people. Never mind any rhetoric about equality or classless societies – if you are rich enough, even Britain will let you in. Some countries have made this equation overt with special investment/citizenship programmes, while others simply make the whole process quicker and easier for the wealthy. This is normally done by using trading companies; a subsidiary or daughter company is opened in the target country, and employs local people. The proprietor obtains work permits, residency, and finally citizenship.

This is expensive if you are only doing it for the passport, but worthwhile if you already have a business involvement with another country. Countries operating overt business for passport schemes include:

- Australia – the 'Business Migration Programme'; the vetting procedure is said to be quite rigorous.
- Bahamas – a number of programmes; the minimum investment is said to be around £100,000.
- Canada – a minimum investment of about £200,000.
- Chile – a minimum investment of about £15,000 is said to be sufficient.
- Ecuador – a minimum investment of about £20,000.
- Mauritius – a minimum investment of about £30,000.
- New Zealand – a minimum investment of about £200,000.
- Singapore – a minimum investment of about £350,000.

The conditions associated with these schemes vary enormously; in some countries the money need only be invested within the country for two years, and residential property investments may be eligible, while in others the investment may be tied up for a long time in risky operations. Fees vary enormously too. Beware of retirement schemes; a few years ago Costa Rica reneged on such a scheme, and many thousands of United States pensioners were expelled, losing their homes and life savings in the process.

172

Passports for sale

This is a logical extension of the investment schemes covered in the previous section. Why not just sell the passports instead of going through an investment rigmarole? A surprising number of countries do exactly this; costs can be as low as £10,000. It would be a shame to name these countries here as it might damage the schemes, but suffice it to say that not all these countries are pariahs, and usable passports can be obtained in this way. Specialist law firms can advise. One-off opportunities often appear. During the lead up to German re-unification it is said that East German passports and citizenship were sold to individuals from many countries. After re-unification these passports were then traded in for new German ones, and the happy recipients became EU nationals.

Religion

Some countries give nationality to members or officers of certain religions. These include:

- Thailand – Buddhist monks may apply for citizenship after an unspecified period of residence in the country, through the offices of their abbot. This is not as exotic as it sounds – two years as a Buddhist monk in Thailand would be a worthwhile experience for many people.

- Israel – the 'law of return' allows Jewish immigrants to become citizens automatically 90 days after their arrival in the country. A full passport is available in the following year. It is sometimes possible to convert to Judaism easily through the offices of a liberal rabbi.

- Spain – the Spanish will give citizenship to descendants of Sephardic Jews who were expelled from the country in the Middle Ages. Membership of a Sephardic community may be sufficient proof of descent.

- Moslem countries – many Moslem countries will look favourably on applications for nationality made by converts to Islam. Stable and civilized Morocco is a possibility.

Becoming a parent

The main points to note here are that children are normally eligible to apply for citizenship in the country in which they were born, even if their parents are not nationals of that country. The parents of such children may be able to apply for citizenship subsequently.

The Great Train Robber Ronnie Biggs used Brazil's fatherhood laws to avoid extradition. In Brazil, the unmarried father of a Brazilian child is responsible for that child, and thus cannot be extradited until the child becomes an adult.

Quasi-diplomatic status

Successful professionals and businesspeople can sometimes become honorary consuls of countries with which they are connected. These are often political appointments, but the duties are not usually onerous – often only entailing the occasional entertaining of foreign visitors and a little paperwork. The benefit? A diplomatic passport, good for travel in most countries.

Ethnicity

Some countries feel guilty about past persecutions, while others wish to perpetuate historical ties with external groups and states. These include:

• Germany – ethnic Germans and descendants of Germans persecuted by the Nazis get favourable treatment and a speeded-up application process.

• Portugal – Brazilians, Goan Indians, Angolans and nationals of other former Portuguese colonies generally have the application process accelerated.

• Spain – people of Spanish descent and nationals of former Spanish colonies (including the Philippines and most of Latin America) get favourable treatment.

• Denmark – people of Nordic descent should be able to obtain citizenship after two years' residency.

• Some ex-USSR countries – Latvia and Lithuania, for example, are keen to encourage returnees and will issue passports to descendants of exiles fairly easily.

• The Solomon Islands – black people of Melanesian descent can obtain citizenship; the 'blackbirding' trade of the eighteenth century (see page 294) spread Pacific Islanders across the globe. Few records survive, and thus little proof of ethnic origin is needed.

• Turkey – descendants of Turks inhabiting the area covered by the former Ottoman Empire have a good chance of obtaining citizenship. Turkish speakers who can show some cultural connection with Turkey are also looked upon favourably.

The United States – a special case
The complexities of US immigration policies are beyond the scope of this book, and are probably the most publicized in the world. But is US citizenship really desirable? Here are some negative factors.

- The US discourages dual nationality in its citizens, although there are loopholes, and in practice only a formal renunciation of citizenship will result in losing US nationality.

- US nationals are taxed on worldwide income even if they are not resident.

- Various government agencies display an excess of zeal that beggars belief – wealthy people are regularly stripped of their property in one way or another.

Becoming a US national is definitely not the soft option that many people think it to be; if discretion, privacy and anonymity are important to you, look at other countries first.

Passports and the EU
Elements within the EU are supposed to want to introduce an EU passport that really does make you an EU national with full rights in all the member countries (this is not currently the case in practice). My own view is that this is never going to happen, and any approach towards this will not be sustained. I believe that Europe cannot ever be politically united to that degree. What is on the cards, though, is an iron curtain around EU borders as economic power shifts towards the Far East, the Third World gets poorer and the CIS becomes a war zone. Thus, dual nationality with one EU passport and one New World or Asian passport would seem appropriate.

Camouflage passports
A number of companies are selling 'camouflage' passports. These documents look like real passports, and purport to have been issued by obscure countries that either no longer exist (e.g. British Honduras, now the independent Belize) or countries that never existed (e.g. Patagonia). The idea is that they are useful in dangerous areas – if you are stopped by soldiers or bandits, you hand over the camouflage passport, hoping that they are not trained immigration officers. There are plenty of stories of this ruse working in central Asia, Latin America and Africa, but it is clearly not for the faint-hearted.

Other uses include offering a camouflage passport in hotels where they insist on holding a passport but keep them unattended in plain view behind the receptionist's desk. Unless you really do travel in war zones and places where law and order have completely broken down, camouflage passports are probably a liability rather than an asset, and in any case should only be used by experienced travellers.

Pitfalls

Once you obtain dual nationality your problems may not be over. Here are two pitfalls.

1. *Military service* – some countries require all males to do a certain number of years' military service, while others, such as Israel and Switzerland, require annual top-up periods as well. Sometimes you can get exemptions or buy your way out of it, but if you can't, or don't want to, never visit that country, even in transit or on holiday – you may be arrested and rushed off to an army camp.

2. *Revocations* – one regime falls and a new one comes to power; naturalizations are revoked, assets seized and innocents imprisoned. Look at the track record of your second country – is it the kind of place where this has happened in the past?

Gough's three dual nationality rules

Here are some tips on how to use your second passport.

1. **Never take both passports with you across a border**. While it is perfectly possible to acquire dual nationality legitimately, immigration officials at borders tend to take a dim view of people if they discover that they are carrying two passports. Be prepared to do a lot of explaining – and you may have the passports confiscated.

2. **Don't tell anyone you have dual nationality.** This particularly applies in cases where, like the shoe manufacturer earlier in this chapter, you may need to leave a country in a hurry.

3. **Look the part.** Suppose you have acquired citizenship of a small Spanish-speaking country. Make sure you speak Spanish and have a full explanation at your fingertips of how you became a citizen. This will help to avoid long, inconvenient hold-ups when travelling.

Conclusion

Living in one country all your life distorts your view of the world. However civilized and free from propaganda one's home country may be, one tends to absorb the attitude that conditions at home are the same as they are abroad, and if they aren't, then there must be a catch. There is no catch, nor is there paradise on earth, but I hope that this book will help you to prosper and find fulfilment by stepping out of the single-country rut.

THE HAVENS OF
EUROPE

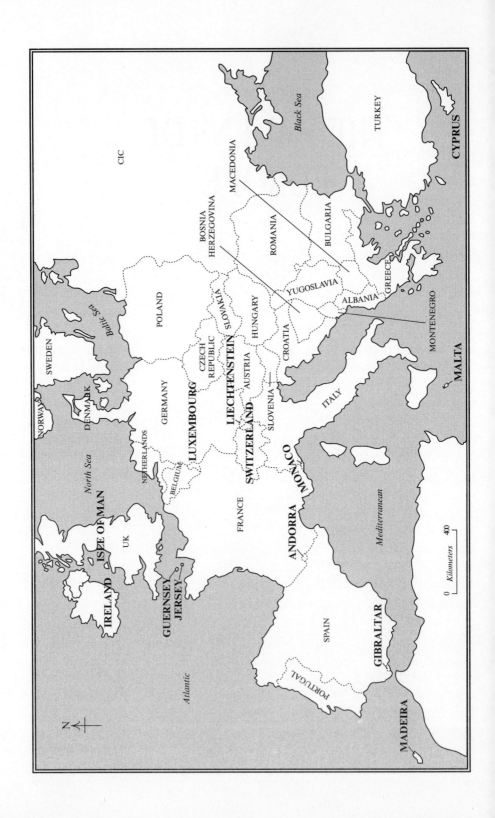

ANDORRA

Essential information

Principality between France and Spain

Capital: Andorra la Vella

Language: Catalan, Spanish, French

Telephone code: 33 628

Voltage: 240 volts AC 50 Hz

Time: GMT +2 hours

Currency: French franc or Spanish peseta

Office hours: *Banks:* Monday to Friday, 9 a.m.–1 p.m., Saturdays, 9 a.m.–Midday. *Shops:* Monday to Saturday, 9 a.m.–8 p.m., Sundays, 9 a.m.–7 p.m.

Driving licence: National driving licences accepted

Climate: Alpine

Health: No certificates required

Visas and passports: Passports must be carried by all except EU nationals with appropriate ID

Customs: There are no restrictions on the import and export of foreign currency. There is no duty on goods.

Background

Andorra is a tiny principality in the Pyrenees between France and Spain, with a population of around 50,000. It is one of the last feudal remnants in Europe (Sark, in the Channel Islands being another) and its joint sovereigns are the Spanish Bishop of Urgel and the French President, but in practice there is a Council General elected by the people. The climate is alpine and harsh. Andorra makes its money out of tourism and duty-free shopping.

Companies and taxation

Andorra has no VAT or Income Tax. There is strong popular feeling against taxation. France breathes heavily down Andorra's neck and it is unlikely to become an offshore haven of any significance. Company formation and obtaining citizenship are severely restricted. Banking is highly

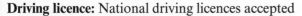

confidential and there are no exchange controls. For the truly dedicated offshore investor, the country does have potential.

CYPRUS (SOUTHERN)

Essential information
Island in the Mediterranean

Capital: Nicosia

Language: Greek

Telephone code: 357

Voltage: 240 volts AC 50 Hz

Time: GMT +3 hours

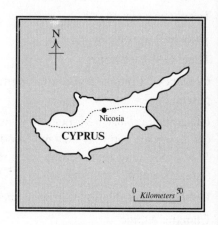

Currency: Cyprus pound (CYP), 100 cents to the pound. CYP notes are denominated as 0.5, 1, 5, 10 and 20 pounds

Office hours: *Banks:* Monday to Friday, 8.15 a.m.–12.30 p.m., afternoon opening at some central banks. *Offices:* Winter – Monday, Tuesday, Thursday and Friday, 8 a.m.–1 p.m. and 2.30 p.m.–5.30 p.m., Wednesdays, 8 a.m.–1 p.m. Summer – Monday, Tuesday, Thursday and Friday, 8 a.m.–1 p.m., Wednesdays, 8 a.m.–1 p.m.

Driving licence: International or national

Climate: Mediterranean

Health: No certificates required

Visas and passports: Visas are not required by most nationals for stays of up to three months. Passports must be carried by all.

Customs: There are no restrictions on the import or export of foreign currency, but it should be declared. You can import up to 200 cigarettes or 50 cigars and 1 litre of spirits.

Airport: Larnaca. Five miles out of the town of Larnaca. No departure tax. 24-hour bureau de change.

History
Cyprus has been inhabited since the New Stone Age. About 1500 BC it was under the control of Egyptian pharaohs, but during the next millennium it was mainly under the influence of the Greeks. Phoenician colonies

appeared on Cyprus about 800 BC, and in the following centuries it came successfully under Assyrian, Egyptian and Persian domination. Commercial trade was important during all these periods. Surrendering to Alexander the Great, Cyprus passed into the hands of Ptolemy, one of his generals, who became king of Egypt in 323 BC. The Roman empire annexed the island in 58 BC. Jewish and early Christian communities were active on the island.

After the Roman empire was divided in two in AD 395 Cyprus became part of what became the Byzantine empire. Following the rise of Islam in the seventh century Cyprus became a border land, passing frequently between Byzantine and Arab control. In 1191 Richard the Lionheart conquered the island, sold it first to the Knights Templar and then bestowed it on Guy de Lusignan, the crusader king of Jerusalem who had been driven out by the Saracens. Guy started a monarchy which survived until the fifteenth century as one of the last bastions of the crusading movement. It then passed into the Venetian empire and a century later the Ottoman empire took it over. At first its rule was liberal and enlightened, but as the Ottomans became moribund their rule became oppressive.

In 1878 Britain took over the government of the island by treaty, although it remained Ottoman in name. Britain annexed it at the outbreak of World War 1.

In the 1930s the Greek part of the population began to demand 'enosis' (union with Greece), and after World War 2 found their champion in the person of Archbishop Makarios. A Greek terrorist organization, EOKA, became active in the 1950s and in 1960 Cyprus became a republic with Britain retaining military bases there. Ethnic divisions continued to cause trouble, and in 1975 Turkey invaded Northern Cyprus, which remains under Turkish military rule. Because of its geographic location, Cyprus has always been a region of intense activity and rivalry between many ethnic groups and political powers.

Geography

Cyprus is in the region where Europe, Asia and Africa meet. Not far from the coasts of Turkey and the Levant, Cyprus plays an important role in the life of the Middle East. Although it is an island, Cyprus has clear skies, low rainfall and plenty of sunshine, owing to its close proximity to large land masses. There are bad droughts every ten years or so. Winters are mild. The capital is Nicosia, in the middle of the island, and the main ports are at Limassol and Larnaca.

People

The population of 700,000 are three-quarters Greek, the remainder being predominantly Turkish. Greek and Turkish are the official languages, and English is widely understood.

Government

Cyprus is an independent country and has membership of the Common-wealth, the UN and the non-aligned countries. It is an associate of the EU. It has a democratically elected President and House of Representatives and elections are held every five years. The legal system is based on English law.

Economy

The capital of Cyprus, Nicosia, is its commercial centre while Limassol is the main industrial and commercial centre. Despite the political problems with Turkey, there are now over 100,000 offshore enterprises on the island and 22 foreign banks, including Barclays. Some banks are believed to be used as vehicles for funding sanction-breaking activities in Serbia. Agriculture is the main employer, but manufacturing is the biggest foreign exchange earner. Tourism is important.

Offshore companies

Offshore enterprises are not allowed to do business on the island, though they may be based there, can tranship goods through Cyprus and hold bank accounts on the island in foreign currency. The main points regarding offshore companies are:

- Tax is currently at 4.5 per cent of profits.
- Offshore branches which are managed from abroad are exempt from tax.
- No Capital Gains Tax is payable.
- There is no withholding tax on dividends.
- There are no exchange controls.
- Shipping activities are exempt from tax.
- Non-residents must obtain exchange control permission before purchasing shares in a company.
- Off-the-shelf companies are not available.
- There is no minimum capital for a company.
- Shares cannot be in bearer form.
- Nominee shareholders are allowed.

- Details of companies are publicly available through the Registrar of Companies.

Double-taxation treaties

Cyprus has some 21 double-taxation treaties, and provided that an offshore company has its management in Cyprus it can take advantage of these.

International trusts

As a common law country Cyprus recognizes trusts; they are not subject to exchange controls and may be moved to and from Cyprus. There are no registration or reporting requirements, but if a bank account for the trust is opened on the island the Central Bank must be informed. The International Trusts Law gives the following rules for an international trust, which is defined as one where the settlor is not a permanent resident of Cyprus and at least one of the trustees is a permanent resident.

- No beneficiary other than a charity can be permanently resident in Cyprus.
- Cypriot immovable property cannot form part of the trust's assets.
- An international trust can last for 100 years.
- The trustees may put the trust funds into any kind of investment anywhere in the world.
- No inheritance or succession law of any country will affect any transfer, disposition or validity of a Cyprus international trust.
- No income tax, Capital Gains Tax or estate duty is chargeable in respect of trust assets.
- Stamp duty of approximately £300 is payable on creation of a trust.
- A beneficiary who is not a Cypriot can retire on the island and yet be exempt of tax, as long as it is an international trust where the trust property is settled abroad and the income derives from abroad.

Whether a local or an international trust, trust funds are not subject to tax. Resident beneficiaries would be taxed on income from a local trust.

GIBRALTAR

Essential information
South-western tip of Spain
Capital: Gibraltar

Language: English, Spanish

Telephone code: 350

Voltage: 220/240 volts AC 50 Hz

Time: GMT +2 hours

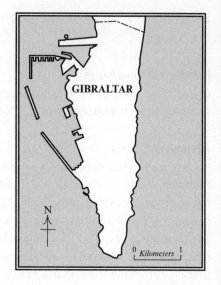

Currency: Gibraltar pound (GIP), 100 pence to the pound. GIP notes are denominated as 1, 5, 10, 20, 50 and 100

Office hours: *Banks:* Monday to Thursday, 9 a.m.–3.30 p.m. Fridays, 9 a.m.–3.30 p.m. and 4.30 p.m.–6 p.m. *Offices:* Monday to Friday, 9 a.m.– 1 p.m. and 3 p.m.–6 p.m. *Shops:* Monday to Friday, 10 a.m.–7 p.m., Saturdays, 10 a.m.–1 p.m.

Credit cards: Major credit cards and travellers' cheques are widely accepted

Driving licence: International and national driving licences accepted

Climate: Dry Mediterranean climate

Health: No certificates required

Visas and passports: Visas are required for everyone except EU nationals. Passports must be carried by all except EU nationals with appropriate ID and UK nationals with a British Visitors Passport

Customs: There are no restrictions on the import of foreign currency provided that it is declared on arrival; you can export up to the amount you declared on importation. You can import up to 200 cigarettes or 50 cigars and 1 litre of spirits and 2 litres of wine.

Airport: Gibraltar North Front, half a mile out of the city centre. No departure tax. Bureaux de change open 8.30 a.m.–9.30 p.m.

History

Well-known in the ancient world as one of the 'pillars of Hercules' which marked the limit of the Mediterranean, Gibraltar seems not to have been heavily populated until the Moslem conquests. The name 'Gibraltar' is a corruption of the Arabic 'Jebel Al Tariq', (Tariq's mountain) and was so called by the Arabs after its capture in 711 by Tariq ibn Zaid. It was held as a fortress by the Arabs for centuries until it was captured in 1309 by Castile. It changed hands back and forth several times until it finally passed into Spanish hands in 1462. During the next 50 years it was so heavily fortified that it was generally regarded as impregnable.

In 1704 during the War of the Spanish Succession a British and Dutch fleet under a British admiral was sent to attack Toulon in France, but after setbacks attacked Gibraltar instead and captured it. Political manoeuvring resulted in the withdrawal of the Dutch in 1713, leaving Gibraltar to the British. The fortifications had become very dilapidated and public opinion in Britain was that Gibraltar was worthless. Continuing hostilities and Spanish demands for its return followed, and in 1726 Spain attacked the fortress unsuccessfully. For the next 50 years the Gibraltar question lay dormant, but in 1779 Spain took advantage of the American Revolution to besiege Gibraltar. The siege lasted four years but the fortress was not captured, and regained its mediaeval reputation for impregnability.

In 1830 Gibraltar became a Crown Colony. Spanish demands for its return became intense in the 1880s, and have remained a live issue ever since.

Geography
The Rock of Gibraltar is a mountain on an isthmus projecting from the Spanish province of Andalusia into the Mediterranean. It is about two and a half miles long and half a mile wide. Consisting mainly of limestone, the Rock has few wells, and most water must be obtained by collecting rain water in reservoirs. There are few large trees, but many small plants flourish in Gibraltar; migratory birds stop there, but there is only one mammal, the famous Barbary Ape, which was imported from North Africa.

People and language
Gibraltarians, as they are known, number 30,000 and are mainly descended from Spanish, Portuguese, Maltese and Italian settlers. Most people speak both Spanish and English, but English is the official language.

Government and legal system
As a Crown Colony, Gibraltar is self-governing except for defence, internal security and foreign affairs, which are administered by the UK. It is governed by a Council of Ministers and also has a 17-member House of Assembly, the majority of whom are elected.

Economy
Political squabbling between Britain and Spain over Gibraltar's future stunted its economy for many years, but since 1985, when Spain opened the border, the economy has improved. Tourism, shipping and offshore finance are main sources of income; bank deposits are now in the region of £2.7 billion and banks are attracting clients from the rest of Europe and the

GAZETTEER

US. Tax incentives to attract high net worth individuals include a flat rate of tax irrespective of income. Following the scandals of Barlow Clowes and BCCI, Gibraltar has introduced a Financial Services Commission to regulate the financial industry. When the UK joined the EU in 1973 Gibraltar was included under Article 227 of the Treaty of Rome. Gibraltar obtained an exclusion from the EU's common customs tariff, the CAP and VAT. The inhabitants have the right of free movement and establishment in the EU. Agreements between the UK and Spain allow the free movement of people, vehicles and goods between Gibraltar and Spain.

Offshore companies

Following Spanish moves against offshore companies holding property in Spain, the rate of company incorporations in Gibraltar has slowed. Gibraltar has four kinds of company:

1. Companies limited by shares.
2. Companies limited by guarantee without share capital.
3. Companies limited by guarantee which have share capital.
4. Unlimited companies with or without share capital.

Most offshore investors form companies limited by shares. Features include:

- Bearer shares are allowed.
- Companies can have one shareholder.
- Only one director is required.
- Annually audited accounts must be filed.

It is possible to form a company which is exempt of tax:

- A company owned by non-residents and doing no business with residents can apply for exempt status.
- Exempt status exempts the company from any taxes for 25 years, unless profits are remitted to Gibraltar.
- Public files do not show whether or not a company is exempt.

Exempt companies can apply for 'qualifying' status instead, which means that the company chooses to pay a rate of tax on profits of between 2 per cent and 18 per cent, not less than 2 per cent and not more than 18 per cent. This is done to prove the payment of tax. For example, relief under a double-taxation treaty is only available if there is evidence that a specified amount of tax has been paid somewhere.

Gibraltar 1992 Holding Companies take advantage of EU directive 90/435 which deals with dividends paid by subsidiaries to parent companies.

- A subsidiary company in one EU country can pay dividends to its parent company in another EU country without withholding tax, subject to certain rules.

- The Gibraltar 1992 Holding Company pays normal tax at 35 per cent on all income, except that dividends are not taxed on arrival. Dividends from EU subsidiaries are free of tax on arrival in Gibraltar and then subject only to a 1 per cent withholding tax if the Holding Company pays out a dividend.

Double-taxation treaties
Gibraltar has no double-taxation treaties. Individuals pay 30 per cent Income Tax, rising to a 50 per cent higher rate, on income arising in Gibraltar or received there.

Trusts
Gibraltar recognizes trusts in the following way:

- The perpetuity period and the accumulation period are both 100 years.

- Trust income is tax free where the settlor and the beneficiaries are non-resident.

GUERNSEY, ALDERNEY AND SARK

Essential information
Part of the Channel Islands

Capital: St Peter Port

Language: English, French

Telephone code: 44 481

Voltage: 240 volts AC 50 Hz

Time: GMT +1 hour

Currency: Sterling

Office hours: As UK

Driving licence: National driving licences accepted

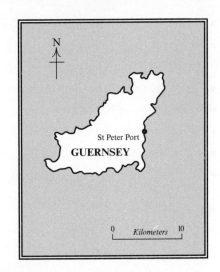

Climate: Temperate

Health: No certificates required

Visas and passports: Passports must be carried by all except EU nationals with appropriate ID

Customs: There are no restrictions on the import and export of foreign currency.

Background

While less developed than Jersey, Guernsey is an important offshore centre with a good reputation to protect – 'poor-quality' business will be turned away. British nationals have the right of abode in the islands, but the housing market is controlled and expensive. The Bailiwick of Guernsey, which includes the smaller islands of Alderney and Sark, is not part of the UK but is ruled by the Queen. All three islands have their own parliaments which are democratically elected, and make their own domestic laws without reference to Britain. There are no political parties. Guernsey is not a member of the EU and is not obliged to adopt EU directives or proposals regarding direct or indirect taxation. The population is about 55,000, some of whom are French speakers. Interest on bank deposits is not taxable, and while there is no compensation scheme in case of a banking collapse, standards of regulation are high.

Offshore companies

Forms of company are the same as those available in the UK, except for the exempt company, which is free of corporation tax and the following conditions apply:

- Authorization to form a company must be obtained.
- Shares must have a par value.
- There is no minimum share capital.
- There are no off-the-shelf companies.
- A minimum of two shareholders is required.
- AGMs must be held in Guernsey.
- Exempt companies need not file annually audited accounts.
- Very little information is on public record.

Tax

Guernsey residents are taxed on worldwide income at 20 per cent. Non-residents are taxed on income from Guernsey only. There are no exchange

190

controls, VAT or death duties. Bank interest is not taxed. Guernsey residents must not have an interest in exempt companies except as nominees. There is no withholding tax on exempt companies. Guernsey has a double-taxation treaty with the UK, but exempt companies fall outside this agreement.

Trusts

Guernsey recognizes trusts. The main rules are:

- The maximum perpetuity period is 100 years.
- Trusts in Guernsey may be moved to another jurisdiction.
- Trust deeds need not be registered.
- Trusts with non-resident settlors and beneficiaries are only taxed on income from Guernsey.

IRELAND

Essential information

Island west of Britain

Capital: Dublin

Language: English

Telephone code: 353

Voltage: 220 volts AC 50 Hz

Time: GMT +1 hour

Currency: Irish pound (IEP), 100 pence to the pound. IEP notes are denominated as 5, 10, 20, 50 and 100

Office hours: *Banks:* Monday to Friday, 10 a.m.–12.30 p.m. and 1.30 p.m. – 3 p.m. *Shops:* Monday to Saturday, 9 a.m.– 5.30 p.m.

Credit cards: Major credit cards and travellers' cheques are widely accepted

Driving licence: International and national licences accepted

Climate: Temperate, changeable

Health: No certificates required

Passports: Passports must be carried by all except for EU nationals with appropriate ID

Customs: There are no restrictions on the import of foreign currency. Export of foreign currency worth over IEP1,200 requires approval and cannot be exported as bank notes.

Airports:
Cork – three miles out of Cork. No departure tax.
Dublin – five miles out of Dublin. No departure tax.
Shannon – 16 miles out of Limerick. No departure tax.

History

Ireland was entirely dominated for many centuries by a small, often oppressive, minority (which was English and Protestant) until 1800, when it was unwillingly incorporated into the UK. In 1846 and 1847 a disease of the potato crop, then the staple food of the inhabitants, caused a devastating famine in which millions died or emigrated, and the population fell by about 25 per cent in five years to 6.5 million. Following the famine political agitation was subdued for 20 years, but emigration continued and land reforms worsened the condition of the people.

A secret revolutionary society, the Fenians, arose, intent on secession from the UK, and was the chief cause of the disestablishment of the Protestant Church (the majority of the people were Catholics) in Ireland in 1869. In 1870 the first Irish Land Act went some way to securing land rights. Charles Parnell, a landowner and Member of Parliament, became head of a Land League dedicated to further reforms, and brought about large rent reductions. The Fenians gave their support to Parnell, whose aim was for Irish home rule, and in 1886 the British Prime Minister Gladstone introduced a home rule bill to Westminster, but was defeated. Parnell was subsequently disgraced by a divorce case, but did not resign his leadership of his Home Rule party, and progress diminished.

In 1900 a new party, Sinn Fein, was formed which demanded that Irish MPs refuse to attend Westminster. At about the same time land reforms were finally carried through by Prime Minister Balfour which transferred land ownership to tenants on easy terms, the intention being to 'kill home rule with kindness'. The county of Ulster, largely Protestant, strongly opposed moves towards home rule, forming the Ulster volunteer force in preparation to defend themselves against nationalism. By the time of the outbreak of World War 1, Ireland was on the verge of civil war, but some 200,000 men volunteered for the British army. In 1916 armed rebellion broke out in Dublin (the Easter Uprising), but was suppressed.

The introduction of army conscription in 1918 increased the popular support for Sinn Fein, which was demanding independence, and a savage civil war broke out. Several political solutions were tried during the next few years, until in 1921 four-fifths of Ireland became the 'Irish Free State', remaining part of the Commonwealth, while the remaining fifth became what is now known as Northern Ireland, a part of the UK. The Irish Free State became an independent republic, known as Eire, or Ireland, in 1949. Difficulties between Eire and Northern Ireland continued, and from the 1960s a campaign of terrorism was waged on both sides, but notably by the republican IRA, both in Ireland and on the mainland of Britain. Hopefully a peaceful settlement will come out of the current talks.

People
The population of Ireland is about 3.6 million. English is the official language. Irish, a Celtic language, is not widely spoken.

Government and legal system
The Republic of Ireland has two Houses of Parliament, the Dail, whose members are elected, and the Senate. The government is elected from the Dail. Ireland is a Catholic country, and legislation reflects this – divorce and abortion are difficult.

Economy
With a small population for its size, Ireland is a net receiver of money from the EU. Agriculture, industry and tourism are its main sources of income. Except for its International Financial Services Centre and certain exempt companies, Ireland is not a tax haven.

International Financial Services Centre (IFSC)
Dublin's International Financial Services Centre has emerged as a rival to other quasi-offshore centres, in particular to Luxembourg, since it was set up in 1987. Among the major companies with a presence there are:

- John Govett (fund management)
- London Life and General Reinsurance of Canada (reinsurance)
- The Bank of Bermuda (services to overseas fund groups)
- Danisco Finance of Denmark (managing the group's financial transactions)
- Gacalux of Luxembourg (captive insurance management)
- Asahi Fire and Marine Insurance of Japan (management of surplus funds)

- Daiwa
- Morgan Grenfell
- IBM
- Porsche
- Coca-Cola
- Hitachi
- Seagram.

Many of these companies use the IFSC for captive insurance and corporate treasury activities. Companies setting up in the IFSC are offered:

- 10 per cent Corporation Tax guaranteed by the EU until 2005. Companies must not deal in the local currency or trade with individuals or companies resident in Ireland. Permitted activities include banking/ asset financing, corporate treasury management, mutual fund management, insurance and ancillary services.
- Exemption from local municipal taxes for 10 years.
- 100 per cent deduction for tax purposes of the capital cost of commercial buildings.
- No withholding taxes on interest and dividends.
- Income arising from active trading in stocks, shares, and other securities by a financial institution is normally to be treated as trading income and is not liable to Capital Gains Tax.

Over 70 captive insurance operations are based in the IFSC. The IFSC is also attractive to companies as a site for offshore corporate treasury activity. Treasury functions that can be carried on include:

- Managing exchange rate and interest rate risk.
- Funding group companies' fixed and floating capital requirements.

The Irish government hopes that the IFSC will provide employment and rejuvenate the docks area of Dublin.

Incentives for companies
Ireland has a history of high unemployment, and therefore offers incentives to companies in manufacturing and export-related services. These include:

- grants
- relief from municipal taxes

- tax allowances
- 10 per cent corporation tax.

The special tax status of these companies is available until 2010. More than 1,000 international companies use Ireland for manufacturing and services.

Non-resident companies
Non-resident companies, defined as companies with no permanent establishment in Ireland, pay no Corporation Tax on profits earned overseas. In other respects, though, they are as tightly regulated as any 'onshore' company. Rules include:

- Shareholders must not be resident in Ireland.
- There must be a registered office in Ireland.
- Non-resident companies do not benefit from double-taxation treaties.
- Central Bank permission is needed to issue bearer shares – applications are usually refused.

Double taxation
Ireland has more than 20 double-taxation agreements, including many of the other EU members, Australia and the United States.

Trusts
Trusts are fully recognized under Irish law, and need not be registered. They get no favourable tax treatment, however, and pay Capital Gains Tax and Income Tax.

JERSEY

Essential information
One of the Channel Islands
Capital: St Helier
Language: English, French
Telephone code: 44 534
Voltage: 240 volts AC 50 Hz
Time: GMT +1 hour
Currency: Sterling

GAZETTEER

Office hours: As UK

Driving licence: National driving licences accepted

Climate: Temperate

Health: No certificates required

Visas and passports: Passports must be carried by all except EU nationals with appropriate ID

Customs: There are no restrictions on the import and export of foreign currency.

Background

Jersey is the largest of the Channel Islands, with an area of 45 square miles. It has a population of 80,000. The financial services industry is the biggest contributor to the island's economy. About 70 banks operate on the island, with deposits of more than £54 billion. Jersey has no bank deposit compensation scheme, but has a strict vetting procedure for banks; BCCI was refused a licence in the 1970s. Jersey wants to attract 'quality' business, and wants to preserve its reputation as a reputable international centre. There is no banking secrecy, but confidentiality is good.

Government

Jersey is ruled by the British Crown but is not part of the United Kingdom and is not subject to UK law. It has a parliament, the States, which has 53 elected members. The legal system is based on the English system and ultimate appeals are to the UK's Privy Council.

Offshore companies

Jersey's companies are regulated on similar lines to British ones:

- Bearer shares are not allowed.
- There must be a minimum of two issued shares.
- There must be a minimum of two shareholders.
- Companies must have a registered office in Jersey.
- Except for exempt companies, annually audited accounts are required.

Jersey has introduced the International Business Company (IBC):

- An IBC must be owned by non-residents and not previously have been an exempt or resident company.

- IBCs pay very low taxes on international profits.

- IBCs can be a company incorporated in Jersey, a foreign company managed and controlled in Jersey or a Jersey branch of a foreign company.

- IBCs cannot have Jersey residents as beneficial owners, but they can have a Jersey intermediate holding company.

- An IBC is fully resident for tax purposes in Jersey. It pays tax on profits in the normal way, but is subject to special rates of tax on any profits derived from international business activities. These include inter-company financial activities, industrial and commercial activities and overseas investment.

- There is deduction of Jersey tax from payments of interest from IBC to individuals or companies in other countries.

- Non-resident directors do not pay tax on their fees. It was initially hoped that IBCs could be used to avoid the Controlled Foreign Companies legislation in the UK, but the UK raised the rate of tax required to avoid CFC legislation to three-quarters of the UK rate, making it 5 per cent higher than the full Jersey Income Tax rate. The UK Inland Revenue rarely uses CFC legislation, though, concentrating on attempts to show that the management and control of companies are in the UK.

Any company in Jersey is subject to tax at 20 per cent, unless it elects to apply for exempt status for a particular tax year. Exempt companies must be owned by non-residents and can be managed and controlled in Jersey. They do not pay tax on foreign income or on interest earned in Jersey.

Double-taxation treaties

Apart from its agreement with the UK, Jersey has no double-taxation treaties. There are no withholding taxes, except for a 20 per cent tax on royalties. Jersey has no Inheritance Tax or Capital Gains Tax. Residents are taxed on worldwide income at 20 per cent, with the exception of Jersey bank interest, which is paid gross.

Funds in Jersey

Jersey's importance as a centre for offshore investment derives from its reputation for a well-managed economy, its unchanging tax rates and its sympathetic authorities. There are over 300 funds managing a total of around £16 billion. The island has 'designated territory' status in the UK which means that its institutions can sell certain funds in the UK.

GAZETTEER

Trusts

Trusts are important in Jersey; the island has about 150 trust companies which are said to manage more than £50 billion. As it is a party to the Hague Convention on trusts, Jersey's trusts are recognized as valid in many other countries. The Royal Court of Jersey has jurisdiction over a Jersey trust and over a foreign trust where the trustees are resident in Jersey or where any of its assets are situated or administered on the island.

- The maximum perpetuity period is 100 years.
- There is no fixed accumulation period.
- Trusts cannot hold land in Jersey.
- The trust instrument is signed only by the trustees.
- Trusts need not be registered.
- Oral trusts are legal, if the agreement has been made clear.
- With discretionary trusts, the beneficiaries' interests can be defined or be at the discretion of the trustees.
- The settlor can be a beneficiary, and may retain powers over the trust assets. Protectors are often appointed so that the settlor is not taxed in his own country on the basis of retaining such powers.
- A trust can be made irrevocable wholly or in part.
- Provisions can be made for trustees to act by majority.
- The terms of a trust may provide for trustees to be removed or replaced by the settlor, but under Jersey law the trustees have powers to retain assets after being removed until they have been properly indemnified against liabilities.
- Trusts can be moved from one jurisdiction to another in the case of political or strategic emergency.

LIECHTENSTEIN

Essential information

Capital: Vaduz

Language: German, English widely spoken

Telephone code: 4175

Voltage: 220 volts AC 50 Hz

Time: GMT +2 hours

Currency: Swiss franc (CHF), 100 centimes to the franc. CHF notes are denominated as 10, 20, 50, 100, 500 and 1,000

Office hours: *Banks:* Monday to Friday, 8.30 a.m.–12.30 p.m. and 2 p.m.–4.30 p.m. *Offices:* Monday to Friday, 8.30 a.m. –Midday and 2 p.m.–5 p.m. *Shops:* Monday to Friday, 8.30 a.m.–Midday and 2 p.m.–6.30 p.m. Saturdays, 8.30 a.m. –Midday and 1 p.m–4 p.m.

Credit cards: Major credit cards and travellers' cheques are widely accepted

Driving licence: National licences accepted

Health: No certificates required

Visas and passports: See Switzerland

Customs: There are no restrictions on the import and export of foreign currency.

Airports: There are no airports in Liechtenstein; the nearest one is at Zurich. Few trains stop here either. The best way to get to the country is by the 'postbus' which runs frequently from Buchs and Sargans in Switzerland or by car on Route 16 through Buchs.

History

Populated by Celtic and Teutonic tribes and colonized by the Romans, Liechtenstein's life as a separate political entity began in 1699 when Prince Johann Adam bought the Lordship of Schellenberg, and then, in 1712, the County of Vaduz from German noblemen. Prince Johann owned large estates in the surrounding countries, but needed these territories to qualify for voting membership of the Diet of Princes.

Charles the Sixth, the Emperor of the Holy Roman Empire, declared Liechtenstein a principality in 1719. It remained within the empire until 1820 when it joined the Rhine Confederacy, controlled by Napoleon. After the fall of Napoleon, Liechtenstein became part of the German Confederation until 1866, when it became independent. A constitution was promulgated in 1929, creating a 'Landtag' (parliament) of 15 elected members. Until 1919 the country was closely linked to Austria, but in 1921 it adopted Swiss currency and agreed on customs union in 1924.

Geography
Liechtenstein has an area of 60 square miles, and runs along the east bank of the Rhine between Austria and Switzerland, some 30 miles south of Lake Constance.

People
The country has a population of 30,000, a third of whom are foreigners. The official language is German, but French and English are widely spoken.

Government and legal system
His Serene Highness Prince Johannes Adam von und zu Liechtenstein, the current monarch, has been running the country since 1984, although he did not succeed to the throne until 1989. Much more than a figurehead, the Prince temporarily dissolved parliament in 1989 when it did not support his plans to build an art museum. There are 25 members of parliament, and local areas have a good deal of autonomy, as in Switzerland. Politically, Liechtenstein remains independent of Swiss influence and policies.

Economy
Liechtenstein is well known for its banking secrecy which some say is tighter than Switzerland's, and also for its wise ability to shun publicity. Even after the enormous criticism resulting from the Maxwell pension fund fraud, it has remained silent. Liechtenstein's attractions as a haven are based on its favourable tax structures and its flexible attitude towards company and trust formation, in particular holding companies. The country levies virtually no tax on non-resident companies. It is estimated that there are some 40,000 holding companies in the principality, some 10,000 more than the number of inhabitants. Agriculture also has a role in the economy, and the region produces good wine. Manufacturing is also important.

Companies
Liechtenstein is one of the few countries whose confidentiality laws are entirely credible. Complete anonymity is on offer. Features of the rules include:

- Companies can be formed within five days.
- Bearer shares are allowed.
- Minimal information is required to be filed with the Public Register.
- Shareholders need not reveal their identities in the Public Register.
- Companies must have a legal representative resident in the country.

Liechtenstein has two company types which may be unfamiliar to British readers:

- *Stiftung* – these are 'foundations' which are legal entities in their own right, unlike a trust, but in other respects operate in a similar way to trusts.
- *Anstalt* – these are 'establishments' which are legal entities without shares, but are similar to a company; they are often used as holding companies.

Double-taxation treaties

Liechtenstein has a double-taxation treaty with Austria. It has no with-holding taxes, but does levy 4 per cent on dividends and similar payments made by companies with capital in the form of shares. Holding companies are free of tax if their daughter companies are outside Liechtenstein. Resident individuals pay a maximum 17.5 per cent wealth and Income Tax.

Banking

Liechtenstein has toughened up banking supervision by introducing a new banking regulatory body, the Banking Commission. The new authority has the power to order special audits on banks. The government has also said that it reserves the right to dissolve dubious financial institutions that have no licence without prior warning. Insider trading and drug money launder-ing are criminal offences, but, unlike Switzerland, bankers are not yet required to declare the beneficial owners of bank accounts.

Trusts

Although it is a civil law country, Liechtenstein has a unique body of law and practices governing trusts which closely resembles English common law, but with a number of advantages:

- Trusts may have an unlimited perpetuity period.
- There is no limit on the accumulation period.
- Beneficiaries resident abroad are not taxed on distributions.

Trusts with foreign assets are taxed annually at 1 per cent of capital, with a minimum of 1,000 Swiss francs.

GAZETTEER

LUXEMBOURG

Essential information

Capital: Luxembourg-ville

Language: French, German

Telephone code: 352

Voltage: 220 volts AC 50 Hz

Time: GMT +2 hours

Currency: Luxembourg franc (LUF), 100 centimes to the franc, and the Belgian franc (BEF), 100 centimes to the franc. LUF notes are denominated as 100 and 1,000

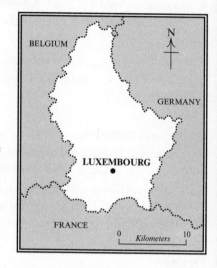

Office hours: *Banks:* Monday to Friday, 9 a.m.–Midday and 1.30 p.m.–4.30 p.m. *Offices:* Monday to Friday, 8.30 a.m.–Midday and 2 p.m.–6 p.m. *Shops:* Mondays, 2 p.m.–6 p.m., Tuesday to Saturday, 8.30 a.m.–6 p.m.

Credit cards: Major credit cards and travellers' cheques are widely accepted

Driving licence: International and national driving licences accepted

Health: No certificates required

Customs: There are no restrictions on the import and export of foreign currency

Airport: Luxembourg, three miles out of the city centre. No departure tax. Bureaux de change open 7 a.m.–8.30 p.m.

History

Inhabited by Celtic tribes, Luxembourg became Romanized in the first century BC, and remained Roman until the Germanic invasions of the fourth and fifth centuries AD. The area which is now Luxembourg became part of the Frankish kingdom of Austrasia, and then part of the empire of Charlemagne. In 963 Luxembourg became an independent principality under Siegfried, count of Ardennes, and in about 1060 his descendant Conrad took the title Count of Luxembourg. Henry the Seventh, who became sovereign of the Holy Roman Empire in the 1300s, was a descendant of Conrad's, and the Luxembourg dynasty remained in control of the empire for 150 years.

Luxembourg was purchased in 1442 by Philip the Good of Burgundy, but was returned to the Hapsburgs (successors to the empire) in 1506. Fifty years later Luxembourg came under Spanish domination, and became part of the Spanish Netherlands, which covered what is now Belgium. In 1713 Luxembourg and Belgium passed back to the Hapsburgs, but, following the French revolution, Luxembourg was annexed by France in 1795. By international agreement, in 1815 Luxembourg once again became an independent state, as a grand duchy belonging to William the First of the Netherlands, but the king managed to incorporate it into his kingdom. Most of Luxembourg joined in the Belgian rebellion against William, and in 1831 the greater part of the country was incorporated into Belgium, while the rest, present-day Luxembourg, was kept by William as a separate state to the Netherlands.

Luxembourg was given a constitution in the 1840s and guaranteed its neutrality in 1867, but was invaded by Germany at the outbreak of World War 1. In 1919 the Grand Duchess Marie-Adelaide, who had shown pro-German sympathies, abdicated in favour of her sister Charlotte. In World War 2 Germany invaded again, but the damage was not great, and Luxembourg regained its prosperity rapidly in the post-war period. Luxembourg's experience of many invasions by various neighbours has resulted in a strong sense of nationality and independence amongst its people.

Geography
The tiny country Luxembourg is surrounded by France, Belgium and Germany and has an area of 1,000 square miles; from north to south it is 51 miles long at its longest point, and it is 35 miles across from east to west. Luxembourg is a country of deep valleys, and its northern region is mountainous and forested, being an extension of the Ardennes.

People and language
The population is about 390,000, of which about a third are immigrants. Almost all of the locals are Catholics, and are bilingual in French and German, as well as speaking their own dialect, Letzeburgesch, a kind of German. French and German have been the official languages since 1830. English is widely understood.

Government and legal system
The Grand Duchy is a constitutional monarchy, and is ruled by a hereditary Grand Duke. Legislative power is shared by the Grand Duke and the Chamber of Deputies, who are democratically elected. The judiciary is independent. The country is governed by the Grand Duke and a Council of Government, whose ministers are appointed by the Grand Duke. In prac-

tice, the Chamber of Deputies must support the appointment of ministers. Luxembourg is a civil law country, and its legal system has been influenced both by the Napoleonic code and German laws.

Economy

Luxembourg has economic and currency union with Belgium and is a founder member of the EU. The clearing house and custodial centre for the enormous Eurobond market are in Luxembourg, as are the EU Courts of Justice, the secretariat of the European Parliament, the European Investment Bank, some offices of the European Community Commission and the European Court of Auditors. Traditionally a private banking centre for the savers of France, Belgium and Germany, Luxembourg has expertise in fund management, custody and administration, reinsurance and shipping. The government has a policy of encouraging foreign investment, and offers certain incentives in addition to the well-known tax breaks. Unlike many tax havens, it is a member of GATT, the OECD and the IMF. Apart from finance, important economic activities in Luxembourg are agriculture and the steel industry, and the service industries surrounding the EU bureaucracies based in the capital, Luxembourg-ville.

Holding companies

Holding companies are of interest to offshore investors as they can:

- Buy shares and bonds of Luxembourg and foreign companies.
- Hold gold and foreign currencies.
- Finance their subsidiaries.
- Hold patents, trademarks and other licencable intellectual property.

They are not allowed to:

- Be brokers or bankers.
- Own property in Luxembourg.
- Provide services.
- Participate in partnerships.

In general, holding companies are used to hold investment portfolios, collect royalties and centralize the control of businesses. Holding companies need not reveal their holdings in their balance sheets. In addition, they may:

- Issue bearer shares.
- Get exemption from Corporation Tax, Income Tax and Capital Gains Tax.
- Get exemption from withholding taxes on dividends and interest payments.

Holding companies are excluded from Luxembourg's double-taxation treaties. The minimum number of shareholders is two, who can be of any nationality; and there must be at least three directors. Annually audited accounts must be filed. There are two special types of holding company:

1. *The Financial Holding Company* – these are used to raise money and lend it to their subsidiaries. Shares must be registered.
2. *The Milliardaire Holding Company* – these must have LUF1 billion of share capital, and are taxed at 3 per cent on interest payments, at a minimum of LUF2 million.

Luxembourg holding companies can act as a clearing house for profits from foreign operations conducted through overseas subsidiaries. The holding company can accumulate profits, reinvest and expand in new countries while paying low rates of tax. Some countries, including Belgium and France, treat payments to a Luxembourg company which receives favourable tax treatment as profit in their country and therefore as fully taxable – this can be avoided by channelling funds through other countries.

Luxembourg and the EU
Luxembourg is under constant pressure from Brussels and the other EU member states to ensure high standards of banking regulation. Its financial authority, the Institut Monetaire Luxembourgeois earned some bad press following the BCCI scandal (see page 128). It is the main centre for pan-European investment funds and has huge potential as a centre for pan-European life assurance, but EU membership has disadvantages, reducing Luxembourg's autonomy. Forthcoming EU tax harmonization may destroy the country's appeal as an investment centre.

Until Switzerland voted against membership of the EU, Luxembourg's bankers argued that EU membership could not possibly be a threat to finance, otherwise the Swiss would not be applying for membership. Money has flooded into the country from Germany after the German authorities imposed a 30 per cent withholding tax on interest. Germany is keen to prevent outflows and is considering an EU withholding tax or a tax on interest accrued outside Germany. EU membership also threatens Luxembourg's confidentiality ethos.

In March 1993, Luxembourg introduced an anti-money laundering law that gives effect to the EU Directive on money laundering. The law requires credit institutions to inform the authorities on their own initiative if they suspect laundering activities. At present its banking secrecy laws prevent bank employees passing on information gained through their work, but there is unease about how the anti-laundering law will mesh with the secrecy laws. There are more than 200 banks in Luxembourg – German banks predominate, but there is also a wide range of Scandinavian, continental European, North American and Far Eastern banks.

Collective investment

The country's fund management industry is growing; most of the money comes from foreign investors. When Luxembourg implemented the EU's UCITS (cross-border funds) legislation in 1988, fund managers moved in, closing or contracting out their operations in offshore havens. There are three types of funds:

- *Fonds communs de placement* (FCP) – unit trusts.
- *Société d'Investissement à capital variable* (Sicav) – variable capital collective investment companies.
- *Fonds speciaux.*

Sicavs and FCPs can be either UCITS or non-UCITS; *fonds speciaux* are for institutional investors only. The most common structure for a UCITS fund is the umbrella so that managers can cater for the preferences of different countries; bonds for Germany, equities for the UK and money funds for France. Most large umbrellas give investors the choice of bearer shares and registered shares. Funds are not liable to Luxembourg's income tax and dividends are not liable to withholding tax. The only tax on funds is a 0.06 per cent annual *taxe d'abonnement* on the value of net assets. No stamp duty is paid on the issue of shares and there is no capital gains tax. Interest on bank deposits is not liable to income tax or withholding tax.

Double-taxation treaties

Luxembourg has double-taxation treaties with many countries including almost all of the EU member states, the United States, Japan and the CIS, but, as mentioned above, exempt holding companies are excluded from these. Dividends and similar payments are subject to a withholding tax of 15 per cent. Residents are taxed on worldwide income, capital gains and inheritance.

Trusts

As a civil law country, Luxembourg does not generally recognize trusts, but since 1983 a bank may be a trustee, but the details of the agreement must be set out in full in the trust instrument. Holding companies can be used for some of the purposes of a trust.

MADEIRA (PORTUGAL)

Essential information

Atlantic islands

Capital: Funchal

Language: Portuguese

Telephone code: 351

Voltage: 220V AC 50 Hz

Time: GMT

Currency: Portuguese escudo (PTE), 100 centavos to the escudo. PTE notes are denominated as 500, 1,000, 2,000, 5,000 and 10,000

Office hours: *Banks:* Monday to Friday, 8.30 a.m.–3 p.m. *Offices:* Monday to Friday, 9 a.m.–1 p.m. and 3 p.m.–7 p.m. *Shops:* Monday to Friday, 9 a.m.–1 p.m. and 3 p.m.–7 p.m. Saturdays, 9 a.m.–1 p.m.

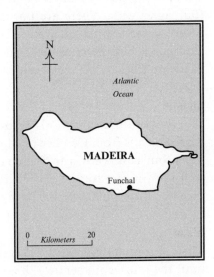

Credit cards: Major credit cards and travellers' cheques are widely accepted

Driving licence: National driving licences accepted

Climate: Subtropical climate

Health: Yellow fever certificate required if coming from an infected area.

Visas and passports: Passports are required except for EU nationals with appropriate ID. Visas are required for stays of up to 90 days by nationals of the EU and many other countries.

Customs: There are some restrictions on the import of foreign currency for investment, and the export of more than 1 million PTE's worth of foreign currency will require proof of importation.

Airport: Funchal.

Geography

Madeira and the smaller island of Porto Santo are inhabited, and there are also two groups of uninhabited rocks, the Desertas and the Selvagens. The islands were formed by volcanoes erupting from the extremely deep ocean floor, but unlike the Canaries, there are no live craters or smoking crevices. Madeira is 36 miles long, and about 14 miles wide at its broadest point. The mountains and gorges of the island are impressive, but little remains of the forest that originally covered the island, although there are large pine plantations.

Porto Santo is 25 miles from Madeira, and is about seven miles long and four miles wide. There are no indigenous land mammals on Madeira. Many varieties of salt-water fish abound. The vegetation is South European, but there are over 100 species of plant which are unique to Madeira. The coast is rocky, and cacti grow widely there.

Climate

The temperature rarely falls below 12°C, even in the coldest time of the year, which is from October to May. Snow falls occasionally in the mountains, but is unknown in Funchal. The air is quite humid. Madeira is well-known as a tourist and health resort, and the climate is said to be excellent for people suffering from chest problems.

History

There is speculation that the Phoenicians knew of Madeira, but it was not until the fourteenth century that seafarers began to alight on the island. Henry the Navigator began their colonization, and the islands have remained in Portuguese hands ever since, except for two short periods of British occupation in the early nineteenth century. Madeira has, since then, had a remarkably peaceful history.

People and language

Madeira was uninhabited when it was discovered, so the 270,000 inhabitants are largely of Portuguese descent. Madeirans are known as hardworking, adaptable, hospitable people, and many work overseas – a large number of Madeirans work as expatriates in the Channel Islands. There is a small expatriate British community on Madeira. Portuguese is the official language but French and English are widely spoken.

Economy

Madeira is reached by air from Lisbon, a journey of about 90 minutes, and there are six daily flights. There are also occasional direct flights to other European cities. Telephone and postal services are good. From its base in agriculture and shipping Madeira hopes to prosper by its quasi-tax haven status within the EU. The island's banking sector has already seen some progress. More than 20 banks are licensed to display the offshore banking sign – Sucursal Financiera Exterior. Most of the offshore banks are Portuguese, and include Banco Espirito Santo e Comercial Portugues,

Caixa Geral de Depositos, Banco Pinto e Sotto Mayor. Foreign banks in Madeira include Manufacturers Hanover, Crédit Lyonnais and Deutsche Bank. Typically, Sucursal Financiera Exterior bank branches offer deposit accounts with interest paid gross. Other services include investments in securities, foreign exchange and money markets transactions, and short- and long-term loans. Deposits come from foreigners as well as Portuguese expatriates. Banks, insurance companies and similar institutions setting up in Madeira's offshore financial centre are exempt from tax until 2011. Exemption from Capital Gains Tax, withholding taxes, stamp duty and Value Added Tax are also on offer. These institutions are also exempt from exchange controls. Communications facilities for business are excellent. Tourism and the export of flowers, Madeira wine and tropical fruits are important to the economy.

Government and legal system
Madeira is an autonomous region of Portugal and is thus a member of the EU. It has five members in the Portuguese parliament, and has its own regional parliament. The islands are a civil law jurisdiction.

Free Zone
In the 1970s Madeira was to set up a consumer free-trade zone, but political events and membership of the EU forced it to abandon the scheme. Madeira has created an industrial free-trade zone instead, for which the Madeira Development Company (MDC) is responsible. It is located at Canical on the east coast and is about an hour's drive from Funchal, the capital. Canical was selected because it is one of the few parts of the island where the land is relatively flat and it has natural port facilities. Any industrial activity can be carried on in the free zone, and there is no tax payable until the year 2011. Products made in the free zone from non-EU materials which are to be sold within the EU are only liable for duty in the EU on the non-EU elements.

Companies
Four kinds of company can be created.

- The private limited company (LDA). LDAs can have a minimum of two partners (the equivalent of shareholders), and a minimum capital of 400,000 escudos.

- A branch of an existing company.

- A joint stock company (SA). SAs can have a minimum of five shareholders and a minimum capital of five million escudos. Preference shares and bearer shares are allowed.

209

- The 'Sociedades Gestoras de Participações sociais' (SGPS), or Portuguese holding company. SGPS, created by legislation in 1988, get a deduction of 95 per cent of their taxable income from dividends they receive, an effective tax rate of 1.8 per cent. Capital gains, however, are taxed at 36 per cent. Non-resident shareholders are exempt from withholding tax. An SGPS can only act as a holding company, and it cannot purchase property except for its own use. It can be formed either as an LDA or as an SA, and there is no restriction on the nationality of shareholders.

Trusts

Although Madeira is a civil law jurisdiction, it recognizes trusts, with the useful benefit that the settlor can choose the trust law under which the trust is to be managed. Trusts may not own property on Portuguese territory.

Double-taxation treaties

Portuguese double-taxation treaties apply. These are with Austria, Belgium, Brazil, Denmark, Finland, France, Germany, Italy, Norway, Spain, Switzerland and the UK. Non-residents can maintain accounts locally in any currency, as may offshore companies, and are not subject to exchange controls.

Comment

As the 'island of eternal spring', Madeira is well known as a temperate paradise floating in the Atlantic. Best known for its fortified wine, Madeira is quite remote, lying 625 miles south-west of Lisbon and 545 miles off the coast of Africa, but these distances may not inhibit its development as an international business centre, given its good communications. Portuguese bureaucracy has a reputation for grinding slowness, so it remains to be seen whether many businesses are attracted there. However, it must be said that Madeira has both the will and the ability to offer first-class offshore facilities.

MALTA

Essential information
Three Mediterranean islands, Malta, Gozo and Comino
Capital: Valletta
Language: Maltese, English, Italian

Telephone code: 356

Voltage: 240 volts AC 50 Hz

Time: GMT +2 hours

Currency: Maltese lira (MTL), 100 cents to the lira. MTL notes are denominated as 2, 5, 10, and 20

Office hours: *Banks:* Monday to Thursday, 8 a.m.–Midday. Fridays, 8 a.m. – Midday and 2.30 p.m.–4 p.m. Saturdays, 8 a.m.–11.30 a.m. *Offices:* Monday to Friday, 8.30 a.m.–12.45 p.m. and 2.30 p.m.–5.30 p.m. Saturdays, 8.30 a.m.–Midday. *Shops:* Monday to Saturday, 9 a.m.–1 p.m. and 4 p.m.–7 p.m.

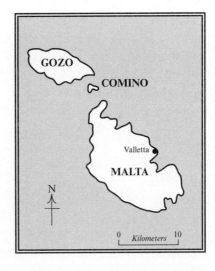

Credit cards: Major credit cards and travellers' cheques are widely accepted

Driving licence: National driving licences accepted

Climate: Mediterranean

Health: Yellow fever certificate required if coming from an infected area

Visas and passports: Visas not required for stays of up to 30 days by nationals of the EU and many other countries. Passports are required for everyone except British Visitor's Passport holders.

Customs: There are no restrictions on the import of foreign currency provided that it is declared on arrival; you can export up to the amount you declared on importation. You can import up to 200 cigarettes or 50 cigars and 1 litre of spirits and 1 litre of wine.

Airport: Malta Luqa, three miles out of Valletta. Departure tax MTL 4. Bureaux de change open 24 hours.

Geography

Malta and its smaller islands, Gozo and Comino, are about 60 miles from Sicily, the nearest land. Malta is approximately 17 miles long and nine miles wide, while Gozo is nine miles by four and a half miles, and Comino has an area of one square mile; there are also two uninhabited rocks in the archipelago. A number of excellent natural harbours make the islands attractive to shipping. The landscape is mainly that of low hills, and is heavily terraced and cultivated. There are no rivers. The vegetation is Mediterranean and includes carob trees, vines, figs and olives. There are huge shoals of fish around Malta, as well as dolphins and seals, and a great variety of bird life.

History

Like much of the Mediterranean, Malta was settled from the earliest times, and there are many Stone Age monuments on the islands. A prosperous trading centre in the classical period, it was captured from the Byzantines by Arabs in 870, who held it for 200 years until it was taken by the Norman master of Sicily. Malta passed through the hands of many feudal overlords until 1530, when the Knights of St John (the Hospitallers), a religious and military order, were granted the islands by the Spanish monarch. Malta then became the seat of their power, funded by war and the possession of vast estates across Europe.

Besieged by the Ottomans, the Knights of St John successfully defended the islands, and subsequently retained control of Malta until it was taken by Napoleon in 1798. Allied with the British, the Portuguese and the Neapolitans, the Maltese defeated the French and subjugated themselves to Britain while retaining their freedom of religion.

Malta became a vital British naval base for the next 250 years. Cultural and political clashes were frequent under the British, and Malta oscillated between short-lived constitutional governments and direct British rule until the 1930s. In World War 2 Malta was an important British outpost, and the island was awarded the George Cross in recognition of its endeavours against heavy aerial attacks and blockades. The country gained independence in 1964 and became a republic in 1974, while Britain kept its military bases there until 1979. In 1970 Malta became an associate of the EU and has applied for full membership.

People and language

The 360,000 Maltese are a mixture of Europeans, North Africans and Arabs. Maltese is a Semitic language closely related to Arabic, and is spoken by almost everyone. About one-sixth of the population also speak an Italian dialect. Today, English and Maltese are the official languages. Most Maltese are Roman Catholic. School is compulsory until the age of 16.

Climate

The climate is temperate and quite windy. The scirocco, an enervating wind, brings mists during the summer. Rain is irregular and it hardly ever snows.

Government

Malta has a parliament with a House of Representatives totalling 65 elected members. The government is run by a cabinet headed by a prime minister.

Legal system

The judiciary is independent of the government and is run along British lines, but with a civil code based on Napoleonic law; business and criminal law is basically English.

Economy

The government and agriculture are the major employers, and there is some manufacturing. Unemployment is relatively low (around 4 per cent), as are wages. The main trade is with the EU. Tourism is a major foreign currency earner. Malta hopes it has oil in the surrounding sea bed and invites tenders for exploration concessions. Contractors' equipment is free of customs duty and income tax on net profits is 50 per cent.

Shipping

Shipping is big business on Malta, and the 1973 Merchant Shipping Act offers benefits to non-resident owners and charterers.

- Exemption from Income Tax on profits earned by a ship registered in Malta.
- Exemption from death, gift and stamp duties on ships and shares in shipping companies.
- Exemption from income tax on loan interest to shipping operations.

To qualify, ships must be not less than 1,000 net tons' capacity. Other benefits include:

- No limits on the sale or transfer of shipping company shares.
- No limits on the nationality of crews.
- No limits on the mortgaging of ships.

Any type of ship may be registered, as long as they are owned by:

- Citizens of Malta.
- Maltese commercial partnerships.
- Offshore Maltese companies.

It is not necessary for owners or ships to visit Malta in order to register. More than 11 million tons of shipping are currently registered as Maltese.

Freeport

In 1998 the Malta Freeport Corporation was founded to administer a customs-free zone at a harbour on the south of the island. The principal activities of the freeport are:

- Breaking down bulk cargo.
- Storing containers.
- Storing and blending mineral oils.
- Warehousing and industrial facilities.

The corporation can issue certificates stating that Malta is the origin of goods that have been processed within the freeport, and can also certify that transshipped goods have not been processed in Malta. It can also issue licences to companies wishing to operate in the freeport. Licensed companies, their shareholders and employees (if not domiciled and ordinarily resident on Malta) are:

- Exempt from Import Tax on most goods.
- Exempt from Income Tax.
- Exempt from death duties.
- Exempt from stamp duties.
- Exempt from exchange controls.

These benefits are guaranteed for 15 years. Licensed companies must produce certified accounts annually.

Residents and non-residents

It is possible to take up temporary residence on Malta without formal permission. People under 60 must renew their tourist visas every 6 months; they must satisfy the authorities that they have sufficient funds for their support. Permanent residents must show the following:

- Income of over £18,000 sterling (approximately) or capital of over £270,000 sterling (approximately).
- A minimum income in Malta of approximately £10,800 sterling for a single person.

Permanent residents must purchase or lease property in Malta within a year. They are liable to Income Tax at 15 per cent on income arriving in Malta, and are subject to 7 per cent stamp duties on local property at death. For the purposes of ownership of offshore companies they are regarded as non-residents.

Non-residents may buy one building worth not less than £27,000 sterling (approximately) for residence purposes.

There is also a special deal for 'investment services expatriates' who are employed by investment funds. For the first ten years' accommodation, relocation costs, travel and a car are all allowable against tax, together with a $700 monthly allowance, medical expenses and school fees. Royalties and interest are also tax-free.

Double-taxation treaties

Malta has double-taxation treaties with over 20 countries, including the UK, Germany, Belgium, Finland, Sweden, Norway, Pakistan, US, Holland, Italy, France, Canada, Australia and Bulgaria. Malta allows unilateral relief from double taxation if overseas tax is paid on income received from a country which does not have a treaty with Malta.

Offshore companies

Malta aspires to become an international financial centre, and to that end has introduced its International Business Activities Act which offers certain advantages to the offshore company. Offshore companies are registered in Malta under the Commercial Partnerships Ordnance and are of two kinds, trading and non-trading.

- General trading companies can be in any business except banking and insurance. The names of shareholders are not publicly accessible, but must be declared to the Malta International Business Authority, although nominees may be used. Corporation tax is at 5 per cent.
- Non-trading companies are restricted to owning and managing property – but immovable property on Malta itself cannot be held. Shareholders can remain anonymous, and there is no corporation tax.

Nominee companies, registered in Malta, exist to service the offshore companies, which must have a nominee company either as a sole director or as a secretary. It is also possible to form an International Trading Company (ITC) which is 'onshore' – it is taxed at 35 per cent, but non-resident shareholders can claim refunds, and pay an effective tax rate of 4 per cent. International Holding Companies (IHCs) are treated in a similar way, with a maximum tax payable by non-resident shareholders of 6 per cent.

Offshore trusts

Trusts can be Maltese or foreign; foreign trusts are governed by the law of their country, which will be recognized by Maltese courts, and do not need to register in Malta. Maltese trusts are governed by Maltese law and must register. Trusts may switch jurisdictions at any time. A trust can have any number of trustees as long as one trustee is a nominee company authorized by the Malta Financial Services Centre. This trustee must file information with the Centre stating:

- The trust's name.
- The name of the settlor, or, in the case of a 'unilateral declaration of trust' by the nominee company, the settlor's name need not be given.
- Information on the beneficiaries, listed by name, class or relationship.

The registration fee is currently MTL200. The settlor of a trust can be a beneficiary also. Trusts may not own property in Malta, or shares or debentures in a local Maltese company. Benefits include:

- The total annual tax chargeable on the trust's income or a beneficiary's income is MTL200.
- There are no death duties.
- There are no stamp duties.
- There is no customs duty on imported property.
- Trust activities are not subject to exchange controls.

Comment

British people with long memories will no doubt recall the troubled times when Mintoff, then Malta's premier, expelled the British miliary in the 1970s. It's a beautiful place, but too small and too reliant on its bigger neighbours to be quite as independent as its rhetoric would indicate. Indeed, Malta's decision to join in on the offshore bandwagon begs the question, 'How long will it last before the rules change again – and when they do, will my assets be safe?' But this is the case with many tax havens. Here's one waspish comment from a senior official in a major tax haven about the government of 'Ruritania' (apparently referring to Malta) setting

> ... its legal draughtsmen to work to crib the appropriate laws governing banking, company formation and administration, trusts and so on. It will then offer permanent or temporary tax concessions and set up the Ruritania Development Corporation and allocate a large amount of money for advertising.

Malta's currently healthy economy, however, relies principally on shipping and manufacturing, and this is likely to continue irrespective of its success as an offshore centre. In addition, the comment quoted above is hardly fair on Malta – most of the newer tax havens have done the same.

Banking on Malta is fairly limited, with only two banks, both Maltese, which have offshore departments. As a relatively cheap place to operate a company relying on trade in the Mediterranean, Malta looks attractive; the nominee companies (there are over 40) are said to vet clients thoroughly, as does the Malta Financial Services Centre (MFSC), which is the regulator. Remember, though, that non-trading companies can protect the anonymity of their shareholders from the MFSC.

ISLE OF MAN

Essential information
Island in the Irish Sea

Capital: Douglas

Language: English

Telephone code: 44

Voltage: 240 volts AC 50 Hz

Time: GMT

Currency: Sterling. The island does issue its own notes and coins are allowed to circulate in the UK

Office hours: As UK

Credit cards: Major credit cards and travellers' cheques are widely accepted

Driving licence: International and national licences accepted

Climate: Temperate, changeable

Health: No certificates required

Visas and passports: As UK

Airport: Ronaldsway, eight miles from Douglas.

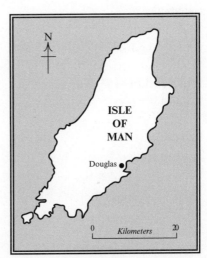

History
The Isle of Man has been inhabited since the Stone Age, and was Christianized early by missionaries following St Patrick. Controlled by Viking jarls (earls) until long after the Norman conquest, Man was ruled under a Scandinavian system which partly survives to this day, as evidenced by its parliament, the Tynwald. In 1266 the king of Norway sold Man to the king of Scotland, but this was resisted by the island's own king – Scotland finally purchased the island some years later. Man passed back and forth several times from England to Scotland. In 1406 Sir John Stanley was granted the title 'King of Man', but diplomatically chose to call himself 'lord of Man' instead, a title which has lasted until today.

Following the Restoration of Charles II, the islanders turned to smuggling in defiance of an attempt to deprive them of their Scandinavian right to permanent freehold of their land. The smuggling trade grew tremendously in the 1700s, and was considered a serious threat to the British Exchequer. Britain purchased the sovereignty of the island in 1762, installing a governor, but during the 1800s a good deal of home rule was restored to the island.

Geography

Man has an area of 221 square miles. It has a mountainous area in the centre (the highest peak is Snaefell) surrounded by low-lying agricultural land. There are few trees. The island boasts rare breeds of sheep and the tailless Manx cat. The island rarely suffers extremes of heat or cold, and rainfall is heavy.

People

About 70,000 people live on the island. Manx, a Celtic language, was widely spoken on the island until the middle of the last century; it is no longer a living language. The Wesleyan church is very well established on the island.

Government and legal system

The Isle of Man is an internally self-governing dependent territory of the British Crown, but is not part of the United Kingdom. The island has a loose relationship with the EU because of Protocol 3 of the Act of Accession of the UK. This places the Isle of Man within Europe for the limited purposes of customs and the free movement of goods, but the island contributes nothing to and receives nothing from the EU funds. The island is not a member or an associate member of the EU; its position cannot be changed without changing the Protocol, which would require a unanimous decision on the part of all EU member states. Features of the Protocol include:

- The EU controls customs and limits on quantities of imports.
- Manxmen do not have the freedom of movement within the EU allowed to member states.
- The other EU provisions on the free movement of capital and services also do not apply.
- The island is not eligible for EU subsidies.

In 1990 uncertainty about the Isle of Man's status with the OECD was removed when the British government declared that the OECD Convention applied to the Isle of Man. This is important because it means that the Isle of Man's financial products and services have access to markets where OECD membership is required. The Tynwald, the island's 1,000-year-old parliament makes its own laws and oversees all internal administration, fiscal and social policies. The UK controls external issues such as defence, and the island makes an annual payment for this. The Manx legal system is based on English common law, but UK law does not extend to the island.

Economy

With manufacturing and tourism in decline, the island relies principally on its status as a major offshore centre.

Offshore companies

There are three types of company:

- Non-resident controlled companies; these pay a £600 annual duty.

- Exempt companies, which are exempt from income tax and pay an annual fee of £300. They must have a resident director and shareholder, and may carry on any activity except manufacturing, retailing, wholesaling, transport, distribution, building, mineral exploration or fishing. In addition, they may not normally be a public company, a bank or an insurance company.

- International companies (ICs), which must be resident in the Isle of Man and not in receipt of income from the island. These pay an annual fee of £300. ICs were created in 1994, and retain the characteristics of an exempt company.

All Manx companies must make an annual return to the Manx Companies Registry; this must be filed on a fixed date, being the anniversary of incorporation. Companies must prepare audited accounts but need not file copies of their accounts, and they need not prepare accounts if they have been dormant since the last accounting period.

Trusts

As a common law jurisdiction, the island recognizes trusts. Important features are:

- Trusts need not be registered and are thus not on public record.
- The accumulation period can be as long as the perpetuity period.

GAZETTEER

219

Tax

Income Tax is at 15 per cent, with a higher rate of 20 per cent worldwide. Allowances for resdents are £6,200 for a single person and £12,400 for a married couple. Companies which are resident on the Isle of Man are liable to 20 per cent Income Tax. There are no death duties, capital transfer or gift taxes, Capital Gains Tax or wealth tax. Low taxation was introduced to the island in the late 1960s. Companies and trusts are generally liable to tax at a flat rate of 20 per cent on their taxable income which, in the case of companies, is essentially their profit after the distribution of dividends. This rate of tax is also levied on all taxable income arising in the Isle of Man to non-residents, although certain income is exempt. There is a system of capital allowances of up to 100 per cent on buildings, plant and machinery. There are currently no exchange controls.

Comment

Man is one of the very few tax havens which have a compensation scheme for bank deposits. The scheme was introduced shortly before BCCI was shut down in 1991. Depositors who had money in the Isle of Man branch of BCCI were able to claim up to £15,000 including non-sterling deposits. Building societies are plentiful, mainly serving expatriates. Under the UK's Financial Services Act, the island has designated territory status, meaning that authorized open-ended schemes can be marketed in the UK. Investors will be compensated up to £48,000 if the manager or trustee of an authorized scheme cannot meet any civil liability in connection with their business. The island has a thriving life assurance business targeted mainly at British expatriates and is allowed to transact business with UK brokers. Captive insurance is important; more than 130 captives are located there. Banks offer current and deposit accounts and all other services normally available from mainland banks. Interest rates are linked to movements in the London money markets. Although the island's currency is sterling, its banks accept deposits and offer competitive returns in all major currencies.

MONACO

History

The Monégasque headland was well known in ancient times to the Phoenicians, Greeks, Carthaginians and Romans. In 1119 it was taken into possession by the Genoese, then a great trading city-state. In 1279 the long reign of the Grimaldi family began, continuing to this day under Prince

Rainier the Third. The Grimaldis have been traditionally allied with France, except for the period from 1524 to 1641 when they were under the protection of Spain. In 1793 the Grimaldis were dispossessed by the French revolutionary regime, which annexed Monaco. Following the downfall of Napoleon Bonaparte the Grimaldis were reinstated in Monaco. In 1848 the principality lost the neighbouring towns of Menton (on the Italian border) and Roc Brun. Monaco and France agreed on a customs union in 1865 which survives to this day, and accounts for Monaco's curious position as a non-EU country within the EU customs area.

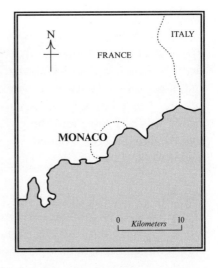

In 1918 an agreement was made with France that if the Grimaldi dynasty should ever die out that Monaco will become an autonomous state under the protection of France. The town has assumed a great importance for lovers of the Grand Prix, minor royalty and the international jet set and has important fiscal structures favoured by the wealthy individual and corporation alike, despite the disfavour in which they are held by the French authorities.

In 1962 a crisis developed with France over Monaco's refusal to impose income tax on its residents, leading to a compromise where some French residents are taxed as are Monégasque businesses doing more than a quarter of their business outside the principality.

Geography
Monaco is a tiny region on the south-east corner of France's Mediterranean coast. With territory of only three-quarters of a square mile, Monaco is about 12 miles east of Nice and about 6 miles west of the Italian frontier. Tucked beneath an escarpment of rocks, Monaco enjoys a pleasant climate in both summer and winter.

People
There are only around 5,000 true Monégasques with the remainder of the population of 30,000 made up of expatriate French, English and Italians. The official language is French.

Government

Monaco is a hereditary monarchy, with Prince Rainier as its sovereign. Its constitution was established in 1962, and Monaco now has an eighteen-member National Council elected by its citizens. A governing council of four, headed by a minister, who must be a French citizen, governs the state, but the Prince has a veto. Essentially the legal and governing power is shared by the Prince and the governing council. The highest legislative body is the Supreme Council, and since 1891 the law has been based on that of France.

Economy

Monaco has a stated aim of attracting companies which will bring 'added value'. International banks fit this profile as they have a high worth and employ a qualified labour force, and cater for the financial needs of the local wealthy. There are now 57 banks and financial services operations in Monaco. Monaco is not a member of the EU and is considered by the EU to be a foreign country. As mentioned earlier, it does have an agreement with France which reduces its attractiveness as a haven for French nationals – French residents established in Monaco since 1963 must pay French tax.

Monaco has been part of the customs territory of the Community since 1984 and EU rules of free circulation of goods apply to Monaco, but there are no agreements with the EU regarding income taxes, taxes on casinos, residences and so on. The principality derives its income from taxes on commercial transactions, state monopolies, sales taxes, TV and radio interests and casino tax. Its chief industry is tourism. Once a *fin-de-siècle* winter resort, Monaco has lost much of its charm, but remains a haven for the wealthy.

Monaco companies

Monaco does not want non-resident companies of the IBC type. Several options are open to foreigners:

- A company limited by shares (*Société Anonyme Monegasque*, or SAM). SAMs must be authorized by the government, and applications are made through notaries. Holding companies are not allowed. Authorization is not a rubber stamp; applicants are thoroughly checked out, and the process takes a long time. It is not usually possible to get an off-the-shelf company. The minimum authorized capital is FF1 million. Shares may be issued in registered or bearer form.

- A general partnership (*Société en Nom Collectif*).

- A limited partnership (*Société en Commandite Simple*).

222

- A partnership limited by shares (*Société en Commandite par Actions*).
- Sole trader.
- Branch of a foreign company (*Succursale*). Authorization is necessary from Monaco, and premises must be secured. Investigations into the founders are thorough. Applications are made through an '*agent responsable*' who is usually a Monaco resident and carries on the business as an agent. Tax returns are filed annually and accounts must be produced on demand.

At least one director of a Monégasque company must be a resident. No one person may be a director of more than eight companies. Assets located in the Principality at the time of the owner's death or at the time that a gift is made are subject to inheritance and gift tax unless protected by a trust.

Tax
There is no Capital Gains Tax or Income Tax on residents of Monaco, but there are gift and inheritance taxes. The rate of tax ranges from zero for transfer of assets to direct heirs and spouses to 16 per cent for transfers to unrelated parties. The taxes are applicable to residents and non-residents alike, regardless of nationality, although they may be minimized through the use of a Monégasque trust (under the current law the settlor is not required to reside in Monaco). This tax advantage is thus in some cases available to foreign nationals residing in France and Italy. Monaco has no double-tax treaties, except that French residents established after 1963 are taxed as if they are in France. Companies are taxed at 35 per cent if more than a quarter of their business is outside Monaco.

Trusts
Although a civil law country, Monaco does recognize trusts, where the settlor's own country recognizes them. The main rules are as follows:

- The settlor's own country must recognize trusts, and a lawyer of that country must submit evidence of this in writing with the trust instrument.
- The trust instrument must be notarized by a Monégasque notary.
- Only trustees approved in Monaco can be used.
- At least one of the trustees must be a trust company.

Trusts are generally used to protect assets from the Monégasque inheritance laws, and non-residents rarely acquire them. There is no inheritance tax on trusts, but a sliding rate of registration fees apply.

GAZETTEER

Immigration and employment

One of the world's most desired possessions is residency in Monaco. All foreigners, except French nationals and bona fide French residents, are required to meet the following conditions:

- Obtained a visa from the French embassy in their current country of residence in order to apply for a non-working residence permit in Monaco.
- Applicants must usually have bought or intend to buy property in Monaco.
- Sufficent funds to support themselves.

The residence permit can take up to three months to obtain though it is much quicker for foreign nationals already resident in France. No social service benefits are available if you have this type of residence, but state education is free to your dependants. After ten years of permanent residence in Monaco privileged residence status may be applied for and then renewed every ten years. Nationality is rarely granted. Residents benefit from banking and professional secrecy, with the sole exception being inspection by customs officials with respect to exchange control. Although in theory Monaco does not differentiate between locals and foreign nationals over the right to purchase or lease property, citizens and, in some cases, established residents are entitled to rent property reserved for this class of privileged persons. While there are no rules prejudicing the employment of foreigners and non-residents in Monaco, there is an order of priority to be followed when considering equally qualified candidates which favours Monégasque citizens and residents.

SWITZERLAND

Essential information

Capital: Berne

Language: German, French, Italian, Romansh

Telephone code: 41

Voltage: 220 volts AC 50 Hz

Time: GMT +2 hours

Currency: Swiss franc (CHF), 100 centimes to the franc. Swiss francs are denominated as 10, 20, 50, 100, 500 and 1,000

Office hours: *Banks:* Monday to Friday, 8.30 a.m.–Midday and 2 p.m.–4.30 p.m.

224

Offices: Monday to Friday, 8 a.m.– Midday and 2 p.m.–5 p.m. *Shops:* Monday to Friday, 8.30 a.m.–Midday and 2 p.m.–6.30 p.m. Saturdays, 8.30 a.m.–Midday and 2 p.m.–4 p.m.

Driving licence: National driving licences accepted

Climate: Northern European/alpine

Health: No certificates required

Visas and passports: Visas are not required by nationals of many countries. Passports are required by all except EU nationals with appropriate ID.

Customs: There are no restrictions on the import or export of foreign currency. You can import up to 200 cigarettes or 50 cigars and 2 litres of alcohol of 15 degrees and 1 litre of alcohol of over 15 degrees and 10 litres of wine.

Airports:

- Basle/Mulhouse, 7 miles from Basle. No departure tax.
- Belp, five and a half miles from Berne. No departure tax.
- Geneva, three miles out of Geneva. No departure tax.
- Zurich, eight miles out of Zurich. No departure tax.

History

Conquered by the Romans in 58 BC, Switzerland prospered for several centuries. A Germanic tribe, the Alemanni, began to invade eastern Switzerland from about 260 AD, and after 400 AD another tribe, the Burgundians, settled in the west, adopting Christianity and the Latin language, thus forming the division between what is now French-speaking (Burgundian) and German-speaking (Alemannic) Switzerland. Switzerland emerged as an independent confederation after 1291, when men from the valleys of Uri, Schwyz and Nidwalden formed the 'Everlasting League' for self-defence against all attackers, but principally against the Holy Roman Empire, of which the area which is now Switzerland formed a part. The Everlasting League specifically agreed not to recognize any external judge or law. After defeating an Austrian army in 1315, other communities (known as cantons) began to join the league, and by 1513 had expanded its territory as far as Milan. Following a heavy defeat by the French and Venetians in 1515, Switzerland renounced expansionism and became a neutral country, a policy it has followed ever since.

During the Reformation, Zwingli and Calvin preached in Switzerland, and many cantons became Protestant. In the seventeenth century some Catholic cantons became allied with France, and the Confederation was in

GAZETTEER

danger of collapse, but ultimately the need for political unity triumphed over religion, and Switzerland became increasingly prosperous as a financial and intellectual centre. In the mid-nineteenth century civil war broke out when Catholic cantons formed a separatist federation, the Sonderbund, which an army from the Protestant cantons defeated in 1847. In 1848 a new constitution was drawn up which has survived to this day, confirming the independence of the cantons while creating a unified state.

During World War 1 the German-speaking cantons sided with Germany, but the country remained neutral, and following a general strike in 1918 workers' rights were improved. Despite its precarious position in World War 2, Switzerland maintained neutrality and was able to prosper quickly during European reconstruction after the war.

Geography

Switzerland is a small country, consisting principally of three large river valleys (the Aar, Rhone and Rhine)in the northern Alps. There are many lakes, the largest of which is Lake Geneva, on the French border. Alpine flora abound, and there are many wild animals, including ibex and chamois.

People and language

The 6.8 million inhabitants of Switzerland include over one million residents who are not citizens (not including the numerous seasonal workers from other countries). The majority of the Swiss (66 per cent) are German-speaking, followed by 18 per cent French speakers, 10 per cent Italian speakers and 1 per cent Romansh speakers. All four languages are official. English is widely understood.

Government

The country is divided into 26 cantons, 6 of which are 'half-cantons'. Each canton has its own constitution and legislative body. The Federation has a two-chamber Assembly; the lower house, the Nationalrat, is elected, with one member per 22,000 citizens, and the upper house, the Standerat, has 46 members (2 per canton and 1 per half-canton). The Assembly elects a 7-man federal council which governs the country. A referendum can be forced with the collection of 50,000 signatures, and legislation can be initiated with the collection of 100,000. Referenda are widely used. Local government is run by communes (Gemeinde), of which there are about 3,000; citizenship is attained through the membership of a commune.

Economy

Switzerland has few nationalized industries; almost all business is in private hands with 60 per cent of the workforce in the service sector, and about 35 per cent are in industry. The country is the fourth largest financial centre after London, New York and Tokyo. Currently Switzerland is not a member of the EU, but most of its foreign trade is with member states. With few natural resources, Switzerland relies on banking and tourism to keep a positive trade balance.

Companies

The main type of company used by foreign investors is the Aktiengesellschaft (Ag), the limited company:

- Ags can be formed within four weeks. No special authorization is needed.
- Formation costs about CHF 7,000.
- Bearer shares are allowed.
- There must be a minimum of three founders, but following formation only one shareholder is necessary.
- There must be a majority of Swiss directors.
- Only one director is required.
- Ags must be registered in a canton and have a registered office there.
- Annual audits are required.

Holding companies get substantial exemptions from tax in some cantons.

Tax

Taxes are levied at federal, cantonal and communal levels.

- There is a federal tax on return on capital of up to 9.8 per cent on world-wide profits.
- Canton taxes vary widely between cantons. There is not usually any Capital Gains Tax.
- There is a federal income tax on individuals' worldwide income of up to 11.5 per cent.
- There is a federal withholding tax of 35 per cent on distributions made by companies.
- Switzerland has many double-taxation treaties.
- Inheritance and gift taxes vary widely between cantons.

GAZETTEER

Banking

In recent years many people were predicting the slow demise of Switzerland as the world's best banking haven. The country is expensive to bank in, and other low tax jurisdictions, such as Luxembourg, offer similar facilities more cheaply. The smart money, however, seems still to support Switzerland. The country has no one factor that makes it a world-beater, but its track record of stability, the fierce defence of its banking clients and general astuteness in money matters, particularly when the rest of Europe is in crisis, still holds good. Switzerland does not have total banking secrecy; criminals will not be protected – although some tax evaders may be – and it is not possible to remain anonymous from one's bankers.

Trusts

As a civil law country, Switzerland does not recognize trusts. It has not ratified the Hague Convention.

THE HAVENS OF
THE CARIBBEAN

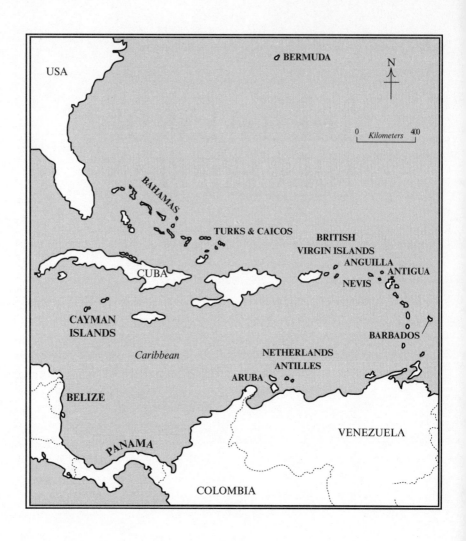

N

0   *Kilometers*   400

USA

BERMUDA

BAHAMAS

TURKS & CAICOS

BRITISH
VIRGIN ISLANDS

ANGUILLA

CUBA

ANTIGUA

NEVIS

CAYMAN
ISLANDS

BARBADOS

Caribbean

NETHERLANDS
ANTILLES

ARUBA

BELIZE

VENEZUELA

PANAMA

COLOMBIA

ANGUILLA

Essential information

Caribbean island

Capital: The Valley

Language: English

Telephone code: 1 809

Voltage: 110/220 volts AC 60 Hz

Time: GMT –4 hours

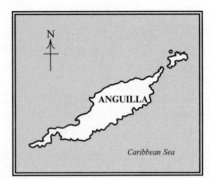

Currency: Eastern Caribbean dollar (XCD), 100 cents to the dollar. XCD notes are denominated as 1, 5, 10, 20 and 100, and there are 1, 2, 5, 10, 25 and 100 cent coins

Office Hours: *Banks:* Monday to Thursday, 8 a.m.–3 p.m., Fridays, 8 a.m.–5 p.m. *Offices:* Monday to Friday, 8 a.m.–Midday and 1 p.m.–4 p.m. *Shops:* Monday to Saturday, 8 a.m.–5 p.m.

Driving licence: National driving licences accepted, or you can obtain a three months' visitors' licence at police stations, hotels and car hire offices on production of your national licence

Climate: Tropical but not very humid. Between June and September there is some rain. Average temperature during the day is 28°.

Health: Yellow fever certificate required if arriving from an infected area within six days

Visas and passports: Visas are required for Haitian and Dominican Republic nationals. Passports must be carried by all except:

1. US and Canadian nationals in possession of a birth certificate, photograph and an ID card or driver's licence.

2. Seaman book holders travelling on duty who are to join their vessels immediately upon arrival on the island.

Customs: There are no restrictions on the import of currency provided that it is declared on arrival; you can export up to the amount you declared on importation. You can import up to 200 cigarettes or 50 cigars and 1.136 litres of wine or spirits.

Background

The tiny coral island of Anguilla is still a British Crown Colony, but has a constitution and is self-governing. The population is under 7,000.

Communications are good. Tourism and the export of salt are the main economic activities.

Offshore companies

There are no direct taxes on income, corporate profits, capital transfers, capital gains or gifts on Anguilla, nor are there value added tax, withholding tax or death duties. Company law is very much on the English model:

- Only public companies may issue bearer shares.
- All companies must maintain a registered office in Anguilla.
- Directors' meetings may be held anywhere.
- Nominee shareholders are allowed.
- Audited accounts must be filed annually.

Incorporation fees and annual charges are low, and same-day incorporations are possible. There are four commercial banks on the island, including Barclays International. There are a number of double-taxation treaties, and the maximum withholding tax is 15 per cent. Anguilla is under pressure to make exchange-of-information agreements with the US.

Trusts

As a common law jurisdiction Anguilla recognizes trusts, which enjoy the tax-free regime.

Comment

Despite its tiny size, Anguilla has managed to attract offshore business. The insistence on audited accounts is strangely comforting – the island would appear to offer anonymity without anarchy!

ANTIGUA AND BARBUDA

Essential information

Caribbean islands

Capital: St John's

Language: English

Telephone code: 1 809

Voltage: 110/220 volts AC 60 Hz

Time: GMT –4 hours

Currency: Eastern Caribbean dollar (XCD), 100 cents to the dollar. XCD notes are denominated as 1, 5, 10, 20 and 100, and there are 1, 2, 5, 10, 25 and 100 cent coins

Office hours: *Banks:* Monday to Thursday, 8 a.m.–2 p.m., Fridays, 8 a.m. –2 p.m., 3 p.m.–5 p.m. *Offices:* Monday to Friday, 8 a.m.–Midday and 1 p.m.–4.30 p.m. *Shops:* Monday to Saturday, 8 a.m.–12 p.m., 1 p.m.– 4 p.m. (some early closing on Thursdays and Saturdays).

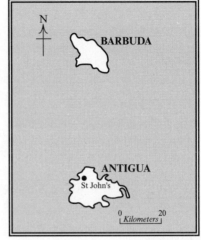

Credit cards: Major credit cards, travellers' cheques and US dollars are widely accepted

Driving licence: National driving licences accepted, or you can obtain a three months' visitors' licence on production of your national licence for a fee of XCD 50.

Climate: Pleasantly tropical but not very humid. Some rain from September to December.

Health: Yellow fever certificate required if arriving from an infected area within six days

Visas and passports: Visas are required for everyone except:

1. British subjects (citizens of United Kingdom and Colonies)

2. Commonwealth citizens.

3. Nationals of Argentina, Austria, Belgium, Brazil, Denmark, Eire, Finland, France, Germany, Greece, Italy, Japan, Liechtenstein, Luxembourg, Malta, Mexico, Monaco, Netherlands, Norway, Peru, Portugal, San Marino, Spain, Suriname, Sweden, Switzerland, Turkey and Venezuela.

Passports must be carried by all except:
US and Canadian nationals, and British subjects (citizens of United Kingdom and Colonies) who have the right of abode in the UK. You must be in possession of proof of identity. A ticket out of the island must be held on entry.

Customs: There are no restrictions on the import of currency provided that it is declared on arrival; you can export up to the amount you declared on importation. You can import up to 200 cigarettes or 50 cigars and 1 litre of wine or spirits.

Airport: Antigua V.C. Bird International, four miles out of St John's. Taxi to town approximately US$7, 15-minute journey.

History

Discovered in 1492 by Christopher Columbus, Antigua was named after the church of Santa Maria la Antigua in Seville, Spain. Colonized by the British in 1632, Antigua has remained British ever since. The United States established a military base there in the 1940s. Barbuda, colonized at about the same time as Antigua, was owned by the Codrington family for some 200 years before reverting to the Crown in the last century and remains underpopulated. Until 1956 Antigua was part of the British colony of the Leeward Islands, which was defederated at that time.

Geography

Unlike the other Leeward Islands, Antigua is low-lying and deforested. There are no rivers and few springs, so droughts can cause problems. With an area of 108 square miles, Antigua offers good shelter for ships with its intricate coastline and plethora of natural bays and harbours. Barbuda, 25 miles north of Antigua, is a coral island with many woods, but is also low lying. The climate is constant at around 21° and has low rainfall and plenty of sea breezes.

People and language

There are some 65,000 people on the islands, almost all of them of African descent. The official language is English.

Government

After independence on 1 November 1981, Antigua remained part of the British Commonwealth. It is also still a monarchy with Queen Elizabeth II as the head of state, and keeps a Governor-General as her representative. The government is modelled on the British parliamentary system with two houses, a House of Representatives and a senate. Representatives are elected, while Senators are appointed. Antigua boasts a high degree of political stability.

Legal system

The system is common law, with a high court upholding acts of parliament.

Economy

The economy depends almost entirely on tourism, although there is some light manufacturing. Most goods are produced for local consumption. Residents of Antigua are not taxed directly; there is no Income Tax,

Capital Gains Tax or Inheritance Tax. Companies are taxed at 40 per cent, but IBCs (see below) are exempt. Acquiring residence is fairly easy and there are no requirements to purchase property. There are some 11 offshore banks with a total on deposit of US$339 million. There are also 15 captive insurance operations and around 1,400 offshore companies.

Double-taxation treaties

Antigua has only one double-taxation treaty, which is with the UK, but IBCs (see below) are not subject to it.

International Business Companies

International Business Companies (IBCs) are the usual form for foreign investors. IBCs are:

- not subject to exchange controls
- not subject to restrictions on the name of the company except when using 'bank', 'trust' or 'insurance' in the name
- not subject to minimum capital requirements (except for banks, trust companies and insurance companies)
- allowed to issue bearer shares and shares are not required to have a par value
- allowed to have only one shareholder
- required to hold their AGMs in Antigua, but a written document signed by all the shareholders which deals with AGM matters is acceptable
- required to have a minimum of one director – company secretaries and chairmen are not required
- required to have a registered office in Antigua, but this can be a private home or at the office of an agent
- not required to produce audited accounts
- entirely exempt of tax for 50 years following incorporation
- bearer shares are allowed.

The incorporation laws on the island are derived from the corporate codes of Delaware, the UK, the Netherlands and Florida.

Offshore trusts

As a common law country, Antigua recognizes trusts. Offshore trusts are not subject to tax.

Comment

Owing to the influx of offshore businesspeople, prices are high for this otherwise ideal tropical paradise, but not so much so as to make living difficult.

The collapse of the Antigua-based European Union Bank in August 1997 highlights the dangers of keeping more than insignificant sums of money in small banks in the less heavily regulated tax havens. The bank, which had changed ownership frequently since its inception in the mid-1980s, had been marketing itself on the Internet and offering very high rates of interest on deposits (which is almost invariably a danger signal for investors). The owners, two Russians with alleged mafia and KGB links, are reported to have fled with investors' money. Other Russian-owned banks on the island have also been closed down by the authorities.

ARUBA

Essential information

One of the Leeward Islands in the Caribbean

Capital: Oranjestad

Language: English, Dutch, Spanish, Papiamento

Telephone code: 2978

Voltage: 110 volts AC 60 Hz

Time: GMT –4 hours

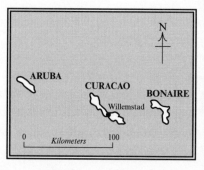

Currency: Aruban guilder (AWG), 100 cents to the guilder. AWG notes are denominated as 5, 10, 25, 50 and 100, and there are 5, 10, 25, 50 and 100 cent coins.

Office hours: *Banks:* Monday to Friday, 8 a.m.–12 p.m., 1 p.m.–4 p.m. *Offices:* Monday to Friday, 8 a.m.–5 p.m. *Shops:* Monday to Saturday, 8 a.m.–12 p.m., 2 p.m.–6 p.m.

Driving licence: International or national licences are accepted

Climate: Tropical

Health: Yellow fever certificate required if arriving from an infected area within six days

Visas and passports: Visas are not required for stays of up to 90 days if carrying an onward or return ticket. For stays of over 90 days, a Temporary

Certificate of Admission is necessary. Passports must be carried by all except US and Canadian nationals if holding other means of identification.

Customs: There are no restrictions on the import and export of foreign currencies. You can import up to 200 cigarettes or 50 cigars and 2 litres of wine or spirits.

Background

One of the Caribbean Lesser Antilles islands, Aruba broke away from the rest of the Netherlands Antilles in 1986, but retains many of the features of Antilles corporate law, which derives from Dutch company law. Unlike the other islands in the group, Aruba has a large proportion of indigenous Carib Indians in its population of 60,000. Dutch is the official language, but English, Spanish and Papiamento are widely spoken. The country is still a 'kingdom partner' in the Kingdom of the Netherlands.

Offshore companies

Antilles corporations still take the Dutch NV structure. Aruba now has its own tax-free corporations, but in other respects is almost identical to the Netherlands Antilles. Features include:

● Bearer shares are allowed.

● Annually audited accounts are not required.

Tax

Aruba has no Income Tax on individuals and no Corporation Tax on exempt companies. There are no double-taxation treaties.

BAHAMAS

Essential information

Caribbean islands

Capital: Nassau

Language: English

Telephone code: 1 809

Voltage: 120 volts AC 60 Hz

Time: GMT –4 hours

Currency: Bahamian dollar (BSD), 100 cents to the dollar. BSD notes are denominated as 1, 3, 5, 10, 20, 50 and 100 dollars, and there is a 50 cent note.

Office hours: *Banks:* Monday to Thursday, 9.30 a.m.–3 p.m., Fridays, 9.30 a.m.–5 p.m. *Offices:* Monday to Friday, 9 a.m.–5 p.m.

Credit cards: Major credit cards, travellers' cheques and US dollars are widely accepted

Driving licence: National driving licences accepted for up to three months

Climate: Less hot than the other Caribbean islands. Warm in winter, hot in summer. There is a risk of hurricanes from June to November, most often occurring in August or September.

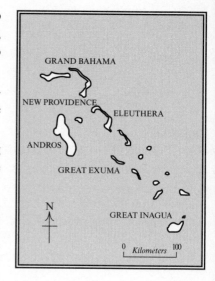

Health: Yellow fever certificate required if arriving from an infected area within seven days

Visas and passports: Visas are not required for short stays by nationals of most countries. Passports must be carried by all except US and Canadian nationals on short visits with appropriate ID.

Customs: There are no restrictions on the import and export of foreign currency. Permission from the Central Bank of the Bahamas is needed for the export of Bahamian dollars over BSD70. You can import up to 200 cigarettes or 50 cigars and 1 litre spirits (2 litres if 1 litre is a Caribbean product). Firearms are forbidden.

Airport: Nassau International, 10 miles out of Nassau. Departure tax is BSD 13. Lockers are available. Banks are open 9.30 a.m.–3 p.m. Monday to Friday.

History

Christopher Columbus is thought to have landed in the Bahamas in 1492, and during the next ten years some 40,000 of the inhabitants, Arawak Indians, were taken as slaves to work in Hispaniola (the modern Haiti and Dominican Republic), and by the mid 1500s the islands had become uninhabited. In 1645 British settlers from Bermuda arrived, but did not prosper until reinforcements arrived a decade later. Law and order was lax for many years, and the settlers turned to piracy. In 1717 the islands were surrendered to the Crown, and in the following year 1,000 pirates surrendered and were pardoned, while eight were hanged. In 1776 the US navy captured Nassau for a few days, and in 1782 the islands were surrendered to Spain, but were restored to Britain in the following year.

The American War of Independence drove loyalists out of the US, and many of them settled in the Bahamas on favourable terms. The islanders strongly resisted the abolition of slavery, which came about in 1834, and until 1869 there was great antagonism between Nonconformists and the wealthy supporters of the Church of England. Since then the Bahamas have had a peaceful history.

Geography

The 700 islands of the Bahamas stretch for 760 miles between Florida and Cuba. Thirty islands are inhabited, and New Providence, although one of the smaller islands, has the capital Nassau. The climate is pleasant, with much sunshine, and the temperature stays the same throughout the year. The islands are flat, and there are still some indigenous forests remaining, as well as mangrove swamps on the coasts.

People

Some 250,000 people live in the Bahamas. The official language is English.

Government and legal system

The Bahamas became independent in 1973, and has a two-chamber parliament based on the Westminster model. The country is a Commonwealth member and the Queen is the head of state, with a Governor as her representative.

Economy

Tourism and offshore finance are the main sources of income for the islands. The Bahamas used to be called the 'Caribbean Switzerland', but since the 1970s the Caymans have overtaken them as the Caribbean's biggest banking centre. The Bahamas have some US$160 billion on deposit, as opposed to the Caymans' US$440 billion.

Offshore companies

The Bahamas' International Business Company (IBC) Act 1990 provides for the following:

- IBCs need not hold their records on the islands.
- The address of the IBC must be lodged with the Bahamian Register General of Companies.

- No audits are required.
- No financial returns are required.
- IBCs need not hold AGMs.
- IBCs are exempt of tax.
- Only one director is required.
- There is no need to register beneficial owners.
- IBCs have no minimum capital requirement.
- IBCs may not hold property in the Bahamas.
- IBCs can continue as a company formed under the laws of a foreign country.
- Bearer shares are allowed.
- A minimum of two shareholders is necessary.

Tax
There are no direct taxes in the Bahamas, and no double-taxation treaties.

Trusts
The main features of trusts are:

- Settlors can be beneficiaries of their own trusts.
- There is no restriction on the accumulation period.
- Revocable trusts are allowed.
- Trustees need not be residents.
- Assets need not be held in the Bahamas.
- Trusts need not be registered.
- Trusts cannot last longer than the duration of a named person's life who is alive at the time of settlement, plus 21 years.
- Asset protection legislation protects trusts against creditors and judgements in civil law countries.
- Trusts are exempt of tax.

BARBADOS

Essential information
Caribbean island (part of the Windward Islands)

Capital: Bridgetown

Language: English

Telephone code: 1 809

Voltage: 110 volts AC 60 Hz

Time: GMT –4 hours

Currency: Barbados dollar (BBD), 100 cents to the dollar. BBD notes are denominated as 2, 5, 10, 20, 50 and 100 dollars

Office hours: *Banks:* Monday to Thursday, 8 a.m.–5 p.m., Fridays, 9.30 a.m.–4 p.m. *Shops:* Monday to Friday, 8 a.m.–4 p.m., Saturdays, 8 a.m.– Midday.

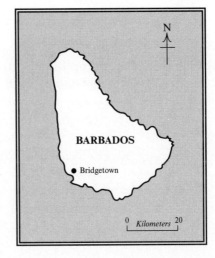

GAZETTEER

Credit cards: Major credit cards and travellers' cheques are widely accepted

Driving licence: International and national driving licences accepted

Climate: Sub-tropical, sunny and dry

Health: Yellow fever certificate required if arriving from an infected area within six days

Visas and passports: Visas are required by all except:

1. British Commonwealth citizens (except India and Pakistan) and US citizens for stays of less than six months.
2. Nationals of Argentina, Austria, Belgium, Colombia, Cuba, Denmark, Germany, Greece, Iceland, Ireland, Israel, Italy, Japan, Liechtenstein, Luxembourg, Netherlands, Norway, Peru, Spain, Sweden, Switzerland and Tunisia for stays of less than three months.
3. Venezuelan nationals with an onward ticket. Passports must be carried by all except US and Canadian nationals on short visits with appropriate ID.

Customs: There are no restrictions on the import of foreign currency, but it must be declared, and you can only export up to the amount declared on entry. You can import up to 200 cigarettes or 50 cigars and 1 bottle of alcohol. Firearms are prohibited.

Airport: Barbados Grantley Adams International, seven miles out of Bridgetown. Departure tax is BBD20. Lockers are available. Banks are open until the last flight leaving.

History

The early history of Barbados is unknown, but it was populated by Arawak Indians and raided by Caribs in pre-Columbian times. By 1518 Spaniards were taking Indians from the island as slaves to work in the colony of Hispaniola, and by 1536 no Indians were left. In the early 1600s the island was settled by the British, in whose hands it remained until independence. In 1627 Charles I granted the island to a Lord Carlisle, but the island was surrendered to Cromwellian forces in 1652, on the condition that the island should not be taxed without its agreement. After the Restoration of Charles II, the Carlisles' claim to the island was revived, resulting in the island reverting to the Crown in return for payments levied by a 4.5 per cent export duty. Until this was abolished in 1838 it was a great source of grievance. In 1876 an attempt at federating Barbados with four other islands led to riots.

Geography

The island is 21 miles long with an area of 166 square miles. Encircled by coral reefs, little of the indigenous forest remains, but there are still indigenous flora and fauna, including some monkeys.

People and language

The majority of the island's 257,000 population are of African descent. The official language is English.

Government and legal system

Since independence in 1966 Barbados has had a two-chamber parliament on the Westminster model. The head of state is the Governor-General, appointed by the Queen. Barbados is a common law jurisdiction.

Economy

For centuries Barbados' principal export has been sugar cane, but tourism and finance are becoming increasingly important in the light of low and fluctuating commodity prices.

Offshore companies

The Barbadian offshore legislation offers:

• Exemption from exchange controls.

• No Capital Gains Tax, estate duties, withholding tax on dividends, interest or royalties, taxes on share transfers and no stamp duties on capital for offshore companies.

- Expatriate employees of offshore companies can get work permits easily and are exempt from tax on up to 35 per cent of their pay.

- Offshore companies can import capital equipment and raw materials free of duty.

- No audited accounts required for companies with assets or turnover of less than BBD1 million.

- Bearer shares are not allowed.

- Companies can have one shareholder.

- Companies can be formed very quickly.

Currently there are around 1,000 International Business Companies (IBCs), paying an initial licence fee of US$510 and US$100 annually. They are taxed at 2.5 per cent on income.

Double-taxation treaties

Barbados has tax treaties, which were concluded by the UK with the US, Switzerland and the Scandinavian countries when Barbados was still a British colony. There are no withholding taxes for IBCs.

Banking

The Offshore Banking Act permits banking in foreign currencies, receiving deposits, sale and placement of securities, making loans, advances and investments. There are capital and reserve requirements and banks must be audited annually. There are currently 16 offshore banking operations with US$2.5 billion on deposit.

Trusts

The main points about trusts are:

- Trusts with non-resident settlors and beneficiaries are exempt of tax.

- Trusts need not be registered.

- Trustees need not be resident.

BELIZE

Essential information

Caribbean coast of Central America

Capital: Belmopan

Language: English, Spanish

Telephone code: 501

Voltage: 110/220 volts AC 60 Hz

Time: GMT –6 hours

Currency: Belize dollar (BZD), 100 cents to the dollar. BZD notes are denominated as 1, 2, 5, 10, 20, 50 and 100 dollars

Office hours: *Banks:* Monday to Thursday, 8 a.m.–1 p.m., Fridays, 8 a.m.–1 p.m. and 3 p.m.–6 p.m. *Offices:* Monday to Thursday, 8 a.m.–Midday and 1 p.m.–5 p.m., Fridays, 8a.m.–Midday and 1 p.m.–4.30 p.m. *Shops:* Monday to Saturday, 8 a.m. –Midday, 1 p.m.–4.30 p.m. and 7 p.m.–9 p.m.

Credit cards: Major credit cards are widely accepted

Driving licence: International and national driving licences accepted

Climate: Sub-tropical, hot and humid. Monsoons June to September, dry January to April

Health: Yellow fever certificate required if arriving from an infected area within six days. There is a risk of malaria.

Visas and passports: Visas are required by all except:

1. British subjects (citizens of the United Kingdom and Colonies).

2. Commonwealth citizens (except India) for up to six months.

3. EU nationals and those of Costa Rica, Guatemala, Iceland, Liechtenstein, Mexico, Sweden, Switzerland, Tunisia, US and Uruguay for stays of less than one month.

Passports must be carried by all, as is an onward or return ticket and sufficient funds for the stay.

Customs: There are no restrictions on the import of foreign currency. Exportation of foreign currency is limited by the Central Bank. You can import up to 200 cigarettes or 50 cigars and 586 ml of alcohol.

Airport: Philip S. W. Goldson International, ten miles out of Belize City. Departure tax is US$11.25.

History

Belize flourished under the Mayas, but when their civilization collapsed around 1,200 years ago it became depopulated. The Spanish left it alone during the conquests of Central America, but in the early 1600s British woodcutters settled on the coast. For the next 150 years these settlers fought periodic battles with the Spanish, culminating in a resounding victory in 1798 over a Spanish naval force. Slaves were less badly treated than elsewhere, and the abolition of slavery caused few problems. In 1847 the native Americans in the Yucatan area of Mexico revolted against the Spanish, and hordes of refugees flooded into Belize. The territory was declared a British colony in 1862, and was governed through Jamaica until in 1884 it became the separate colony of British Honduras. Since the 1850s Guatemala has coveted the territory.

Geography

About half of Belize is less than 200 feet above sea level and the coasts are protected by coral reefs. Most of the country is covered in forest, and there are mangrove swamps on the coast. There is an abundance of Central American flora and fauna.

People and language

The 194,000 people who inhabit Belize mainly live in the towns. There are still native Americans in the interior, and the rest of the people are very mixed, but many are of African origin, some of whom speak Carib, a native American language. Others speak Creole and Spanish, but English is widely understood and is the official language.

Government

Independent since 1981, Belize has a political system based on the Westminster model, with a bicameral parliament consisting of a 29-member House of Representatives and a nine-member Senate. Belize remains a Commonwealth member, and the Queen is the constitutional head of state. The Queen's representative in Belize is the Governor-General, who must be a Belize national.

Economy

Timber has traditionally been Belize's biggest business, with mahogany being the most valuable wood. Chicle, used in chewing gum, is derived from the sapodilla tree. Sugar, tobacco and other cash crops are grown. Tourism is important, particularly the 'green' variety, which is attracted to Belize's magnificent and unique wilderness.

GAZETTEER

Offshore companies

Belize introduced the IBC Act in 1990 which allows the creation of International Business Companies (IBCs), which are exempt of tax on the following:

- Company income.
- Dividends and distributions by the company to individuals.
- Interest, royalties and similar payments made by the company to non-residents.
- Capital gains.

Trusts

Belize's Trusts Act of 1992 includes the following features:

- A perpetuity period of 120 years which is considerably longer than is allowed in most countries.
- The option to convert trusts of finite duration to charitable trusts with indefinite duration.
- Trust registration is optional.
- Exemption from taxes and exchange controls for trusts created by non-residents.
- Facilities to switch trusts from one jurisdiction to another and to adapt local rules to those which prevail in the settlor's country.
- A settlor can make himself a beneficiary of a spendthrift trust to avoid creditors.

Companies and individuals outside the Export Processing Zone (see below) are subject to exchange controls in the form of the requirement of Central Bank clearances on foreign currency transactions.

Comment

Like many small countries dependent on primary commodities, Belize has seen the benefits of introducing tax reforms to boost its foreign income. As well as introducing IBCs, Belize has made tax reforms to attract foreign investment, including the reduction of corporate income tax from 45 to 35 per cent and income tax exemption for public investment companies. Belize has an Export Processing Zone which offers the following:

- Equipment, office furniture and construction materials can be imported free of all taxes and duties.

- Companies within the zone are free of all taxes, including Income Tax and Capital Gains Tax.

- There are no exchange controls.

- Profits may be repatriated freely.

- Work permits easily obtained.

BERMUDA

Essential information

Island in the west Atlantic.

Capital: Hamilton

Language: English

Telephone code: 1 809

Voltage: 110 volts AC 60 Hz

Time: GMT –3 hours

Currency: Bermudan dollar (BMD), 100 cents to the dollar. BMD notes are denominated as 2, 5, 10, 20, 50 and 100 dollars

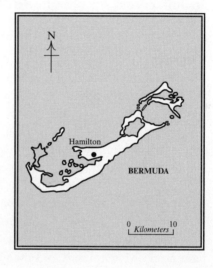

Office Hours: *Banks:* Monday to Thursday, 9.30 a.m.–3 p.m., Fridays, 9.30 a.m.–3 p.m. and 4.30 p.m.– 5.30 p.m. *Offices:* Monday to Friday, 9 a.m.–5 p.m. *Shops:* Monday to Saturday, 9 a.m.–5 p.m.

Credit cards: Major credit cards and US dollars are widely accepted

Driving licence: Visitors are not allowed to drive cars

Climate: Semi-tropical

Health: No certificates required

Visas and passports: Visas are not required except for: nationals of ex-communist or Arab countries, the Phillippines and Sri Lanka. Passports must be carried by all except for UK citizens with a British Visitors' passport (unless travelling via the US), US and Canadian nationals with appropriate ID.

Customs: There are no restrictions on the import of foreign currency but it must be declared. Foreign currency can be exported up to the amount declared on entry. You can import up to 200 cigarettes or 50 cigars and 1.136 litres of wine or spirits.

Airport: Kindley Field, 12 miles out of Hamilton. Departure tax is BMD 20. Bureaux de change are open 11 a.m.–4 p.m. daily.

History

It is not known when the islands were first discovered, but they were uninhabited before European sailors began to visit them frequently in the 1500s. In 1609 a British group of colonists, on their way to Virginia, were wrecked off Bermuda and subsequently settled there – the basis for the plot of Shakespeare's play, *The Tempest*. The islands were in the possession of the Virginia Company until 1684 when they were taken over by the Crown, and are Britain's oldest colony. In 1941 the US was given a 99-year lease for air and naval bases.

Geography

The Bermudas consists of a group of some 300 islands, some of which are only rocks; only about 20 are inhabited, and the main island, Grand Bermuda, is known as the 'mainland'. It is 14 miles long and is linked by bridges to six of the other islands. These bridges surround large areas of sea within which most of the other smaller islands lie. They are coral islands, with low hills and no rivers or lakes. When the Bermudas were first discovered they were thickly wooded, but various tree diseases have wreaked havoc on indigenous species. The most common tree is the Bermuda cedar, a kind of juniper. The islands are in the Atlantic, some 570 miles east of North Carolina; their remote position means that they have no native mammals, but many species of bird stop there on their way across the ocean.

People and language

About two-thirds of the inhabitants are of African origin, and the remainder are of British and Portuguese descent. The population is about 58,000, making Bermuda overcrowded and thus it is difficult for outsiders to settle there. The official language is English.

Government

As a British dependent territory, Bermuda's defence, internal security and external affairs are a British responsibility. Bermuda has its own parliament and a Governor who represents the Crown. Demands for independence appear periodically, and are currently a burning issue – the islands are becoming increasingly dependent on the US economy, and more distant from Britain. As one of the most respectable and well-established of the world's tax havens, Bermuda is likely to remain an important offshore centre even if it is does become independent.

Economy

The financial industry and tourism are Bermuda's main sources of income. Although Bermuda is one of the most densely populated countries in the world, its per capita income is high and there is little unemployment. The island's time zone is advantageous as its working day precedes that of the Far East. With excellent communications and a sound infrastructure, Bermuda is the domicile of more than 7,000 international companies. The central bank is the Bermuda Monetary Authority (BMA); it issues and redeems notes and coins, manages exchange controls, regulates Bermuda's financial institutions and vets applications from companies wishing to incorporate in Bermuda. In recent years the BMA's authority over banks has increased. Bermuda has designated territory status under the UK's Financial Services Act which means that its system of investor protection is acknowledged by the UK to be at least as good as that in the UK. Bermuda is an OECD member.

Offshore companies

Offshore investors may incorporate exempt companies and the following conditions apply.

- Founders must apply to the BMA for permission to incorporate, giving details of the beneficial owners.
- Exempt companies may not carry on business within Bermuda, but can run overseas operations from the island.
- Exempt companies must keep their cash in foreign currency, only holding Bermuda dollars to pay local running costs.
- Other than the above there are no exchange controls on exempt companies.
- Exempt companies may not buy property in Bermuda.
- Bearer shares are not allowed.
- Exempt companies must have a minimum of three shareholders.
- Companies must have a registered office in Bermuda where company records are kept.
- Annual audited accounts are not required for exempt companies.
- There are no taxes on income, profits or distributions in Bermuda.

It is also possible to set up an exempt partnership, which may be limited, on similar terms.

Double-taxation treaties

There are no double-taxation treaties, but Bermuda has an exchange of information agreement with the US. There are no withholding taxes.

Trusts

Bermuda is a common law country, and its trust law is broadly similar to the UK's. Until recently, the administration and management of trusts in Bermuda has been the preserve of three firms of lawyers and three banks, but the Trust Companies Act of 1991 paved the way for additional local applications from professional firms, causing a row between the Bank of Bermuda and the Bermudian finance ministry over the second stage of the trust expansion plan whereby applications were invited from overseas trust companies. The main points on trusts are:

- Trusts need not be registered.

- A settlor can form a private trust company, controlled by associates, to act as a trustee, with the day-to-day management done by an approved corporate trustee.

- There is no accumulation period; the perpetuity period is 100 years.

- The settlor can choose what jurisdiction's law will govern the trust.

Banking and finance

Bermuda's pool of legal, accountancy, banking, insurance and administrative skills are superior to those of most offshore centres. Bermuda has never permitted offshore banking. Its two biggest banks, the Bank of Bermuda and the Bank of BT Butterfield, are indigenous banks, owned primarily by Bermudian individuals. Bermuda Commercial Bank is smaller and has Barclays Bank as a minority shareholder. Bermuda's banks offer a range of private banking services to internationally minded high net worth clients. The country is the world's biggest captive insurance centre, with more than 1,300 captives. Captive insurance formation and management has been an established part of Bermuda's international scene for more than 20 years. The quality of the local infrastructure is endorsed by the fact that many international insurance broking companies use Bermuda for staff training.

BRITISH VIRGIN ISLANDS

Essential information

Islands in the Eastern Carribean

Capital: Road Town

Language: English

Telephone code: 1 809 49

Voltage: 60/110 volts AC 60 Hz

Time: GMT –4 hours

Currency: US dollars.

Office hours: *Banks:* Monday to Thursday, 9 a.m.–2 p.m., Fridays, 9 a.m. –2 p.m. and 4 p.m.–6 p.m. *Offices:* Monday to Friday, 8.30 a.m.– 5 p.m., Saturdays, 8.30 a.m.–12.30 p.m.

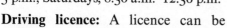

Driving licence: A licence can be obtained for US$10 on production of national licence

Climate: Semi-tropical

Health: No certificates required. Polio and typhoid immunization recommended.

Visas and passports: Visas are required by all except for:

1. British subjects (citizens of United Kingdom and Colonies)
2. Commonwealth citizens
3. EU nationals and those of Turkey, Tunisia, Uruguay and Venezuela. Passports must be carried by all except for US and Canadian citizens.

Customs: There are no restrictions on the import of foreign currency but it must be declared. Foreign currency can be exported up to the amount declared on entry.

History

When Christopher Columbus discovered them in 1493 the British Virgin Islands were inhabited by Carib and Arawak Indians, but slavery and disease wiped them out during the succeeding centuries. The Dutch occupied Tortola in 1648, and the British took it in 1666, remaining there ever since. The BVI were a favourite haunt of pirates during the seventeenth century.

251

Geography
Part of the Virgin Islands, which are divided between the US and the UK, the British Virgin Islands consist of some 60 islands and islets, of which 4 are inhabited. The main island, Tortola, has the capital, Road Town, at a harbour on its the south side. The islands are the peaks of underwater mountains which extend beneath the Greater Antilles.

People and language
The population is about 18,000, the great majority of whom live on Tortola. The official language is English.

Government and legal system
The British Virgin Islands are a British Crown Colony (now known as a 'dependent territory') with a Governor representing the UK government, an executive council and a legislative council. The Governor is responsible for internal security, external affairs, defence, the civil service and many legal matters. The BVI are a common law jurisdiction.

Economy
Agriculture is difficult on the islands because of their rocky soil, and the BVI survive principally on tourism. Offshore finance is becoming increasingly important as the BVI offers a cheap and safe location for offshore companies.

Offshore companies
The British Virgin Islands is the Caribbean's largest company formation centre. It was one of the first offshore centres to target the market for International Business Companies (IBCs) in Hong Kong and other parts of the Far East. Some 35,000 IBCs are formed annually, the majority by Hong Kong residents. The BVI regularly sends delegations to Hong Kong to promote itself. Following the fall of General Noriega in Panama a large number of Panamanian offshore companies moved to the BVI. The main features of IBCs are:

- IBCs may not do business with BVI residents.
- IBCs may not own property in the BVI.
- Minimum registration costs are $750, with annual fees of $650
- Bearer shares are allowed.
- A minimum of one shareholder is allowed.
- The names of directors need not be disclosed to the Registrar of Companies.

- A BVI agent is required.
- No annual audit is necessary.
- Information on shareholders need not be registered.

The BVI's rules are a blueprint for IBC laws in other havens, for example those in the Bahamas.

Tax

Residents are taxed on worldwide income, while non-residents are taxed only on income from the BVI. There is no Capital Gains Tax. The tax rate on individuals varies between 3 and 20 per cent, depending on the size of income. IBCs are exempt of tax, including withholding taxes. The BVI has a double-taxation treaty with Switzerland, and one with the US is in the pipeline.

Banks

The BVI is a small banking centre with some US$300 million on deposit. There are no exchange controls.

Trusts

The main features of trusts are:

- Trusts must be registered unless an IBC is involved.
- The accumulation period is as long as the perpetuity period of 100 years.
- Trusts are not taxed, except on income deriving from the BVI.

CAYMAN ISLANDS

Essential information

Caribbean islands

Capital: Georgetown

Language: English

Telephone code: 1 809

Voltage: 110 volts AC 60 Hz

Time: GMT –5 hours

Currency: Cayman Islands dollar (KYD), 100 cents to the dollar. KYD notes are denominated as 1, 5, 10, 25, 50 and 100 dollars.

Office hours: *Banks:* Monday to Thursday, 9.30 a.m.–2.30 p.m., Fridays, 9.30 a.m.–4.30 p.m.. *Offices:* Monday to Friday, 8.30 a.m.–5 p.m. *Shops:* Monday to Saturday, 9 a.m.–5 p.m.

Driving licence: Local required

Climate: Pleasant warm climate

Health: No certificates required. Polio and typhoid vaccinations recommended.

Visas and passports: Visas are not required by nationals of most First World countries. Passports must be carried by all except US, Canadian, British and British Dependent Territory citizens on visits of up to six months with appropriate ID.

Customs: There are no restrictions on the import or export of foreign currency. You can import up to 200 cigarettes or 50 cigars and 1.136 litres of spirits or 4 litres of wine.

Background

The Cayman Islands are a group of three Caribbean islands 480 miles south of Miami, Florida, comprising Grand Cayman, Little Cayman and Cayman Brac. Grand Cayman, site of the capital Georgetown, is the largest island, measuring 7 miles at its widest point and 28 miles in length. It is hot all year. The coasts generally have coral reefs and none of the islands have rivers. The Caymans were discovered in 1503 by Christopher Columbus, but were not colonized until the British came in the eighteenth century, principally from Jamaica. During the heyday of the Caribbean pirates, the Caymans were often used as a base, especially by Edward Teach, the infamous Blackbeard.

People and language

The population is about 28,000. English is the official language.

Government and legal system

Cayman is a British Crown Colony. Laws are made by the Legislative Assembly, which comprises 12 members elected every 4 years, and 3 official members appointed by the Governor who acts as the president of the Assembly. The Governor is appointed by the Queen.

Economy

Sea-going turtles used to be the main source of income for the islanders, but these have been supplanted by tourism and international finance. The islands have no Income Tax, Capital Gains Tax, Corporation Tax or death duties and are a major centre for captive insurance and offshore trusts. There are no exchange controls or regulations on the import and export of precious metals.

Offshore companies

The main points for offshore companies are:

- Exempt companies can issue bearer shares.
- There are no minimum capital requirements.
- Companies may have one shareholder only.
- Exempt companies need not have a registered office.
- Exempt companies file an annual declaration that they have complied with the Companies Law, but do not file details of their ownership or annual audited accounts.

Banking

There are more than 500 banks in the Cayman Islands, of which around 70 have offices there. Offshore bank deposits amount to some US$427 billion. Licences issued by the Banking Supervision Department can be either Category A or Category B – these are for both banks and trust businesses. Category B businesses are allowed to deal only with clients outside the Caymans and some are restricted to named persons. The Caymans have a Mutual Legal Assistance Treaty with the US, agreeing to co-operate with the US in investigations of any offence which is a crime in the Caymans, and also some offences which aren't, such as racketeering, insider trading, foreign corrupt practices and fraudulent securities activities.

Double-taxation treaties

Cayman has no double-taxation treaties or withholding taxes.

Trusts

Exempt trusts, which have non-resident beneficiaries, are subject to the following:

- Trusts must be registered.
- The maximum perpetuity period is 100 years.
- Accumulation periods can be as long as the perpetuity period.
- There are no taxes on trusts.
- Creditors cannot have trusts set aside without proof.

NETHERLANDS ANTILLES

Essential information

Islands in the Caribbean

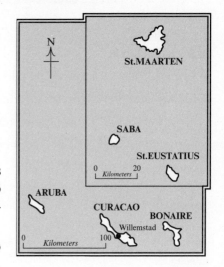

Capital: Willemstad

Language: Dutch, English, Spanish

Telephone code: 599

Voltage: 110/220 volts AC 50 Hz

Time: GMT +4 hours

Currency: Netherlands Antilles guilder or florin (ANG), 100 cents to the guilder. ANG notes are denominated as 5, 10, 25, 50, 100 and 250

Office Hours: *Banks:* Monday to Friday, 8.30 a.m.–Midday and 1.30 p.m. –4.30 p.m. *Offices:* Monday to Friday, 8 a.m.–Midday and 1.30 p.m.–4.30 p.m. *Shops:* Monday to Saturday, 8 a.m.–Midday and 2 p.m.–6 p.m.

Driving licence: International and national driving licences accepted

Climate: Tropical

Health: Yellow fever certificate required if coming from an infected area within 6 days.

Visas and passports: Visas are not required by anyone staying for up to 14 days. Passports are requried by all except:

1. National identity card holders of Belgium, Brazil, Germany, Luxembourg, Monaco, Netherlands, San Marino, Trinidad and Tobago and Venezuela.

2. Holders of a British Visitor's Passport being a 'citizen of the United Kingdom and Colonies'.

3. Nationals of Canada with apropriate ID.

Passports are required for everyone.

Customs: There are no restrictions on the import or export of foreign currency. You can import up to 400 cigarettes or 50 cigars and 2 litres of alcohol.

Background

The Netherlands Antilles are two groups of islands in the southern Caribbean. The southern group, which lie 60 miles off Venezuela and includes Curacao, were discovered in 1499 by the Spanish, but became Dutch in 1634. The islands were important posts in the trade with the New World in the seventeenth and eighteenth centuries, but declined during the nineteenth century. Venezuelan oil improved their fortunes and the islands boast important oil refineries. They are long standing tax havens, set up when Dutch companies fled Nazi control in World War 2, and deal equally fluently with Dutch, English and Spanish speakers.

People
The population is about 275,000, the majority of whom live on Curacao. Dutch is the official language, but Spanish, English and Papiamento are widely spoken.

Government
The Dutch Antilles is an independent 'partner' in the Kingdom of the Netherlands. They have a Governor-General representing the Queen of the Netherlands, and a parliament and council of ministers who govern the islands' internal affairs.

Economy
Oil, tourism and international commerce are the principal economic activities.

Companies
Companies must obtain authorization to be formed, but offshore companies rarely experience difficulties in obtaining permission. Rules include:

- Companies which are resident in the Antilles and own a minimum of 25 per cent of the shares of a Dutch company enjoy reduced withholding tax of 7.5 per cent in Holland.
- Bearer shares are allowed.
- Companies need to have a registered office in the Antilles.
- A company can change its domicile from the Antilles to another jurisdiction at any time.
- Annually audited accounts are not required.
- Offshore companies are taxed at 2.4 –3 per cent on offshore income, and are exempt of Capital Gains Tax.

Double-taxation treaties
The Antilles have the equivalent of a tax treaty with Holland. There are no withholding taxes. Non-resident individuals are free of tax on most foreign income.

Trusts

Trusts are not recognized, but Antilles residents may act as trustees of a foreign trust.

Comment

The Antilles suffered some setbacks in the 1980s when the US authorities took specific measures aimed at reducing foreign purchase of US property and closing down Antilles-based Eurobond finance subsidiaries of US companies. The UK also tightened up its rules with regard to the islands, which are gradually becoming more like the other havens of the Caribbean.

NEVIS

Essential information

Caribbean island

Capital: Charlestown

Language: English

Telephone code: 1 809

Voltage: 230 volts AC 60 Hz

Time: GMT –4 hours

Currency: Eastern Caribbean dollar (XCD), 100 cents to the dollar. XCD is denominated as 1, 5 , 10, 20 and 100.

Office hours: *Banks:* Monday to Thursday, 8 a.m.–6 p.m. Fridays, 8 a.m.– 5 p.m. *Offices:* Monday to Saturday, 8 a.m.–Midday and 1 p.m.–4 p.m. *Shops:* Monday to Saturday, 8 a.m.–Midday and 1 p.m.–4 p.m.

Driving licence: International and national driving licences accepted

Climate: Tropical

Health: Yellow fever certificate required if coming from an infected area within six days

Visas and passports: Visas are not required by many nationals. Passports are required by all except US and Canadian nationals with appropriate ID.

Customs: There are no restrictions on the import of foreign currency but it must be declared. Export allowed up to the amount declared on importation. You can import up to 200 cigarettes or 50 cigars and 1.136 litres of alcohol.

Background
Nevis was discovered by Christopher Columbus, but was not colonized until the British arrived in 1628. The population is approximately 8,000. Nevis is a virtually circular island that has the appearance of a cone from the sea. A British colony from 1628 to 1983, Nevis is now independent and has joined the federation of St Kitts and Nevis. The federation is an active member of the British Commonwealth with a democracy based on the British parliamentary system.

Economy
Sugar exports are a major part of the economy, but are troubled by price fluctuations. Tourism, fishing and manufacturing are being expanded, as are offshore incentives.

Offshore companies
The Nevis Business Corporation Ordinance of 1984, modelled on the laws of Delaware in the US, includes comprehensive provisions for the transfer of a foreign company to the island. Offshore companies are exempt from all forms of Nevis taxation. They must pay an annual fee of 450 dollars. Company formation is fast – the company exists as soon as the capitalization tax is paid to the Register of Companies. Off-the-shelf companies are available. While Nevis corporate law has its foundation in US law, it does have similarities with UK law. Important features are:

- No taxes are levied on income, dividends or distributions of a Nevis company which are not earned on the island.
- Corporate financial returns need not be filed in Nevis.
- Shareholders, directors and officers may be of any nationality and reside anywhere.
- No annual or other reports by shareholders or directors are required to be filed in the public records of Nevis.
- Changes of shareholders, directors or officers need not be reported to the Registrar of Companies.
- Shares may be in registered or bearer form.
- Shares with par value may be denominated in any currency.
- Shareholders and directors may act with unanimous consent without a meeting.

- The company's records and its principal office may be located anywhere.
- Any corporation formed in another jurisdiction may redomicile in Nevis.

Trusts

An important change in Nevis' life as an offshore centre is its enactment of some of the most attractive asset protection trust laws ever devised. Features include:

- A settlor can be a beneficiary and a protector of the trust and retain some control of the trust's assets.
- The trust remains valid even if fraudulent transfers are determined to have taken place.
- Foreign judgements regarding APTs are not recognized in Nevis courts.
- The statute of limitation on challenging an APT is one year.
- The burden of proving fraudulent intent lies with the plaintiff.
- Anyone starting an action in Nevis against a Nevis trust must lodge a bond of US$25,000 first.
- Trust documents need not be filed and are not a matter of public record.
- Trusts must be registered, but the only information required is the name, the date of creation and the name of the representing trust company.
- Fees are 200 dollars on registration and again annually thereafter.

PANAMA

Essential information

Central America

Capital: Panama City

Language: Spanish, English

Telephone code: 507

Voltage: 120 volts AC

Time: GMT –5 hours

Currency: Balboa (PAB), 100 centesimos to the balboa. There is no paper money. US dollars accepted.

Office hours: *Banks:* Monday to Friday, 8 a.m.–1.30 p.m. *Offices:*

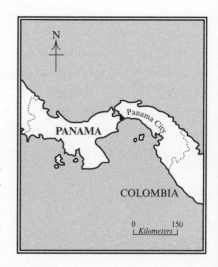

Monday to Friday, 8 a.m.–Midday and 2 p.m.–5 p.m. *Shops:* Monday to Saturday, 8 a.m.–6 p.m.

Driving licence: National driving licences accepted

Climate: Semi-equatorial; hot and humid

Health: Yellow fever certificate recommended. Danger of malaria.

Visas and passports: Visas are not required by many nationals who may purchase a Tourist Card valid for 30 days for US$2. Passports are required by all except US nationals with appropriate ID.

Customs: There are no restrictions on the import or export of foreign currency. You can import up to 500 cigarettes or 50 cigars and 3 bottles of alcohol.

Airport: Panama City Tocumen International 17 miles out of Panama City. Departure tax US$15. Bureau de Change 8.30 a.m.–8 p.m.

History

Parts of the coast of Panama were explored from the time of Christopher Columbus; the region was inhabited by native tribes, who successfully prevented much colonization, although a small settlement was established by the Spanish on the western shore of the Gulf of Darien in the early 1500s. The village of Panama grew in importance because of its strategic location between the two oceans, and throughout the 1500s much of the gold trade passed through the area, attracting the attention of privateers such as Drake. In the 1600s pirates flourished, and the notorious Sir Henry Morgan managed both to capture the port of Porto Bello and Old Panama city in 1671. As the gold trade declined Panama became less important throughout the eighteenth century.

In 1821 Panama declared its independence from Spain after Simon Bolivar had defeated loyalist forces, but soon joined a union with Colombia. In 1845 a treaty was signed with the US guaranteeing the neutrality of the isthmus and free transport of goods across it. In 1849 the California Gold Rush caused the building of a railway, completed in 1855, across the isthmus. Soon there was pressure to build a canal, but international politics and practical problems – in particular the possibility of an alternative route through Nicaragua – meant that plans came to nothing.

In 1903 Panama revolted, with some assistance from the US, and proclaimed independence from Colombia. The Hay-Bunau-Varilla treaty of 18 November 1903, gave the US the exclusive use, occupation and control of the planned canal zone, over which Panama would have no sovereign powers, in return for payment.

261

Building the canal was a tremendous undertaking, and was one of the greatest engineering feats ever attempted. It took ten years to build, and much further construction work has been necessary since its completion in 1914. The relationship between Panama and the US has been stormy ever since, and Panama has gradually regained some rights over the canal zone, which is of vital strategic importance to the US. Recently, General Noriega's spectacular falling out with the US Administration over his indictment on money-laundering and drug-dealing charges led to the American 'Just Cause' invasion of 1989.

Geography
Much of Panama is mountainous. There are mangrove swamps and palm forests along the coasts, and in the west of Panama there are large rain forests. There are numerous species of land animals, and an abundant sea-life.

People
The population is over 4 million, and is very mixed, consisting of Native American, European and African strains. Spanish is the official language but English is spoken widely. There are still native tribes who are allowed to live under their own laws.

Government and legal system
Panama is a republic with an elected National Assembly, a president and two vice presidents. It has no military forces.

Economy
The strategic importance of the Panama Canal is the lifeblood of the country's role in international shipping, and the free trade zone at Colon (on the Atlantic side) takes advantage of this. Over 30 ships a day pass through the canal. Agriculture and manufacturing have a minor role in the economy by comparison with the commercial services sector, including a vigorous international banking centre. Panama has no exchange controls and is to the Americas what Hong Kong has been to Asia.

Companies
Panama allows various types of partnership, but most offshore investment comes through companies. Important features include:

- The minimum number of shareholders is two, who can be of any nationality. Once the company has been formed the number of shareholders can be reduced to one.

- It is not necessary to come to Panama to set up a company.
- Off-the-shelf companies are available.
- Bearer shares are allowed.
- There must be a Panamanian registered agent.
- It is not necessary to have a registered office in Panama.
- Companies that are not doing business in Panama need not file audited accounts.
- Companies that are not doing business in Panama are not subject to tax.
- Invoicing from the Panama office, receiving dividends from foreign companies and initiating business that is settled elsewhere are all considered activities outside the rule on doing business in Panama.
- Branches of foreign companies can be set up in Panama.

Trusts
Panama recognizes trusts:

- Trusts can be settled in respect of future property.
- A trust must have a Panamanian trustee.

Comment
Panama's recent history has been marked by the number of corporations fleeing its tax-favoured shores. Noriega was flushed out of hiding, and so have many offshore companies, using the 'flee and continuance' features of Panamanian law to head for the British Virgin Islands. Most Panamanian incorporation agents now also have offices in the BVI capital, Tortola, and continue to assist with the tax-efficient businesses that have fled Panama. Under US pressure Panama is making efforts to introduce a code of ethics and self policing among financial services operators, focusing particularly on 'know your customer' rules. It is still a substantial financial centre, with 106 offshore banks holding deposits worth over US$31 billion and more than 300,000 offshore business companies.

TURKS AND CAICOS

Essential information
Caribbean islands
Capital: Cockburn Town (Grand Turks)

Language: English, Creole

Telephone code: 1 809

Voltage: 110 volts AC

Time: GMT –4 hours

Currency: US dollar (USD), 100 cents to the dollar

Office Hours: *Banks:* Monday to Friday, 8 a.m.–1 p.m. Saturdays, 8 a.m.–Midday. *Offices:* Monday to Friday, 8 a.m.– 1 p.m. and 2 p.m.– 4.30 p.m. Saturdays, 8 a.m.–Midday.

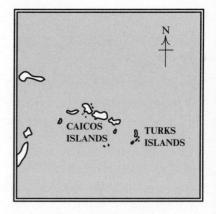

Driving licence: International and national driving licences accepted

Climate: Tropical

Health: No certificates required

Visas and passports: Visas are not required except by nationals of former Communist bloc countries. Passports are required by all except US and Canadian nationals with appropriate ID.

Customs: There are no restrictions on the import or export of foreign currency. You can import up to 200 cigarettes or 50 cigars and 1.136 litres of alcohol.

Background

Geographically the Turks and Caicos (TCI) are part of the Bahamas; they consist of some 14 islands, but only some are inhabited. The Turks are named after a cactus that grows there that resembles a Turkish fez. Grand Turk is the principal island. The islands were discovered in 1512 by Juan Ponce de Leon but were not settled until British settlers from Bermuda came in 1678. The TCI became a British Crown Colony in 1960. The UK is responsible for the government of the islands, their defence and foreign relations. The TCI have a democratically elected internal self-government with the stated aim of achieving economic independence for the islands. The population is about 10,000 and the official language is English.

Offshore companies

The main company type used by offshore investors is the International Business Company (IBC), of which there are more than the population of the islands.

- Annual fees can be prepaid for periods of 5, 10 and 15 years at a discount, reducing the standard annual fee of US$4,500 over 15 years to US$2,000 per year.

- IBCs can be limited by shares, limited by guarantee or have members with unlimited liability, or a combination of these. This allows great flexibility for tax purposes.

- Companies can be formed in one day.

- IBCs are not subject to direct taxation.

- A company's objects may be restricted.

- It is not required to report to the Registrar details of its directors, shareholders or other officers.

- An IBC's register of shareholders is not open to inspection.

- IBCs are not required to hold AGMs.

- Bearer shares are allowed.

- An IBC may issue shares with or without par value in any currency.

- IBCs may change their domicile to another jurisdiction.

Turks and Caicos also offers the Limited Life Company (LLC) with US investors in mind:

- An LLC maintains the tax advantages of partnerships while retaining the limited liability aspects of a corporate entity.

- An LLC is set up as a holding company. When dividends are received from a foreign partner they pass through the LLC and return to the US without any corporation tax liability. Although you are being taxed as a partner, you are avoiding personal or individual liability, since the LLC is a company.

Trusts

Turks and Caicos has revised its trust law in the area of fraudulent dispositions and asset protection trusts. Purpose trusts are also being examined and the outcome is as follows:

- Trusts that are set up with the primary intention of defeating justified claims against them are forbidden.

- There is no tax on trusts.

Comment

Turks and Caicos are eager to dispel the scandals of the 1980s when Chief Minister Norman Saunders was arrested for his involvement in a drugs scandal. New laws have been introduced including a banking law, regulations for the creation of the Turks and Caicos Offshore Finance Centre Unit, a Trustee Licensing Law and regulations governing company formation. It is claimed that TCI's new regulations are better than the Caymans', being cheaper and simpler. No taxes apply and there is no obligation to supply shareholder records or company accounts.

THE HAVENS OF THE REST OF THE WORLD

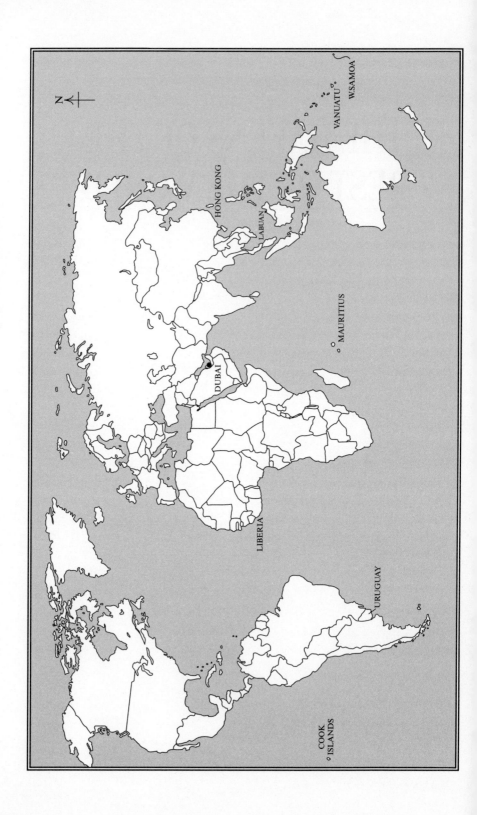

COOK ISLANDS

Essential information

South Pacific

Capital: Avarua on Rarotonga

Language: Maori, English

Telephone code: 682

Voltage: 230 volts AC 50 Hz

Time: GMT –10 hours

Currency: New Zealand dollar (NZD), 100 cents to the dollar. NZD notes are denominated as 5, 10, 20, 50 and 100 dollars.

Office Hours: *Banks:* Monday to Friday, 9 a.m.–3 p.m. *Offices:* Monday to Friday, 8 a.m.–4 p.m. *Shops:* Monday to Friday, 8 a.m.–4 p.m., Saturdays, 8 a.m.–Midday

Driving licence: Local required

Climate: Hot and rainy

Health: No certificates required

Visas and passports: Visas are not required except for business visitors. Passports must be carried by all except New Zealand nationals for stays of up to 31 days.

Customs: There are no restrictions on the import or export of foreign currency, but it should be imported through banking channels. You can import up to 200 cigarettes or 50 cigars and 2 litres of spirits or wine.

Airport: Rarotonga, two miles out of Avarua. Departure tax NZD20.

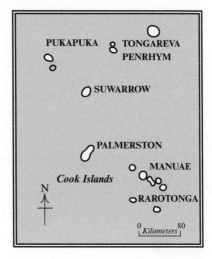

Background

A group of 15 islands divided into a northern and a southern group, the Cook Islands have a total land area of 93 square miles. The biggest island is Rarotonga, site of the capital Avarua. Rarotonga is volcanic and has a lagoon around it, as do many of the islands, which are variously volcanic, coral islands or atolls. Rarotonga is some 2,000 miles from New Zealand and 600 miles from Tahiti. Many explorers visited the Cook Islands – they are named after Captain Cook – but colonization was effectively in the hands of missionaries until they were claimed as a British protectorate in 1888.

Annexed to New Zealand in 1901, in 1956 they became independent, but remain closely associated with New Zealand – islanders have New Zealand citizenship and are British subjects. These are the classic South Sea islands of popular fancy – extremely remote, beautiful and romantic, crime-free and with full employment.

People
The islanders, numbering 18,000, are Polynesian, closely related to the Maoris of New Zealand. Literacy is claimed to be almost 100 per cent. English is the official language, but most inhabitants also speak Maori.

Government and legal system
The Cook Islands have a parliament on the Westminster model. There is a Queen's Representative to give the royal assent by proxy. The judiciary is independent, with a final appeal to the UK's Privy Council.

Economy
The islands have few natural resources; agriculture, fishing, tourism and offshore finance are the main sources of income. There are no foreign exchange controls.

Offshore companies
Following their association with the bankrupt entrepreneurs Alan Bond and Bruce Judge, the islands are seeking to improve their reputation. Most offshore business came from Australia and New Zealand in the 1980s, but anti-tax avoidance legislation introduced in those countries has virtually killed this business. Since then, the islands have been targeting emigrants from Hong Kong to North America who are retaining ties with Hong Kong and China. Features of the offshore regime include:

- The Cook Islands are the only Pacific centre to which listed Hong Kong companies can be redomiciled and remain listed on the stock exchange (the Caymans and Bermuda share this advantage).
- There are no taxes or foreign exchange controls.
- Companies formed within the offshore centre are outside domestic laws.
- They can purchase their own shares.
- Bearer shares, bearer warrants and bearer debentures are allowed.
- In most cases a single shareholder is allowed. No record of who the shareholders are need be filed.

- There is no minimum share capital requirement.
- 'No liability' companies can be formed.
- Only one director is necessary.
- Companies must have a registered office on the islands.
- Companies must have a company secretary resident on the island who is an officer of a trust company.
- Companies can move their domicile to and from the Cook Islands – prior approval, valid for three years, should be obtained.
- Audited accounts are not required.

There are also strict secrecy provisions which, if breached, may result in imprisonment. Hong Kong and Shanghai Bank own a small trust company in Rarotonga, while Standard Chartered own a larger one, European Pacific. These acquisitions have helped the Cook Islands regain some credibility following the Bond debacle.

Double-taxation treaties
There are no double-taxation treaties.

Offshore trusts
In 1991, the islands amended their International Trust Act 1984 providing retroactive protection for trust beneficiaries. If a trust has been domiciled in the islands for more than two years, any legal action against its assets will be dismissed. Other features include:

- The perpetuity period is a maximum of 100 years.
- Foreign bankruptcy is not recognized or given any effect in the islands.

Comment
The Cook Islands are growing in appeal and are thought to have the most rigid and protective laws on asset protection trusts, the controversial vehicle designed to shield US-based trust beneficiaries from creditors. For individuals, the Cook Islands represent a safe repository of funds.

DUBAI (UNITED ARAB EMIRATES)

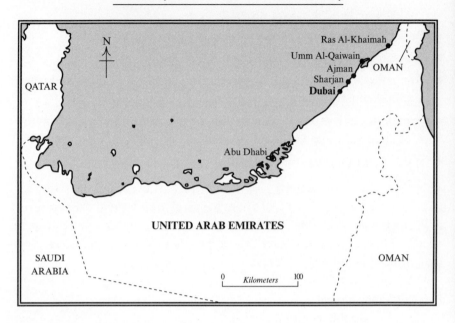

Essential information

Federation of Gulf States: Abu Dhabi, Ajman, Dubai, Fujaira, Ras al Khaima, Sharja, Umm al Qaiwain

Capital: Abu Dhabi

Language: Arabic, English

Telephone code: 971

Voltage: 220/240 volts AC 50 Hz

Time: GMT +4 hours

Currency: Dirham (AED), 100 fils to the dirham. Dirhams are denominated as 1, 5, 10, 50, 100, 500 and 1,000.

Office hours: *Banks:* Saturday to Wednesday, 8 a.m.–Midday. Thursdays, 8 a.m.–11 a.m. *Offices:* Saturday to Wednesday, 7 a.m.–1 p.m. and 4p.m.–7.30 p.m. Thursdays, 7 a.m.–Midday.

Driving licence: International and national driving licences accepted

Climate: Very hot, low rainfall

Health: No certificates required

Visas and passports: Nationals of other Gulf states and Britain do not need visas, but all other nationals do. Passports are required by all.

Customs: There are no restrictions on the import or export of foreign currency. You can import up to 2,000 cigarettes or 2 kg of tobacco. Alcohol prohibited.

Airports: Abu Dhabi International, 21 miles out of Abu Dhabi. No departure tax. Bureaux de change open 24 hours.

Dubai International, three miles out of Dubai. No departure tax. Bureaux de change open 24 hours.

Sharjah, six miles out of Sharjah. No departure tax. Bureaux de change open 24 hours.

Background

Dubai is the most vibrant city in the Gulf. In 1793 the Bani Yas, ancestors of the modern ruling families of Dubai, moved into the area from the desert. A general peace was imposed on the Gulf tribes by the British navy during the nineteenth century, but the area was a backwater, and the few merchants that passed through were mainly Indian and Persian. The discovery of oil changed everything. Concessions began to be granted in the 1930s, but it was not until the 1960s that the surrounding emirates began to grow wealthy. Dubai is the second richest state in the United Arab Emirates after Abu Dhabi, but its prosperity derives from trade, not oil. Though not in the strict sense an offshore finance centre, Dubai is the leading trading centre of the Middle East. Its own markets are small, but its position gives it a strategic importance, and Dubai is seen as a key location by the international financial services business. Dubai is one of the seven emirates comprising the United Arab Emirates; the ruler of each emirate is sovereign in his own territory, but there is also a federal government presided over by Sheikh Zayed of Abu Dhabi. Dubai is the most resistant of all the emirates to further integration.

Economy

Despite a population of only half a million, Dubai's annual imports exceed US$10 billion; Dubai is the major re-export centre for the region and some 70 per cent of goods are re-exported. There is great demand for all kinds of foodstuffs, high-tech equipment and luxury products. Dubai is also a gateway to the poorer but more densely populated markets of India, Pakistan, Iran and East Africa.

Offshore companies

Dubai welcomes outsiders and there are many thousands of expatriates in the region, drawn by a booming economy and no income taxes. Dubai is a

GAZETTEER

free market, and there are no exchange controls, quotas or trade barriers. Import duties are very low and many products are exempt. The country is free of exchange controls. To form a company there are two options; onshore in Dubai city itself under the regulations of the municipality and the UAE federal government, or offshore under the regulations of the Jebel Ali free zone.

- Onshore companies can operate through various structures ranging from setting up a representative or branch office to establishing a limited company with majority share ownership by UAE nationals.

- The main requirement for any type of business in Dubai is a municipality licence. These come in three major categories – trade, professional and industrial. A service agent or partner can help with the necessary procedures to have this licence processed by the authorities. Once issued it is the passport to securing all essential permissions for doing business in Dubai including renting premises and securing visas for staff.

HONG KONG

Essential information

South China coast

Capital: Victoria

Language: Cantonese, English

Telephone code: 852

Voltage: 200 volts AC 50 Hz

Time: GMT +8 hours

Currency: Hong Kong dollar (HKD), 100 cents to the dollar. HKD notes are denominated as 10, 20, 50, 100, 500 and 1,000.

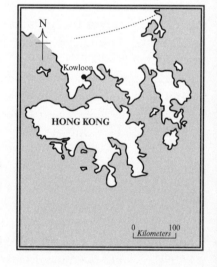

Office hours: *Banks:* Monday to Friday, 9 a.m.–4.30 p.m. Saturdays, 9 a.m.– Midday. *Offices:* Monday to Friday, 9 a.m.–5 p.m. Saturdays, 9 a.m.–12.30 a.m.

Credit cards: Major credit cards and travellers' cheques are widely accepted

Driving licence: International licences required

Climate: Subtropical. Rainy from May to September

Health: No certificates required

Visas and passports: Visas are required for everyone except UK nationals, citizens of Commonwealth countries. Passports must be carried by all.

Customs: There are no restrictions on the import and export of foreign currency. You can import up to 200 cigarettes or 50 cigars and 1 litre of spirits.

Airport: Hong Kong International, three miles out of Kowloon. Departure tax HKD 150. Bureaux de change open 8.30 a.m.–4.30 p.m.

History

The earliest inhabitants of Hong Kong are believed to have been of Chinese origin, migrating towards Indonesia and the Philippines in the second millenium BC. Settled by various Chinese people, Hong Kong became a pirate base for many centuries. The Ming dynasty had its last stand here against the Manchus in the seventeenth century. The British began to use the harbour in the early nineteenth century and launched the first Opium War from Hong Kong in 1839. Realizing its strategic value, the British obtained the island in perpetuity from China in the Treaty of Nanking 1842. The Kowloon peninsula, on the mainland opposite Hong Kong, was a constant source of danger, and in 1860 Britain took possession of it, extended its dominion over other areas of the mainland and some islands collectively known as the New Territories, which were leased for 99 years from China in 1898.

After the overthrow of the Manchus and the foundation of the Chinese Republic in 1911, Hong Kong became a place of refuge for many Chinese. Relations improved in the 1930s when Japan invaded Manchuria, but in 1941 the Japanese captured the colony after bitter fighting. Hong Kong was liberated by the British in 1945 and has prospered enormously in the post-war period. A joint declaration made by Britain and China in 1985 stated that all of Hong Kong would become a special administrative area of China after 1997 (when the New Territories lease expired). China promises to maintain the capitalist system in Hong Kong for at least 50 years.

Geography

The area of Hong Kong is 400 square miles, of which Hong Kong island itself has only 29 square miles. The island is only one mile from Kowloon at its closest point. The climate is subtropical, with monsoon seasons in winter and summer.

GAZETTEER

People and language

The vast majority of the population of six million are Chinese. Most of these are from Kwangtung. Many Chinese languages and dialects are spoken, but Cantonese is universally understood and English is spoken in business. Chinese and English are the official languages.

Doubt following the handover

In the sections below you will find information relating to the rules prior to the 1997 handover of Hong Kong to China. At the time of writing (August 1997) it is unclear whether these rules will remain in operation for long. For this reason, it is plainly unwise to initiate any kind of long-term plan based on the use of Hong Kong companies or trusts which could be overturned by a Chinese government in the future.

Hong Kong's current situation perfectly illustrates the need for flexible, international strategies when operating offshore; when one regime falls, an investor must be able to get out quickly before the new incumbents can move the goalposts.

Economy

With few natural resources, Hong Kong relies on commerce and manufacturing for its prosperity. Opinion is divided over the future of Hong Kong, but if China's promises hold good, Hong Kong's way of life will remain intact until 2047 and it will continue to be a major international centre. The Sino-British joint declaration provides for the retention of the English common law system, the free movement to and from Hong Kong of people, goods and capital, a freely convertible Hong Kong dollar and Hong Kong's autonomy in external commercial relations. Those who believe that China will keep its word make the following points:

- Communist China is accepting features of capitalism, especially in the south of the country, where Hong Kong companies have become big employers.
- China has stock exchanges in Shanghai and Shenzen.
- China wants to develop, and must keep Hong Kong open for business to accelerate the process.

The risks for residents are enormous, however, and Hong Kong nationals have taken steps to acquire dual nationality and spread assets across the world. Some are distrustful of the Beijing government, citing the Tiananmen Square massacre in 1989. China has conducted a campaign of vilification against the Hong Kong Governor Chris Patten after he proposed democratic reforms in 1992.

Companies

Hong Kong is the world's tenth largest trading economy, and is a popular domicile for company incorporation in the Far East. The main features of company operation include;

- No exchange controls.
- No minimum capital required.
- Public companies can issue bearer shares.
- Companies must have a minimum of two shareholders.
- Annually audited accounts must be filed.
- Companies are only taxed on income earned in Hong Kong; the current rate is 16.5 per cent.

Most companies incorporated in Hong Kong are for commercial use within the territory so Hong Kong offshore companies are not generally regarded as tax avoidance vehicles by other countries' authorities.
Types of company include:

1. *Trading companies.* These are often used by non-residents who use Hong Kong's facilities to trade with China. The company may receive a commission for the trading, or it may trade in its own right so that the ultimate importing company in a high-tax area can open a transferable letter of credit in favour of the Hong Kong company and that company can arrange a partial transfer of credit to the manufacturer. If purchases and sales are negotiated and concluded outside the Hong Kong, the company can still maintain banking facilities and process its shipping documentation within the territory without it being regarded as having Hong Kong source income.

2. *Administration companies.* These are used as regional headquarters or for administration by international companies, and pay tax on a nominal part of profits. Over 1,300 international businesses have administration companies in Hong Kong.

3. *Holding companies.* Hong Kong imposes no Capital Gains Tax, so companies can sell their subsidiaries for gain; dividends received from subsidiaries are not assessed for Hong Kong tax.

4. *Licensing companies.* These can be used to shift profits on intellectual property into Hong Kong's low-tax environment.

GAZETTEER

Double-taxation treaties

Hong Kong has a double-taxation treaty with the US limited to shipping. There are no withholding taxes. Individuals' salaries are taxed between 2 per cent and 25 per cent after allowances, or at a flat rate of 15 per cent of gross salary, whichever produces the lower liability.

Trusts

As a common law jurisdiction, Hong Kong recognizes trusts. They need not be registered and are not subject to tax.

LABUAN (MALAYSIA)

History

The island of Labuan was ceded to the British by the Sultan of Brunei in 1846 so that they could use it as a base from which to operate against pirates. It became a British Crown Colony in 1848. Between 1890 and 1906 is was administered by North Borneo, and in 1946 it became part of the colony of North Borneo, now called the state of Sabah and part of Malaysia. Labuan's main town, Victoria, was demolished during the war, but has been rebuilt. In the early sixties there was a period of serious confrontation between

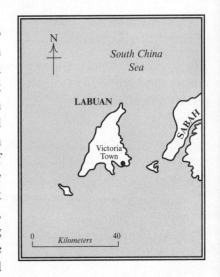

Indonesia, under Sukarno, and Malaysia, and Labuan became the headquarters of the Commonwealth defence forces.

Geography

Labuan island lies at the mouth of Brunei Bay opposite Sabah and faces the South China Sea. It covers 38 square miles and has a deep natural harbour. The flight from Kuala Lumpur takes about two hours and there are daily flights. The climate is tropical and rainfall is heaviest in the monsoon periods from April to June and from September to December. The island has beautiful beaches and a rich flora and fauna.

People

More than 60 per cent of the 54,000 population are Malays, the rest being mainly Chinese. English is widely spoken.

Government

The Labuan Federal Territory is an administrative area directly governed by Malaysia. Malaysia was created out of an amalgamation in 1963 of four former colonies: Malaya, Sarawak, North Borneo and Singapore. In 1965 Singapore seceded to become an independent state. Labuan has one member in the Malaysian House of Representatives. Malaysia itself is a constitutional monarchy, and the federal government legislates except where Islamic or native laws still prevail. It consists of nine states governed by hereditary rulers and four states headed by appointed governors. Malaysia has a senate and house of representatives. The press is privately owned but heavily restricted.

Economy

Labuan's main town, Victoria, is a freeport and the chief transhipment point for Brunei and Northern Sarawak. Low lying and well cultivated, its main agricultural products are rubber, copra and sago. Its airport is currently only served by Malaysian airlines. The only multistorey office and commercial complex in Labuan is the 11-storey Wisma Oceanic. This houses Bank Negara (the central bank), the Registrar of Companies and the Department of Inland Revenue, as well as five offshore banks and two offshore insurance companies. A financial park is under construction. In 1989 the Malaysian government declared Labuan to be an international offshore financial centre in order to diversify, widen and strengthen Malaysia's financial system. Progress has been modest, although about 90 offshore companies are incorporated or registered in Labuan. These comprise eight offshore banks including Mitsubishi, Hong Kong and Shanghai and Standard Chartered, two offshore insurance companies and 80 offshore entities. They operate in areas such as trading, asset management, investment holding and financial consultancy. Improving the infrastructure is Labuan's main priority, and progress is accelerating rapidly.

Offshore companies

Companies formed under the Malaysian Companies Act are not treated as offshore companies. To enjoy offshore status, a company must be incorporated under the Offshore Companies Act of 1990. There are two types:

GAZETTEER

1 The offshore company.

2 The foreign offshore company.

The main features of these companies are:

- A minimum of two shareholders.

- Except for Malaysian banks, insurance companies and certain Islamic banks, shareholders may not be Malaysian.

- A registered office in Labuan is required.

- A company must have a minimum of one director and a secretary who is an officer of a trust company.

- Except for banks and insurance companies, companies need not file audited accounts, but they must submit an annual return.

- Taxation is 3 per cent of net profits or RM20,000 a year.

- There are no foreign currency restrictions for offshore companies.

- Companies may buy assets in Labuan.

- Companies classified as 'non-trading', meaning that they simply hold assets and investments, pay no tax, and must submit an annual declaration to that effect.

Tax

Residents of Labuan are taxed on income generated in Malaysia or brought into the country. Rates vary from 4 to 35 per cent, while non-residents pay 35 per cent. Expatriate employees of offshore companies are exempt, until 1997, of tax on half of their salary. Royalties paid by one offshore company to another or to a non-resident individual are not subject to withholding taxes, and nor, in most cases, is interest paid in the same circumstances. There are no customs and excise duties on petroleum products.

Banks and insurance companies

The regulatory regime for offshore banks operating in Labuan is generally liberal and relaxed. However, the Malaysian Ministry of Finance says that entry will be strictly controlled to ensure that only reputable international banks operate there. The Banking and Financial Institution Act of 1989 and the Islamic Banking Act of 1983 which regulate financial institutions in Malaysia do not apply to offshore banks operating in Labuan. The Offshore Insurance Act of 1990 legislates on the licensing and regulation of captive and direct insurance, reinsurance and related activities such as underwriting and broking.

Offshore trusts

Under the Labuan Trusts Act 1990, trusts are recognized, and need not be registered to have full force. They may hold shares in offshore companies.

LIBERIA

Essential information

West African country

Capital: Monrovia

Language: English, Krou, Bassa, Kpelle

Telephone code: 231

Voltage: 110 volts AC 60 Herz

Time: GMT

Currency: Liberian dollar (LRD), 100 cents to the dollar; US dollars in notes are used since LRDs do not circulate in note form.

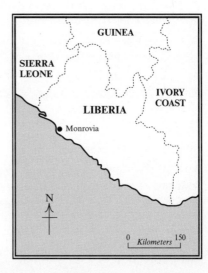

Office hours: *Banks:* Monday to Thursday, 9 a.m.–Midday, Fridays, 8 a.m.–2 p.m. *Offices:* Monday to Friday, 8 a.m.–Midday and 2 p.m.–4 p.m. *Shops:* Monday to Saturday, 8 a.m.–1 p.m. and 3 p.m.–6 p.m.

Driving licence: Temporary licences issued on presentation of national driving licences

Climate: Tropical

Health: Yellow fever certificate required by all. Risk of malaria, polio and typhoid.

Visas and passports: Visas are not required by nationals of many African countries. Passports are required by all.

Customs: There are no restrictions on the import or export of foreign currency.

Airport: Roberts International, 36 miles from Monrovia. Departure tax LRD20.

History

French settlers operated settlements on what is now the coast of Liberia between 1364 and 1413, but little is known of their history. In 1461 the country was explored by the Portuguese Pedro de Cintra, and remained under Portuguese domination for over a century. The main trade was in gold, slaves and pepper. Other colonial powers moved in in the seventeenth century, and in the 1800s both France and Sweden considered colonizing the area. With the abolition of slavery, Cape Mesurado, part of Liberia was chosen as a location for repatriated ex-American slaves, but the numbers that went were small and there were conflicts with the indigenous tribes. Liberia became independent in 1847. Border disputes followed with the Ivory Coast and Sierra Leone which were resolved in the late nineteenth century. Some slave trading apparently continued until 1931.

Geography

Liberia is a plateau with dense forests and has an abundance of West African flora and fauna. Coconut, rubber and oil palm trees grow widely. Although the country has many rivers, only one, the Cavalla, is navigable from the sea for any distance because of rapids.

People and language

The population of over two and a half million are mainly descended from the indigenous peoples. Many African languages are spoken, but English is the official language.

Government and legal system

The government is a republic, modelled on that of the US. It has a House of Representatives and a Senate. Only black Africans can become citizens. The judiciary is independent, and modelled on the US system.

Economy

Rubber and iron ore are the main sources of foreign currency, and many other commodities are also exported. As the main 'flag of convenience' country, Liberia's shipping industry is also important.

Shipping

Many of the major shipping operations use vessels registered in Liberia, and any kinds of ships or boats can be registered. Vessels must be owned by a Liberian company, but this can be non-resident and exempt of tax.

Offshore companies

Companies are quick to form and cheap to run:

- Bearer shares are allowed.
- There is a minimum of one shareholder.
- A registered office in Liberia is not required.
- Non-resident companies need not file annually audited accounts.
- Non-resident companies are not subject to tax.

Double-taxation treaties

Liberia has double-taxation treaties with Canada, Sweden and Germany. There are no exchange controls.

Trusts

As a common law jurisdiction, Liberia recognizes trusts. Non-resident trusts are not subject to tax.

MAURITIUS

Essential information

Island in the Indian Ocean

Capital: Port Louis

Language: English, French, Creole

Telephone code: 230

Voltage: 220/240 volts AC 50 Hz

Time: GMT +4 hours

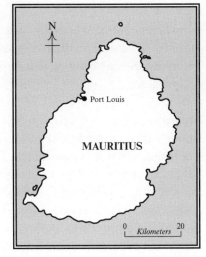

Currency: Mauritius Rupee (MUR), 100 cents to the rupee. MUR notes are denominated as 5, 10, 20, 50, 100, 200, 500 and 1,000.

Office hours: *Banks:* Monday to Friday, 9.30 a.m.–2.30 p.m. Saturdays, 9.30 a.m.–11 a.m. *Offices:* Monday to Friday, 9 a.m.–4 p.m. Saturdays, 9 a.m. –Midday.

Credit cards: Major credit cards and travellers' cheques are widely accepted

Driving licence: International and national driving licences accepted

Climate: Tropical

Health: Yellow fever certificate required if coming from an infected area within six days. Danger of malaria

Visas and passports: Visas not required for stays of up to 90 days by nationals of many countries. Passports are required for everyone.

Customs: There are no restrictions on the import of foreign currency provided that it is declared on arrival; you can export up to the amount you declared on importation. You can import up to 200 cigarettes or 50 cigars, 1 litre of spirits and 2 litres of wine.

Airport: Sir Seewoosagur Ramgoolam International, 30 miles out of Saint Louis. Departure tax MUR 100.

History

Probably visited by Arab and Malay traders in the Middle Ages, Mauritius was 'discovered' in the early 1500s by Portuguese explorers. The Portuguese set up no settlements on the island, and the Dutch took possession of it in 1598; never numbering more than a few hundred on the island, the Dutch finally abandoned it in 1710, having exploited the island's forests of ebony and introduced sugar cane, cotton and domestic animals. In 1715 France claimed Mauritius, calling it Ile de France, and it was governed by the French East India Company until 1767, when the French government took over direct control. The island prospered economically, and the production of cloves, nutmeg and other high-value spices was introduced.

During the war between Britain and France in the early 1800s, Mauritius became a serious threat to British merchant shipping, and Britain captured it in 1810. Under the Treaty of Paris in 1814 the islanders were allowed to keep their own laws, religion and customs, and thus the culture of the island remains partly French to this day, while its name reverted to Mauritius, given it by the Dutch. Following the emancipation of slaves in 1834, labourers from India were brought in to work on the plantations, and the island has continued to prosper ever since as a major sugar producer, despite many natural catastrophes, such as pests and drought. Following World War 2, the British recognized the inevitability of self-government, and Mauritius finally achieved independence in 1968, becoming a member state of the British Commonwealth.

Geography

Formed by volcanoes aeons ago, Mauritius has always been an oceanic island, not linked to any continent, and thus boasts unusual fauna – the most famous of which is the extinct dodo, a flightless bird. The island's vegetation consists mainly of species introduced since colonization; the ebony forests have all but disappeared, and in their place are sugar cane plantations and heathland. The island is surrounded by a coral reef. Mauritius also possesses several tiny islands scattered across the Indian Ocean, which means that its territorial waters are surprisingly large.

Climate
The south-east trade winds reach Mauritius between April and November, producing mild, sometimes chilly, weather. For the rest of the year the weather is very hot and humid, with the occasional cyclone. Rain is possible at all times of the year.

People
The one million or so people of Mauritius are all immigrants or the descendants of immigrants. Some two-thirds are Indian, the majority of which derive from the northern Indian state of Bihar. About a quarter of the population are of Creole (mixed) descent from African, Indian and European parentage, about 3 per cent are Chinese and 2 per cent French. English is the official language, but French, several Indian languages and Chinese dialects are spoken. Creole, a French-based patois, is understood by most people. Very few traces of African culture remain among the people, but Hinduism, Islam and Roman Catholicism coexist peacefully. Literacy is high (claimed to be over 95 per cent) and education is compulsory up to the age of 11.

Government
Mauritius became a republic on 12 March 1992. Its constitution is based on Westminster's, and the legal, executive and judicial powers are kept separate. The Mauritian National Assembly has 70 members, 62 of whom are elected. The head of state and commander-in-chief is the President, whose role is similar to that of the Governor-General when Mauritius was a colony. The prime minister is the chief executive of the government.

Legal system
As mentioned earlier, Mauritius has a legal system based on both English and French law. Company law, criminal and civil litigation is basically English, while substantive law is based on the Napoleonic Code. The highest court of appeal is the Judicial Committee of the Privy Council in the UK.

Economy

Sugar is still Mauritius' main way of earning foreign currency, but is closely followed by the export of manufactured products through the island's Export Processing Zones (EPZ), which were founded in 1970. Tourism is also an important source of funds. The Mauritian economy is said to be growing at an average of 6 per cent per annum. The government is keen to continue healthy growth by the development of its stock exchange and off-shore business centre. In 1991 monetary policy was relaxed, liberalizing interest rates, capital movements and limits on bank credit. The stock market was created in 1989, consisting of an official market, and over-the-counter market and a debt securities market. Mauritius is a GATT signatory, and has trade agreements with various countries, including:

1. *The Lomé Convention* – this treaty promotes trade co-operation between the EU and various developing nations. The EU guarantees free access to the majority of Mauritian goods and exemption from duty. Under the special Sugar Protocol, Mauritian sugar is promised free access to the EU indefinitely.

2. *The Preferential Trade Agreement* – this is a mutual help treaty between countries in Africa and the Indian Ocean. Mauritian exports to PTA countries are significant.

Mauritius is keen to expand its economy, and there are a number of tax break schemes for industrial investment, including the Export Enterprise (EE) Scheme which gives exemption from import levies and customs duties on machinery and equipment. Corporation tax is at 15 per cent, imports of raw materials and components are tax free; dividends are exempt from income tax for the first 20 years and foreign investors may repatriate their investment without capital transfer tax or prior approval of the central bank.

The incentives for high-tech companies include 15 per cent corporate tax rate for the first 10 years, tax exempt dividends for 10 years, exemption from tax on visiting staff, and a 50 per cent tax credit for two expatriate staff.

Shipping

Shipping is an important activity on the island, and Mauritius' rules offer some possibilities for the entrepreneur. A ship may be registered as Mauritian if it is wholly owned by a Mauritian national, or by a company registered in Mauritius. A ship can be registered as Mauritian in a port out-side the country, in which case it would receive a temporary (six months) certificate. Ships can be used as collateral for loans. It is possible for a ship to have a parallel (i.e. dual) registration with Mauritius and another country.

The island offers incentives to shipping companies, including exemption from income tax for:

- owners of foreign vessels
- owners of local vessels operating outside Mauritian territorial waters
- dividends paid to shareholders not resident on the island on profits made from operating foreign vessels
- sailors.

There is no duty on ship's stores or consumables, and no work permit is necessary for people working on a Mauritian vessel.

Freeports

Freeport zones have been set up at Port Louis and the airport. They are defined as not being areas within Mauritian territory and are used principally for the warehousing, processing and assembly of goods. Operations within a freeport require a licence, and are exempted from duty, import levies and Sales Tax on goods destined for re-export. Licensees are also exempted from Income Tax.

Offshore companies

The Mauritius Offshore Business Activities Authority (MOBAA) regulates most offshore business activities with the exception of banking, which is governed by the island's central bank. MOBAA grants offshore certificates to companies and trusts, and is the body through which all official applications are made. Offshore business can be conducted by companies or trusts, exclusively with non-residents, and in foreign currencies. Attractive exemptions include:

- Documents are not available for public inspection.
- A notarized deed is not necessary for the registration of a company.
- No requirements on the nationality of a director.
- Annual returns are not required.
- Offshore companies are exempt from most state duties, levies and charges.

Offshore companies are forbidden to:

- hold land or buildings in Mauritius.
- have an account in a domestic Mauritian bank, except for day-to-day transactions.

GAZETTEER

- hold shares, debentures or interests in companies in Mauritius other than foreign companies, offshore companies or offshore trusts.

Since December 1992, well over 1,000 offshore companies have been registered. Two kinds of offshore company are allowed, the international company (see below) and the ordinary offshore company. This latter obtains the benefits of double-taxation treaties by getting a tax residence certificate. Offshore companies, which must have some management actually in Mauritius, take on average 15 days to incorporate. Tax certificates are granted by MOBAA on a case-by-case basis. A US$1,500 fee is payable to the government on registration. Full incorporation costs including a tax certificate should be around US$3,000. Ordinary status companies must declare beneficial ownership, provide bank references and declare the origin of company funds. The annual licence fee payable to the authority is US$250 for an exempt company and US$1,500 for an ordinary one.

Double-taxation treaties

Mauritius currently has double-taxation treaties with the UK, France, Germany, India and South Africa. Treaties have been signed, but not yet ratified, with Italy, Sweden, Malaysia and Zimbabwe. Treaties with other countries are in the process of being negotiated. Key points of the UK/Mauritius treaty include:

- A Mauritius company controlling 10 per cent or more of the voting rights in a UK company is not liable to UK tax.
- A Mauritius resident who is entitled to the tax credit that a UK resident would be in the same situation is taxable at only 15 per cent on dividends and tax credits received from the UK company.
- A UK company which controls 10 per cent or more of the voting rights of a Mauritian company is taxable at only 10 per cent on the dividend received.
- In any other case, dividends are taxable at 15 per cent.

Mauritius soaked up much of the deluge of international cash rushing into India's liberalizing economy, and by the middle of last year its seven offshore banks had assets of US$400 million on the island. All this interest is due mainly to the double-taxation agreement between Mauritius and India. By employing a Mauritian offshore company, investors can avoid India's 45 per cent Capital Gains Tax and pay 5 per cent withholding tax on dividends rather than 20 per cent. Currently, the growth areas are non-resident Indians and companies who are setting up ventures in India.

International companies

The International Companies Act (1994) provides a separate regime for international business activities carried out in foreign currencies. Excluded activities are:

- Banking and insurance.
- Investment funds.
- Nominee and trust services.

International companies (ICs) are not regarded as tax-resident in Mauritius. Shareholders must also be non-resident. The main points for ICs are:

- A single shareholder and a single director are permitted.
- An IC must have a registered office and a registered agent (which may be a bank or offshore company) in Mauritius.
- An IC can be continued in another jurisdiction.
- The life of an IC can be limited to 50 years, then make further extensions up to a total of 150 years.
- ICs are exempted from duties, taxes and fees and also from exchange controls. There is no requirement to file documentation.
- ICs are exempt from Capital Gains Tax, Income Tax and tax on dividends, royalties, rents, interest and similar payments made to non-residents.
- ICs cannot hold land or buildings in Mauritius.
- ICs cannot have an account in a domestic Mauritian bank, except for day-to-day transactions.
- ICs cannot hold shares, debentures or interests in companies in Mauritius other than foreign companies, offshore companies or offshore trusts.
- ICs can issue bearer shares, and there are few restrictions on types of shares or their denominations.

International companies can be bought off the shelf – it costs about US$500 to set one up, plus a US$100 fee to the MOBAA. Annual fees are between US$850 and US$1700.

Offshore trusts

Offshore trusts must be registered with the MOBAA. To be operative, such a trust must:

- have a settlor who is non-resident during the life of the trust.
- have no property in Mauritius, or any shares, debentures or interests in local companies.
- have two trustees, if individuals, one of whom must be a Mauritian resident, or a single trustee who is an offshore bank or a recognized offshore company.

The chargeable income of a trust is the difference between its income from investments and its management expenses and distributions to beneficiaries. The chargeable income is taxed at 0 per cent, but a trustee can opt to pay up to 35 per cent tax. Non-resident beneficiaries pay no income tax on dividends. Only a handful of trusts have been formed after the introduction of the Offshore Trusts Act 1992; asset protection trusts are not allowed. A creditor has two years from the formation of a trust in which to challenge it. Formation fees are US$1,000, plus around US$1,250 in annual fees.

Offshore banks

Any bank, insurance company or manager handling third party funds must set up as an offshore company under Mauritian law. The company must file fully audited accounts with MOBAA and have at least two directors and two shareholders. Offshore banks can be licensed to conduct banking business with non-residents in foreign currencies, including:

- Offshore fund management and advisory services.
- Trusteeship of offshore trusts.
- Offshore lending.

Such banks must hold net free assets, and must have capital or paid-up capital of not less than MUR25 million, but this capital need not be domiciled in Mauritius. Secrecy is provided for. Offshore bans are exempt from exchange controls and state taxes and duties. Income tax is 0 per cent, but banks can choose to pay up to 35 per cent tax if they wish. Some seven banks have so far been given licences; these are:

- Barclays Bank
- the Hong Kong and Shanghai Banking Corporation
- State Bank International (a joint venture between the State Bank of India and the State Bank of Mauritius)
- Bank of Baroda

- Banque Internationale des Mascareignes (a joint venture between the Mauritius Commercial Bank and Credit Lyonnais)
- Banque Internationale de Paris Intercontinentale
- Banque Privée Edmond de Rothschild (Ocean Indien).

Comment

The Indian Ocean island of Mauritius has achieved remarkable economic growth by Western standards, and its success seems likely to continue. Mauritius is a harmonious, multiracial society and in spite of its colonial origins, its culture is Indian rather than Western. The island possesses a highly sophisticated infrastructure in an environment of sun, sea and sand. The largest bank was established more than 150 years ago. The country has a busy network of banks and insurance companies, and boasts hundreds of accountants, lawyers and other graduates from the local and overseas universities. There is no Capital Gains Tax except on certain sales of land and no Inheritance Tax. Income Tax is payable up to a top rate of 30 per cent, and there is a Gift Tax ranging from 12.5 to 45 per cent. No disclosure of beneficial ownership is required for exempt companies and there is therefore total anonymity.

URUGUAY

Essential information

South American country

Capital: Montevideo

Language: Spanish

Telephone code: 598

Voltage: 220V 50 Hertz AC

Time: GMT –3 hours

Currency: New Uruguayan peso (UYP), 100 centimos to the peso. Notes are denominated as 50, 100, 500, 100, 5,000 and 10,000 pesos.

Office hours: *Banks:* Monday to Friday, 1 p.m.–5 p.m. *Offices:* Monday to Friday, 8.30 a.m.–12 a.m. and 2.30 p.m.–6.30 p.m. *Shops:* Monday to Friday, 9 a.m.–12 a.m. and 2 p.m.–7 p.m., Saturdays, 9 a.m.–12.30 a.m.

Driving licence: International licences must be obtained locally

Climate: Temperate

Health: No certificates required

Visas and passports: Visas are not required for many nationals. Passports are required by all.

Customs: There are no restrictions on the import or export of foreign currency.

History

The region was explored by Juan Días de Solis in 1516, but with few minerals, Uruguay was not settled until 1680 by the Portuguese. The Spanish followed, and a long struggle between the two powers ensued. Occupied by Britain in 1807, it was returned to Spain, but in 1811 a war of independence began, and in 1828 Uruguay became an independent state. The rivalry between the Spanish and the Portuguese was continued by that of Argentina and Brazil over the country, which was torn by civil strife until 1870. A succession of military regimes followed, culminating in a civil war in 1904. Political problems have come and gone over this century, largely following the periodic economic crises.

Geography

With an area of 72,000 square miles, Uruguay is the smallest country in South America. A land of plains and plateaus, it has a temperate climate and is mainly covered by prairie grasses.

People

The population is about three million, most of whom live in towns and cities. The official language is Spanish, but English is widely understood.

Government

Uruguay is a republic with a democratically elected government. The two main parties, traditional rivals since the last century, are the Colorados and the Blancos.

Companies

The type of company most often used by offshore investors is the Foreign Investment Corporation (SAFI). Some of the conditions applied to them are as follows:

- They must not do business within Uruguay.
- Bearer shares are allowed.
- Founders of SAFIs need not be the beneficial owners.
- There is a minimum of one director, who can be non-resident.
- Annually audited accounts are required.
- They cannot be listed on local stock markets.
- They must not bring more than 5 per cent of their paid-up capital and reserves into the country each year.

Double-taxation treaties
There are no double-taxation treaties. There is no income tax on individuals. Dividends to non-residents are subject to a 30 per cent withholding tax.

Trusts
Although it is a civil law country, Uruguay recognizes foreign trusts.

VANUATU

Essential information
South Pacific islands

Capital: Port Vila

Language: French, English, Pidgin

Telephone code: 678

Voltage: 240 volts AC 50 Hz

Time: GMT –11 hours

Currency: Vatu (VUV), 100 centimes to the vatu. Vatus are denomiated as 100, 500 and 1,000.

Office hours: *Banks:* Monday to Friday, 8 a.m.–3 p.m. *Shops:* Monday to Friday, 7.30 a.m.–11.30 a.m. and 2 p.m.–5 p.m. Saturdays, 7.30 a.m.–11 a.m.

Driving licence: National driving licences accepted

Climate: Tropical

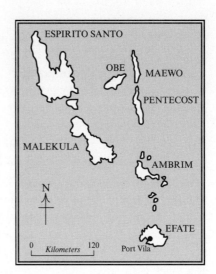

293

Health: No certificates required

Visas and passports: Visas are not required by nationals of many countries. Passports are required by all.

Customs: There are no restrictions on the import or export of foreign currency. You can import up to 200 cigarettes or 50 cigars and 1.5 litres of spirits and 2 litres of wine.

History

Known as the New Hebrides until independence, Vanuatu was discovered by Captain Cook in 1774. The islands had been populated since prehistoric times by a succession of peoples, and by the time of the European discovery the inhabitants consisted of cannibal tribes, constantly at war with one another. The islands had been visited by Portuguese and French explorers before Cook, but it was not until the 1820s that they began to be exploited commercially; the sandalwood forests, then growing widely on some islands, were cut down for the Chinese market, and had disappeared from the archipelago by 1868. Next came 'blackbirding', the practice of abducting islanders for long periods of forced labour elsewhere. This nefarious practice was resisted by Presbyterian missionaries, who had established themselves as the dominant Christian sect on the islands.

European diseases killed 90 per cent of the islanders during the nineteenth century; from a population estimated at one million in the first half of the century, only some 100,000 remained by 1900, and by 1935 the numbers had halved again. In 1853 France annexed the neighbouring islands of New Caledonia, and the Presbyterian Church lobbied the British parliament to declare the New Hebrides a protectorate; this was rejected, however, on the grounds of cost and unprofitability.

The British settlers on the islands fell into a decline, and in 1882 an Irishman, John Higginson, was able to purchase a fifth of the cultivable land on the islands within a period of weeks. By 1905 his company, Société Francaise des Nouvelles Hebrides (SFNH), owned 55 per cent of the cultivable land. The French now outnumbered the British, and an intense rivalry developed amidst an atmosphere of lawlessness. An Anglo-French condominium was set up in 1906 in order to deal with this, it being agreed that British and French settlers would retain citizenship of their respective countries with equal rights, leaving the indigenous population stateless. A joint court was established to govern the island, with one French, one British and one neutral judge. Under the condominium's ineffective rule cannibalism survived until the 1960s and the opium trade until the 1940s. Occupied by the US military during World War 2, the islands received a huge economic boost, and a large number of cargo cults grew up, one of which, the Jon Frum cult, survives as an important force to this day. Vanuatu achieved independence in 1980, following extreme unrest and attempts at secession by some areas.

Geography

The islands are volcanic, and are still rising at the rate of a millimetre every two years. There are seven active volcanoes on land and two under the sea. The archipelago extends for over 620 miles, and lies some 105 miles from the Solomon Islands, to the north, and 142 miles from New Caledonia to the south-west. Vanuatu has some 14 large islands, and another 60 smaller ones which are inhabited. Including all islets and rocks, Vanuatu has some 344 islands in total. Marine life is abundant, and many of the islands are still covered by rain forest, boasting many rare species, including 40 kinds of orchid.

Climate

The northern islands of Vanuatu are tropical, while the southern ones are subtropical. The dry season is from May to October and this is the time considered best for visitors. The summer is from November to April, and is humid with heavy showers. Humidity is highest in the early mornings, and during the summer temperatures average 30°C. There is an average of one cyclone a year; Cyclone Uma caused widespread damage to buildings at Port Vila, the capital, in 1987.

People

The people of Vanuatu are ethnically diverse: there are Melanesians (94 per cent) who are the indigenous people; Polynesians, who came from other Pacific territories belonging to France; Europeans, who live mainly at Port Vila and Luganville; and Chinese. The population now stands at 155,000, but the birth rate is one of the highest in the world. Education is in either English or French, while many islanders also speak a form of pidgin English called Bislama. About 90 per cent of the islanders receive primary education, but few go on to further education and adult literacy is about 60 per cent. Traditional ideas about property ownership mean that outsiders can only lease land for 75 years. Disputes are common. Pagan beliefs surrounding sorcery and taboos are common and many traditional beliefs and practices survive. About 84 per cent of the inhabitants are Christian, however, and there is a church in every village.

Government

Vanuatu is a republic, achieving independence from France and the UK in 1980. It is a member of the United Nations, the Commonwealth and the South Pacific Commission. It has a parliament with 46 members based on the Westminster system. The legal system is based on British law, with a lower level system of six island courts presided over by tribal chiefs. Unlike many Third World countries, Vanuatu has only 1.7 per cent of the population working in the public sector, half the Third World average. Port Vila, the capital, is the financial centre and the seat of government. In the constitution it is stated that British and French laws will continue unless the parliament alters them.

Economy

About 15 per cent of Vanuatu's population of 150,000 live in Port Vila. The economy is based on subsistence farming; raising coconut plantations for copra is the only commercial activity in many areas. Government revenue is raised from import and export duties, airport tax, and a tourist tax on restaurant and hotel charges, but the greatest earner of foreign exchange is still agriculture: copra, coffee and cocoa being the principal cash crops, followed by the export of frozen beef. This dependence on commodities makes the economy vulnerable to the fluctuations in world prices. Few mineral deposits have been found, and there is little manufacturing. Tourism is becoming increasingly important, the majority of it coming from Australia and New Zealand. An offshore financial centre was established at Port Vila in the 1970s, and is attractive because there is no income tax on individuals or companies. Flights from Sydney take about three and a half hours. There are about 100 offshore banks in Vanuatu and 900 offshore companies. Captive insurance is a small but significant business.

Offshore companies

In 1993 Vanuatu introduced an International Companies Act designed to make it competitive with other tax havens such as the British Virgin Islands and the Turks and Caicos Islands. Together with the Companies Act of 1986 and the Vanuatu Banking, Insurance, Stamp Duties and Trust Companies Regulations, these form the basis for the administration of the offshore centre by the Registrar of Companies. The types of business entity are:

1. Partnerships and sole traders. Limited partnerships are available.
2. The local company, used by investors for trading in the islands. These have a memorandum and articles of association, and need permission to

incorporate. Local companies take two weeks to form. Bearer shares are permitted.

3. The exempted company, specifically for banks, insurance companies and trust companies.

4. The international company (IC).

International Companies (ICs)

ICs offer the following benefits:

- Formation costs US$900.

- Annual fees are US$300.

- ICs are exempt of any tax on income, profits, capital gains, distribution, estate gift or stamp duty for 20 years from the registration of the company.

- ICs have a constitution rather than a memorandum and articles of association. They do not have the concept of authorized capital and may be limited by shares, guarantee or both.

- ICs can have their official name in any language.

- Directors need not be named in an IC's constitution.

- Incorporation can be done in a day.

- An IC can do what it likes with its assets as long as it remains solvent.

- An IC need not appoint a company secretary or other officers, nor does it need to hold annual general meetings or file annual returns.

- It can keep its accounts, minutes, registers and records anywhere in the world but they must be brought to Vanuatu if the Registrar of Companies orders it.

- The company must have one or more directors who may reside anywhere in the world.

- It may make loans to directors, subject to a solvency test.

- It may hold meetings anywhere in the world and in any manner as long as the members can hear and recognize each other's voices.

- The company may apply to the Vanuatu court for permission not to recognize shares in the company acquired by force, confiscation, imposition of tax, assessment or other foreign government charge.

- It has all the powers of a natural person, but must have a registered agent in Vanuatu.

- An IC need not issue share certificates, and may issue bearer shares.

- Subject to a test of solvency enshrined in Vanuatu's International Companies Act, an IC may distribute its net assets to its owners or gift them, purchase its own shares and even cancel shares.

The two limitations on ICs are that:

- It may not trade in Vanuatu itself, except with other ICs.
- An IC cannot offer its shares or debentures to the public and may be struck off if it no longer qualifies as an IC.

Trusts

Trusts can be created for people resident anywhere in the world. A trust deed must be in writing and signed by the settlor. It need not be registered, and is not subject to taxes. The perpetuity period is 80 years. A stamp duty, minimum US$75, is payable when it is established.

Tax

Vanuatu has no double-taxation treaties, withholding taxes or any kind of direct taxation on individuals or companies. Exchange controls are absent. Indirect taxes include:

- A 10 per cent Tourist Tax from hotels and restaurants.
- A 15 per cent tax on rental turnover.
- A 5 per cent stamp duty on transfer of a local land lease, and a further 2 per cent on registration.
- Import duties on all imported goods.

Shipping

Vanuatu has a busy shipping industry, with laws based on US maritime law. The shipping register is run in New York, while company formations are done in Vanuatu. Ships can be registered under the Vanuatu flag if they are owned by a Vanuatu company, but exemption can sometimes be granted. Crews can be of any nationality and a ship can be registered without coming to Vanuatu.

Immigration

You can retire to Vanuatu, or go there as an investor or an employee. The length of time that you can stay is linked to the amount of investment. For example, an investment of US$100,000 will let you obtain a three-year residence permit which can be renewed. Retirees must purchase a bond to cover repatriation and medical expenses, and show that they have enough income to live. Permits take about two months to obtain. You can apply for citizenship after being resident for 10 years on the islands. The cost of living is high for those that rely on imported goods. All land belongs to the traditional owners, and leases are generally between 50 and 75 years. Port Vila has some office blocks and a good standard of residential accommodation.

WESTERN SAMOA

Essential information
South Pacific island

Capital: Apia

Language: Samoan, English

Telephone code: 685

Voltage: 240 volts AC 50 Hz

Time: GMT –11 hours

Currency: Tala (WST), 100 Sene to the tala. Talas are denominated as 2, 5, 10, 20, 50 and 100.

Office hours: *Banks:* Monday to Friday, 9 a.m.–3 p.m. Saturdays, 8.30 a.m.–12.30 p.m. *Offices:* Monday to Friday, 8 a.m.–Midday and 1p.m.–4.30 p.m. *Shops:* Monday to Friday, 8 a.m.–Midday and 1.30 p.m.–4.30 p.m. Saturdays, 8 a.m.–12.30 p.m.

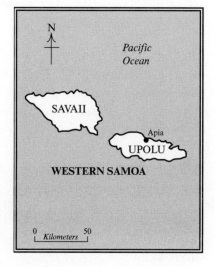

Driving licence: International driving licences accepted

Climate: Tropical

Health: Yellow fever certificate required if arriving from an infected area within six days

Visas and passports: Visas are not required by visitors for up to 30 days. Passports are required by all.

Customs: There are no restrictions on the import or export of foreign currency. You can import up to 200 cigarettes or 50 cigars and 1.5 litres of spirits and 2 litres of wine.

Airport: Faleolo International, 21 miles out of Apia. Departure tax WST20. Bureaux de change open during flying hours.

History

The islands of Samoa were discovered by Europeans in the eighteenth century, although it had been inhabited by Polynesians since about 1000 BC. Germany, Britain and the US all became interested in the islands in the nineteenth century, and in 1899 Britain agreed to withdraw from Samoa in return for rights in Tonga and the Solomon Islands. The US had its main interests in the eastern islands of the archipelago, while the Germans had interests in the western ones, now known as Western Samoa. Germany controlled Western Samoa until World War 1, when, in 1914, New Zealand troops occupied the island. After the war Western Samoa was put under the mandate of New Zealand and in 1947 it became a trust territory by the UN with New Zealand as the administering authority. In 1962 Western Samoa became independent.

Geography

Nine of the islands in the Samoan archipelago make up Western Samoa. Only four are inhabited and all are volcanic. The islands are rocky and there is little level land for agriculture. Rainfall is heavy and there are many hurricanes, but the climate is pleasantly tropical for much of the year.

People

The population of approximately 60,000 people are mainly Polynesian and are closely related to the Maoris and Hawaiians. The official languages are English and Samoan. Most of the people are Christians.

Government

Western Samoa has a single-chamber parliament on British lines at the capital, Apia. Local affairs are governed by officials nominated by the villages. The islands are a common law jurisdiction based on English law.

Economy

There are no minerals, timber or oil on the islands. Agriculture is the biggest foreign currency earner, and the main products are copra, cocoa beans and bananas. After a bad period of high inflation in the 1980s and two serious cyclones in 1990 and 1991 the islands are getting back on their feet and tourism is growing.

Offshore companies

The offshore centre in Western Samoa was set up in 1988 and is based on a legal framework comprising:

- The International Companies Act 1987
- The Offshore Banking Act 1987
- The International Trusts Act 1987
- The Trustee Companies Act 1987
- The International Insurance Act 1988.

The International Companies Office administers these laws and supervises all offshore entities registered under them. It was set up as an autonomous unit within the Central Bank of Samoa, and comprises a registrar and support staff. The operations of the International Companies Office are overseen by a steering committee of government officials – the financial secretary, the general manager of the Central Bank and attorney general. The Western Samoa jurisdiction aims to continually update its offshore laws in line with trends and developments of the international financial scene and to remain competitive with other finance centres. Since 1990 three series of amendments have been enacted including substantial amendments in 1991 to the International Companies Act 1987, which were modelled on the British Virgin Islands' jurisdiction. The most notable of the amendments relate to international companies and became effective on 1 February 1993. These changes are expected to make the offshore finance centre more cost-effective.

1. The abolition of annual renewal certificates of incorporation in favour of certificates with no expiry dates.

2. The payment of annual renewal fees on a fixed date (30 November) each year and not on the annual anniversary of the company's incorporation. In the transitional period some companies will benefit financially from the change. For instance, a company incorporated or registered after 1.2.93 will pay its first renewal fee on 30.11.94 instead of 1.2.94. The above amendments will substantially reduce the administration involved in managing international companies and will streamline office procedures.

3. The introduction of a new breed of international company; a long-term company which can be registered for 5, 10 or 20 years. This is envisaged as a progressive trend and is expected to attract further offshore business. Paying one fee for a long-term company – US\$1,000 for five years, US\$1,500 for 10 years and US\$2,000 for 20 years – is considerably cheaper than paying the normal fee of 300 US dollars each year. Also, clients and trustee companies do not have to worry about paying renewal fees every year.

4. The abolition of the requirement that international companies with bearer shares specify the date of their annual general meetings in their articles of association.

Tax

The islands tax resident individuals and companies on their worldwide income and there are exchange controls. There are no double-taxation treaties. International (offshore) companies are exempt of tax.

Offshore trusts

As a common law country, Western Samoa recognizes trusts. They fall into one of two categories.

- International trusts.
- Local trusts.

International trusts are exempt of tax and exchange controls.

USEFUL ADDRESSES

In countries where official bodies are easily approached their addresses have been given, and where this is not the case, addresses of banks or trust companies are given instead, but this is not intended to be an endorsement of their services.

ANDORRA

Banc Internacional d'Andorra
PO Box 8
Andorra la Vella
Andorra

Credit Andorra
19 Av. Princep Beniloch
Andorra la Vella
Andorra

Banc Agricoli Comercial d'Andorra
PO Box 49
Andorra la Vella
Andorra

ANGUILLA

KPMG
PO Box 136
The Valley
Anguilla

ANTIGUA

Antigua Overseas Bank
PO Box 1679
High Street
St John's
Antigua

Swiss American Bank
St John's
Antigua

Antigua Management and Trust
PO Box 1679
High Street
St John's
Antigua

Caribbean Management and Trust Co
60 Nevis Street
St John's
Antigua

Guardian International Bank
Long Street
St John's
Antigua

ARUBA

Chamber of Commerce and Industry
Zoutmanstraat 21
Oranjestad
Aruba

Department of Economic Affairs
L.G. Smith Boulevard 82
Oranjestad
Aruba

Aruba Foreign Investment Agency
85 Nassaustraat
Oranjestad
Aruba

Centrale Bank van Aruba
Havenstraat 2
Oranjestad
Aruba

First National Bank of Aruba
Caya GF (Betico) Croes 67
PO Box 184
Oranjestad
Aruba

Corporate Trust (Aruba) NV
Oranjestad
Aruba

BAHAMAS

Bahamas Chamber of Commerce
PO Box N–665
Nassau
Bahamas

Registrar General
PO Box N–532
Nassau
Bahamas

Swiss Bank Corporation
Claughton House
Shirley and Charlotte Streets
PO Box N7757
Nassau
Bahamas

BARBADOS

Barbados Industrial Development Corporation
Harbour Road
Bridgetown
Barbados WI

Ministry of Finance
Treasury Building
Bridgetown
Barbados WI

Registrar of Companies
Coleridge Street
St Michael
Barbados WI

Central Bank of Barbados
PO Box 1016
Bridgetown
Barbados WI

BELIZE

Belize Corporate Services Ltd
60 Market Square
Belize City
Belize

Deloitte and Touche
40A Central American Boulevard
PO Box 1235
Belize City
Belize

BERMUDA

Bermuda Monetary Authority
Hamilton HM12
Bermuda

Chamber of Commerce
PO Box HM 655
Hamilton HM CX
Bermuda

Registrar of Companies
30 Parliament Street
Hamilton HM 12
Bermuda

Ministry of Finance
Government Administration
Building
30 Parliament Street
Hamilton FM 12
Bermuda

The Bank of Bermuda
PO Box HM 1020
Hamilton HM DX
Bermuda

BRITISH VIRGIN ISLANDS

Barclays Bank Plc
PO Box 434
Road Town
Tortola
British Virgin Islands

Bank of Nova Scotia
PO Box 438
Road Town
Tortola
British Virgin Islands

Corporate Trusts (BVI) Ltd
Abbott Building
2nd Floor
PO Box 933
Road Town
Tortola
British Virgin Islands

CAYMAN ISLANDS

Registrar of Companies
Government Administration
Building
Grand Cayman
Cayman Islands BWI

Bank of Bermuda (Cayman) Ltd
PO Box 513
George Town
Grand Cayman
Cayman Islands BWI

Banking Supervision Department
Cayman Islands Government
Grand Cayman
Cayman Islands BWI

Swiss Bank and Trust Corporation
PO Box 852
George Town
Grand Cayman
Cayman Islands BWI

Euro Bank Corporation
PO Box 1792
George Town
Grand Cayman
Cayman Islands BWI

Lloyds Bank International (Cayman)
PO Box 857
George Town
Grand Cayman
Cayman Islands BWI

Schroder Cayman Bank and Trust
Company Ltd
PO Box 1040
West Wind Building
George Town
Grand Cayman
Cayman Islands BWI

COOK ISLANDS

European Pacific Trust Company
European Pacific Centre
Tutakimoa Road
PO Box 25
Rarotonga
Cook Islands

Investment and Legal Trust
Corporation
Legal Chambers
PO Box 821
Avarua
Rarotonga
Cook Islands

Westpac Banking Corporation
Main Road
Avarua
Rarotonga
Cook Islands

Bank Gutzwiller, Kurtz, Bungener
PO Box 666
Avarua
Rarotonga
Cook Islands

Cook Islands Development Bank
PO Box 113
Avarua
Rarotonga
Cook Islands

CYPRUS

Central Bank of Cyprus
PO Box 5529
Nicosia
Cyprus

Credit Libanais SAL
PO Box 3492
Limassol
Cyprus

Cyprus Development Bank
PO Box 1415
Nicosia
Cyprus

Bank of Cyprus
86–90 Phaneromeni Street
Nicosia
Cyprus

Federal Bank of the Middle East
PO Box 5566
Nicosia
Cyprus

Byblos Bank
PO Box 218
Limassol
Cyprus

DUBAI

Barclays Bank
Ahmed Mohammed Burhaima
Building
Clock Tower Roundabout
PO Box 1891
Dubai
United Arab Emirates

British Bank of the Middle East
PO Box 66
Dubai
United Arab Emirates

Standard Chartered Bank
PO Box 999
Dubai
United Arab Emirates

Emirates Bank International Ltd
PO Box
2923
Dubai
United Arab Emirates

Finexco Dubai
PO Box 7000
Dubai
United Arab Emirates

Middle East Bank
PO Box 5547
Dubai
United Arab Emirates

GIBRALTAR

Hambros Bank (Gibraltar) Ltd
PO Box 375
Hambro House
Line Wall Road
Gibraltar

**Hong Kong Bank and Trust
Company Ltd**
PO Box 19
Library Street
Gibraltar

Coutts & Co (Gibraltar) Ltd
PO Box 709
National Westminster House
57–63 Line Wall Road
Gibraltar

Anglo-Swiss Fiduciary Trust
Haven Court
5 Library Ramp
Gibraltar

Algemene Bank Gibraltar Ltd
PO Box 100
2–6 Main Street
Gibraltar

GUERNSEY

Bank of Bermuda
PO Box 208
St Peter Port
Guernsey

Guinness Flight
Guinness Flight House
La Plaiderie
St Peter Port
Guernsey

**Hambros Channel Islands Trust
Corporation**
PO Box 86
St Peter Port
Guernsey

NM Rothschild and Sons (CI) Ltd
St Julian's Court
St Julian's Avenue
St Peter Port
Guernsey

Royal Bank of Scotland
PO Box 62
22 High Street
St Peter Port
Guernsey

HONG KONG

Trade Department
G/F Ocean Centre
5 Canton Road
Kowloon
Hong Kong

Inland Revenue Department
Windsor House
11 Gloucester Road
Causeway Bay
Hong Kong

**Hong Kong Trade Development
Council**
Convention Plaza
Office Tower 36th–39th floors
1 Harbour Road
Wanchai
Hong Kong

Registrar of Companies
Queensway Government Offices
13th–14th floors
66 Queensway
Hong Kong

BZW Investment Management Ltd
18th Floor, 2 Pacific Place
88 Queensway
Hong Kong

Credit Lyonnais
6th Floor
3 Exchange Square
8 Connaught Place
Central
Hong Kong

Kleinwort Benson
40th Floor Gloucester Tower
The Landmark
11 Pedder Street
Central
Hong Kong

Tyndall International (Asia) Ltd
505 Bank of America Tower
12 Harcourt Road
Central
Hong Kong

IRELAND

Dublin Chamber of Commerce
7 Clare Street
Dublin
Ireland

Ireland Industrial Development Authority
Wilton Park House
Wilton Place
Dublin 2
Ireland

AIB Custodial Services Ltd
Bankcentre
Ballsbridge
Dublin 4
Ireland

Financial Services Department
Industrial Development Authority
Wilton Park House
Wilton Place
Dublin 2
Ireland

Investment Bank of Ireland
IFS Centre
1 Harbourmaster Place
Dublin 1
Ireland

Pfizer International Bank Europe
Alexander House
Earlsfort Centre
Earlsfort Terrace
Dublin 2
Ireland

ISLE OF MAN

Commercial Development Officer
Commercial Development Division
Government Offices
Douglas
Isle of Man
British Isles

Coutts & Co
PO Box 59
33 Athol Street
Douglas
Isle of Man
British Isles

Freeport Centre
Ballasalla
Douglas
Isle of Man
British Isles

Royal Skandia
Skandia House
Finch Road
Douglas
Isle of Man
British Isles

Warburg Asset Management
12–13 Hill Street
Douglas
Isle of Man
British Isles

JERSEY

BankAmerica Trust Co
Union House
Union Street
St Helier
Jersey

Citibank (Channel Islands) Ltd
PO Box 104
St Helier
Jersey

Flemings
PO Box 73
Queen's House
Don Road
St Helier
Jersey

Hambros
13 Broad Street
St Helier
Jersey

Swiss Bank Corporation
40 Esplanade
St Helier
Jersey

LABUAN

Public Bank
Lot B
Level 5
Wisma Oceanic
Jalan OKK
Awan Besar
87007 Labuan
Malaysia

Hong Kong and Shanghai Banking Corporation
First Floor, No 4
Jalan Merdaka
87007 Labuan
Malaysia

Standard Chartered Labuan International Offshore Centre
No 151 Jalan Tun Mustapha
PO Box 111
87008 Labuan
Malaysia

Ernst and Young Trust SDN. BHD
PO Box 80123
87011 Labuan
Malaysia

LIECHTENSTEIN

Liechtensteinsche Landesbank Staatsgarantie
Fl–9490 Vaduz
Stadtle 44
Postfach 384
Liechtenstein

Verwanltungs-und-Privat-Bank Ag
Fl–9490 Vaduz
Postfach 885
Liechtenstein

Bank in Liechtenstein
Herrengasse 12
PO Box 85
Fl–9490 Vaduz
Liechtenstein

Liechtensteinische Landesbank
Stadtle 44
PO Box 384
Fl–9490 Vaduz
Liechtenstein

Bil Treuhand Ag
Stadtle 18
Postfach 683
Fl–9490 Vaduz
Liechtenstein

LUXEMBOURG

Kredjetbank SA Luxembourgeoise
43 Boulevard Royal
L–2955
Luxembourg

Banque International a Luxembourg
2 Boulevard Royal
Luxembourg

ING Bank (Luxembourg) SA
64–66 Av. Victor Hugo
L–1750
Luxembourg

Banco di Roma International
PO Box 692
L–2016
Luxembourg

Bank of Boston SA
PO Box 422
L–2014
Luxembourg

Banque de Gestion Edmond de Rothschild
PO Box 474
L–2014
Luxembourg

Banque International a Luxembourg
2 Boulevard Royal
L–2953
Luxembourg

Credit Suisse (Luxembourg) SA
PO Box 40
L–2010
Luxembourg

Hauck Banquiers Luxembourg SA
PO Box 414
L–2014
Luxembourg

MADEIRA

Caixa Geral Depositos
Av. Arriage 17–3
9000 Funchal
Madeira
Portugal

Madeira Management Companhia
Rua dos Murcas 68
PO Box 7
9000 Funchal
Madeira
Portugal

Madeira Development Company
Rua Imperatrix D Amelia
PO Box 4164
9052 Funchal Codex
Madeira
Portugal

Madeira-Fiducia Management LDA
Rua de Janeiro 81A–58E
9000 Funchal
Madeira
Portugal

Castro Barros Sobral e Xavier
9000 Funchal
Madeira
Portugal

MALTA

Malta International Business Authority
Palazzo Spinola
PO Box St Julians 29
Malta

Malta Development Corporation
House of Catalunya
Marsamxetto Road
Valletta
Malta

Bank of Valletta International
86 South Street
Valletta
Malta

Malta Trust Group
Wisely House
First Floor
206 Old Bakery Street
Valletta
Malta

Mid-Med Bank Ltd
233 Republic Street
Valletta
Malta

MAURITIUS

**Offshore Business Activities
Authority**
2nd Floor
Deramann Tower
30 Sir William Newton Street
Port Louis
Mauritius

Mulitconsult Ltd
c/o De Chazal Du Mee
Vigux Conseil Street
Port Louis
Mauritius

**International Management
(Mauritius) Ltd**
Rogers House
PO Box 60
5 President John Kennedy Street
Port Louis
Mauritius

MONACO

Compagnie Monégasque de Banque
Les Terrasses
2 Avenue de Monte Carlo
Monte Carlo
Monaco

Crédit Foncier de Monaco
17 Boulevard Albert Premier
PO Box 6
Monte Carlo
Monaco

Perspectives Financières
5 Avenue de Grande Bretagne
98000 Monte Carlo
Monaco

Secoma
57 Rue Grimaldi
Monte Carlo 98000
Monaco

NETHERLANDS

ABN Bank
32 Vijzelstraat
Amsterdam
Holland

Bank Mees and Hope NV
548 Herengracht
PO Box 293
1000 AG Amsterdam
Holland

Rabobank Nederland
Croselaan 18
3521 CB Utrecht
Holland

NETHERLANDS ANTILLES

First Curacao International Bank
Breedestraat 16
PO Box 299
Willemstaad
Curacao
Netherlands Antilles

Curacao International Trust Company
Handelskade 8
PO Box 812
Willemstaad
Curacao
Netherlands Antilles

Algemene Bank Nederland
Pietermaai 17
Willemstaad
Curacao
Netherlands Antilles

Rabobank Curacao
PO Box 3876
Willemstad
Curacao
Netherlands Antilles

Pierson Heldring and Pierson (Curacao)
PO Box 3889
Willemstad
Curacao
Netherlands Antilles

Bank van de Nederlandse Antillen
Breedestrat 1
Willemstad
Curacao
Netherlands Antilles

NEVIS

Nevis Cooperative Bank Company
PO Box 60
Charlestown
Nevis WI

CAPCO Trust Nevis Ltd
Springates Building
Government Road
Charlestown
Nevis WI

Morning Star Holdings
Memorial Square
PO Box 556
Charlestown
Nevis WI

PANAMA

Caja de Ahorros
PO Box 1740
Panama 1
Panama

Banco Nacional da Panama
PO Box 5220
Panama 5
Panama

Panama International Trust Corporation
PO Box 4881
Panama 5
Panama

Panamercian Management Services
Calle Aquilino de la Guardia
10 Elvira Mendez Street
Panama 5
Panama

Icaza Gonzales-Ruiz and Aleman
Calle Aquilino de la Guardia
No 8 Edificio IGRA
PO Box 850 Panama
Panama

SWITZERLAND

Swiss Bank Corporation
1 Aeschenvorstadt
CH–4002 Basel
Switzerland

Ueberseebank
PO Box 8024
Limmatquai 12
Zurich
Switzerland

Bank Institute Zurich
PO Box 5138
CH–8022 Zurich
Switzerland

Anker Bank
17 Rue de la Mairie
CH–12–7 Geneva
Switzerland

Bank Julius Baer & Co
Bahnhofstrasse 36
Postfach 66
CH–8010
Switzerland

Banque Cantonale Vaudoise
14 Place Saint Francois
CH–1003 Lausanne
Switzerland

Finter Bank Zurich
65 Rue Du Rhone
1204 Geneva
Switzerland

Rothschild Bank Ag
Zollikerstrasse 181
CH–8034
Switzerland

TURKS AND CAICOS

Registrar of Companies
Grand Turk
Turks and Caicos Islands BWI

Superintendent of the Offshore Finance Centre
Finance Department
Grand Turk
Turks and Caicos Islands BWI

Turks and Caicos Banking Company
PO Box 123
Harbour House
Grand Turk
Turks and Caicos Islands BWI

Europe-Americas Trust and Management
Gretton House
Duke Street
PO Box 65
Grand Turk
Turks and Caicos Islands BWI

Caribbean Management Services
PO Box 103
MacLaw House
Grand Turk
Turks and Caicos Islands BWI

VANUATU

Barclays Bank
PO Box 123
Port Vila
Vanuatu
Southwest Pacific

Melanesia International Trust Company
Rue Pasteur
PO Box 213
Port Vila
Vanuatu
Southwest Pacific

Pacific Fund Managers Ltd
PO Box 65
Port Vila
Vanuatu
Southwest Pacific

Pacific International Trust Company Ltd
Box 45
International Building
Port Vila
Vanuatu
Southwest Pacific

European Bank Ltd
PO Box 395
Port Vila
Vanuatu
Southwest Pacific

WESTERN SAMOA

Registrar of International and Foreign Companies
PO Private Bag
Apia
Western Samoa

Bank of Western Samoa
Beach Road
PO Box L–1855
Apia
Western Samoa

European Pacific Trust Company
PO Box 2029
Apia
Western Samoa

Western Samoa International Trust Company
Level 1
Ione Viliamu Building
Falealili Street
PO Box 3271
Apia
Western Samoa

BIBLIOGRAPHY

Jules Abel, *The Rockefeller Millions: The Story of the World's Most Stupendous Fortune* 1967.

Rowan Bosworth-Davis, *Too Good to be True*, Bodley Head 1987.

J. Carswell, *The South Sea Bubble*, Cresset Press 1960.

Hugo Cornwall, *The Hacker's Handbook*, Century Hutchinson 1989.

Richard Eels and Peter Nehemkis, *Corporate Cultures*, Macmillan 1984.

Attitudes of Companies in Britain to Fraud (Consensus Research), Ernst and Whinney 1987.

Leo Gough, *The Financial Times Guide to Business Numeracy*, Pitman Professional Publishing 1994.

Leo Gough, *The Investor's Guide to How the Stock Market Really Works*, Pitman Professional Publishing 1994.

John Guiseppi, *The Bank of England: A History from its Foundation in 1694*, 1966.

S.L. Hays, A.M. Spence and D.V.P. Marks, *Competition in the Investment Banking Industry*, Harvard University Press 1983.

Michael Joseph, *The Conveyancing Fraud*, Michael Joseph 1989.

Michael Joseph, *Lawyers Can Seriously Damage Your Health*, Michael Joseph 1990.

J.M. Keynes, *The General Theory of Employment Interest and Money*, Harcourt 1936.

V.P. Lane, *Security of Computer-based Information Systems*, Macmillan 1985.

L.H. Leigh, *The Control of Commercial Fraud*, Heinemann Educational Books 1982.

Ferdinand Lundberg, *The Rich and the Super Rich*, Thomas Nelson & Sons 1969.

C. Mackay, *Extraordinary Popular Delusions and the Madness of Crowds*, Harmony Books.

Burton G. Malkiel, *A Random Walk Down Wall Street*, W.W. Norton & Co 1991.

Harry Markowitz, *Portfolio Selection: Efficient Diversification of Investments*, Wiley 1959.

C. Northcote Parkinson, *Parkinson's Law*, John Murray 1958.

Patrick Philips, *Inside the Gilt-edged market*, Woodhead-Faulkner.

Anthony Sampson, *The Money Lenders*, Coronet Books.

Fred Schwed Jr., *Where are the Customers' Yachts?*, Simon and Schuster 1940.

Adam Smith, *The Money Game*, Random House 1968.

George Soros, *The Alchemy of Finance*, Weidenfeld and Nicholson.

Edwin H. Sutherland, *White Collar Crime*, Dryden Press 1949.

Alvin Toffler, *Future Shock*, Random House 1970.

Tolley's Tax Guide, Tolley Publishing Company.

John Train, *Preserving Capital and Making It Grow*, Penguin 1983.

Periodicals

The Banker, UK

Far Eastern Economic Review, Hong Kong

Investment International, UK

International Money Marketing, UK

Offshore Investment, Isle of Man

INDEX AND GLOSSARY OF TERMS